791.43   c.1
Corman.
  How I made a hundred movies
in Hollywood and never lost a
dime. $18.95

*How I Made
a Hundred Movies
          in Hollywood and
Never Lost a Dime*

🏠 Random House New York

How I Made
a Hundred Movies
in Hollywood and
Never Lost a Dime

Roger Corman

with Jim Jerome

Library of Congress Cataloging-in-Publication Data
Corman, Roger
How I made a hundred movies in Hollywood and never lost a dime / by Roger Corman with Jim Jerome.
p. cm.   ISBN 0-394-56974-1
Filmography: p.   Includes index.
1. Corman, Roger.   2. Motion picture producers and directors—United States—Biography.   3. Low budget motion pictures—United States.   I. Jerome, Jim.   II. Title.   PN1998.3.C68A3   1990
791.43′0233′092—dc20   89-33766

Manufactured in the United States of America
Designed by J. K. Lambert
98765432
First Edition

To my wife, Julie—my best friend, strongest supporter, and most valued critic. I love you.

Introduction

My career has been an anomaly in Hollywood. I have been called everything from the King of the B's to the Pope of Pop Cinema—directing over 50 low-budget independent motion pictures, and producing and/or distributing another 250 for my own companies, New World Pictures and Concorde/New Horizons. While there's a tradition in Hollywood that no one sees profits on a movie no matter what the box office, I've seen profits on probably 280 of those 300-odd pictures. Despite their low budgets, my films have been shown at prestigious festivals, and I was the youngest director to have retrospectives at the Cinémathèque Française in Paris, the National Film Theatre in London, and the Museum of Modern Art in New York. While I produced R-rated exploitation films through the 1970s at New World, I also imported distinguished art films from abroad—five of which won the Academy Award for Best Foreign Film.

Over the years, the motion picture industry has undergone significant sociological and economic shifts. Drive-ins, once a major outlet for my films, have given way to mall and urban multiplexes. The majors usurped the theatrical market in "exploitation" or "B" genres in the 1970s, throwing giant budgets, top stars and directors, and state-of-the-art high-tech effects at an idiom that had long been the humble domain of the "quickie" artists. As a result, the dominant ancillary market for low-budget features has evolved from TV in its early days to network, syndicated TV, pay TV, and home video. The breakup of the studios' "vertical" monopoly over production-distribution-exhibition in the late 1940s gradually opened up the field to independents. Through these years my company and I have changed with the times. We still stand as one of the leading independent production and distribution companies in the United States.

Because of my notoriety as an "outlaw," a new generation of filmmakers, educated in the 1960s counterculture, saw me as an uncompromised artist/entrepreneur who got his own movies made outside the Establishment. They could learn from me not only the filmmaking skills of preparation, prelighting, dolly movements, "cutting in the camera," composition, and quick pacing; I also grounded them in marketing, advertising, and distribution. A Corman credit in the "minors" was their fastest path to the majors.

In the early days, I directed Robert Towne's first script. Jack Nicholson appeared in eight of my films and I produced three of his screenplays before Hollywood "discovered" him in *Easy Rider*. Francis Coppola and Peter Bogdanovich started out by recutting and reworking Russian science fiction movies I acquired for release before I backed their first features. Dennis Hopper shot second unit for me on *The Trip*.

But it was in the 1970s, when I grew tired of directing and created New World Pictures, that the "Corman School" became an alternative institute of independent filmmaking. Many of those New World "graduates" are powerful directors and producers today, with credits that have netted the majors hundreds of millions of dollars: Martin Scorsese, Jonathan Demme, Ron Howard, Joe Dante, Jonathan Kaplan, Allan Arkush, John Sayles, James Cameron, Jon Davison, Gale Anne Hurd, Frances Doel, and Barbara Boyle.

I never forgot how tough it had been for me to break in to the studio system in the early 1950s, when there were far fewer independents in business. I spent months looking around for work and still needed connections just to get hired as a messenger at Fox. My engineering background at Stanford helped anchor me in meticulous preparation and a passion for efficiency and discipline.

I did many of my movies in one or two weeks for well under $100,000. On a bet, I shot *Little Shop of Horrors* in two days and a night for $35,000. I decided to shoot half of *The Terror* in two days without a finished script simply because I hated to see the wonderful gothic sets for *The Raven* go to waste when we wrapped. I made two films at once, first in Hawaii and then again in Puerto Rico, to cut transportation costs. I hired Hell's Angels, along with their bikes and women, to lend realism to *The Wild Angels* in 1966, and a year later I dropped acid in Big Sur before making a film about the effects of LSD, *The Trip*.

My first seventeen pictures in a row were profitable until I lost money on an art film about racial segregation called *The Intruder*. I learned my lesson and almost never lost money on a film again.

I was even offered a job running a major studio, but the salary was less than I was making. I asked for total control and considered this nonnegotiable. The studio, of course, rejected my request. No single production executive ever has "total control" in the majors, which is why I have remained faithful to my maverick sensibility. Studios thrive on a committee approach that prevents anyone from concentrating power for too long.

As the head of my own company, I favor a small, loosely stratified office environment that rewards dedication and competence and resists excessive bureaucratization. Titles and job descriptions mean virtually nothing. There's an aura through the halls that everybody can—and eventually will—do everything. There is no room for prima donnas or political power plays.

Three very successful filmmakers teamed up on their first feature at New World when my head of promotion, Jon Davison, bet me he could produce a film in ten days for under $90,000. He got my trailer editors, Allan Arkush and Joe Dante, to direct *Hollywood Boulevard*—and won the bet. Examples like theirs still abound. We hired a gofer recently for a four-week shoot and by the end of the first week he had advanced to second assistant director. By the time we wrapped he was first a.d., and two pictures later I asked him to be production manager.

★ **FRANCES DOEL**

I was Roger's assistant and story editor for sixteen years and worked for him probably longer than anyone. He had a most contradictory approach to delegating. On the creative side—writing scripts and directing—he would give tremendous responsibility to young people who basically had no idea what they were doing. And they would learn. But in terms of running the company, he found it very, very difficult, if not impossible, to delegate decision-making authority.

There was never, for instance, in my entire time at New World, a staff meeting. Except once. That was when Barbara Boyle, Roger's vice president, counsel, and chief negotiator, pointed out that most other production-distribution companies and studios actually had staff meetings *all the time.* Roger was very reluctant to do anything like that, but she convinced him to try it once.

This was a great novelty—like instead of starting work on Monday morning and facing the horrific and impossible tasks Roger would ask you to handle alone, we'd have a group meeting. We were all there and he showed up.

We asked Roger all kinds of questions. To which Roger responded by mumbling, "I don't know," "We haven't made a decision yet"—using the royal corporate serious "we"—or he was silent.

The meeting lasted a whole twenty minutes and he didn't really answer one question. He was unwilling to indulge ever again in that kind of a) bureaucracy and b) waste of time.

★ JOHN SAYLES

When you're starting out, most screenwriters write a dozen things and two maybe get made. The important thing about Roger is that he makes movies—he doesn't fuck around a lot. He just decides, "I'm going to pay somebody to write this movie and that means we are making it once the script is in as good a shape as we can for the money and time I've set aside for it." I wrote three screenplays for Roger and all three got made into movies. That's why he is really so incredible. You get the learning, the writing, the story conferencing, and all that. But you also see the whole thing translated into a movie.

Because of the smallness and directness—I mean, there was one boss, which was Roger—you didn't go through a dozen subproducers to get to the guy who was going to say yes or no to a screenplay. With the studios, you're always campaigning for one guy so that he'll hand it off to the next guy, and the other guy might actually respond very differently. So you never really know who your audience is. Five or six people will filter your script through, whereas at New World there was Roger and there was Frances and that was it. So right away you got to talk to the people who were responsible for making your movie.

I did so many fewer drafts working for Roger than for other places, and as far as I'm concerned the extra drafts didn't make for a better movie. It was just that other functionaries in the major studio process were getting to lift their leg up on your work along the way.

★   ★   ★

For an independent, to make a movie and wait to see money is a strategy for demise. It can take, incredibly enough, up to a year for theater owners to get an independent's box-office figures on the books, even though they know to the dollar how much your film has taken in by the time the popcorn is swept up after the last show. Having brought legal action against exhibitors more than once— always getting my checks on the courthouse steps just before a hearing—I know. As an attorney once told me, "At least the exhibitors build nice new theaters on the interest your money earns them."

Still, I'd rather earn that interest myself. Very few independents control their own distribution. Even if you don't, the trick to remaining in business is to get advances from distributors so you can stay in production. I have been in production almost constantly since 1954. The first film I produced—an underwater monster story—cost $12,000 cash with a $5,000 deferment for lab costs and made a profit of $100,000. Before long I had an advance from that film's distributor, which financed my next picture. Then I signed a three-picture deal with what would become American International Pictures. With a steady cash flow—fees, advances, profits on film rentals—to reinvest in production, I was able, for example, to produce/direct eight movies in one year in the late 1950s. The pace hasn't slackened. In 1987, 1988, and 1989 my company produced and released more than sixty films, topping any major studio's output for those three years.

The major challenge has been finding new markets and recouping costs while the majors have dominated the exploitation genres with budgets ten times higher than ours. I made movies about interplanetary adventures when George Lucas was still in grade school. And it was Vincent Canby of *The New York Times* who once wrote, "What is *Jaws* but a big-budget Roger Corman movie?" But when the Spielbergs and Lucases make technically exquisite genre films, they cut deeply into the box-office appeal of our kind of picture. The majors also send out 1,000 to 1,500 prints. No independent distributor can afford the prints and advertising of such a massive release. Also, with one-tenth the budget you're unavoidably getting far less production value.

So in the late 1970s, we had to sell our films to the networks and the emerging pay TV market. Then we began to *presell* the films once we established a track record. This often allowed us to recoup our *entire* cost of production before shooting, as in the cases of *Avalanche* and *Grand Theft Auto*, both of which were sold to network TV for more than $1 million.

A few years later, even that market began to erode because the cable and network markets wanted bigger-budget features. Audiences were simply accustomed to science fiction, horror, or action/ adventure films with a $10 million or $20 million price tag or more. So I moved my company in the direction of home videocassette presales. I can supply many of the home video dealers by signing multipicture deals that guarantee me an ancillary source of cash for virtually every movie I produce or distribute—with a "limited" theatrical release that publicizes the cassette releases and greatly reduces my distribution costs.

It helps that I have a track record of reliability and trustworthiness in delivering films that earn money for the video dealers. I remember one deal especially well. I was having lunch in Germany with an agent and I asked her, "Has anybody shot anything in English that I might pick up for U.S. distribution?"

She mentioned a film about a rock musician that had been shot a few years earlier in Berlin but never finished. The role of the down-and-out American rock promoter was played by Dennis Hopper. I watched half the film and she asked me what I thought. "It's not very good," I said. "It makes no sense at all, really, and you're right, it isn't even finished. I'll buy the American rights for fifty thousand dollars."

This offer startled her. "Roger," she said, "you can't *buy* a film for fifty thousand dollars." But I did buy it—going up slightly in my final offer—and went to work on it back in L.A. I assigned the recutting and finishing of the film to Rodman Flender, my head of advertising, who was in his mid-twenties. But we had two major problems: the film didn't hang together and the German producer hadn't paid Dennis all his money yet. But I saw a way out.

A favorite device of mine when a film makes no sense is to add narration. Suddenly all the disconnected, incoherent scenes fit because you've created narration to match and explain them. I offered to pay Dennis the missing money owed him by the producer, and then deducted *that* money from the purchase price of the film. So I basically got Dennis to read the narration for free. We then cut in some American rock 'n' roll sequences from another film produced by my company and retitled Dennis's movie *Let It Rock*.

All this took about two weeks and $20,000; my total investment was still under $100,000. We sold the film to a home video firm with whom we had a multipicture deal. The price: $450,000. That's what is so amazing about film. There is *always* something there—like a 350 percent profit—if you just find a way to rework, recut, reshoot. That's where an independent filmmaker has a clear edge.

Part of why Hollywood studio features *average* $20 million is the justifiable cost of making big pictures combined with supply and demand for huge box-office stars who command gigantic fees. But another part is simply inefficient or indulgent filmmaking. I can look at a movie with an ostensible $1 million budget and say whether the money was well spent or not. With a $30 million or $50 million picture, I have no frame of reference. Who can tell you what a $50 million picture is supposed to look like? Lucas's *Star Wars* money was brilliantly spent. It was on the screen. The fortunes spent on *Heaven's Gate* or *Ishtar,* for example, clearly were not.

I remember shooting *Atlas* in Greece almost thirty years ago when I was staging the climactic battle in which Atlas leads the troops of Praximedes against the walled city of Thenis. I'd promised a contribution to the Greek Army Charity Fund in return for its providing five hundred soldiers for the battle. On the appointed day only fifty appeared. Possibly someone had misplaced a decimal point. The script called for Praximedes to overwhelm the outnumbered defenders with the size of his army. The only thing I could think of was to abandon my plans for large-scale panoramic shots and shoot the battle in a series of close action shots to hide the size of the army with a flurry of action on the screen. Before shooting I quickly wrote some new dialogue in which Atlas asked Praximedes how he hoped to conquer the city with such a small number of soldiers. Praximedes replied that in his theory of warfare a small band of efficient, dedicated, highly trained warriors could defeat any number of rabble.

That's my theory of filmmaking.

How I Made
a Hundred Movies
in Hollywood and
Never Lost a Dime

Chapter 1

Where does an "outlaw" or "maverick" filmmaker come from? Specifically, in my case, Detroit and Beverly Hills. When I was about fourteen, my family moved from a straight middle-class environment in suburban Detroit to Beverly Hills. In Detroit, I don't think there was one really rich kid in school. At Beverly Hills High, I was immediately aware that some kids in class came from very wealthy families.

But snobbery was not a problem—there was very little of it and I was never without a few close friends. So if I felt awkward around the more aggressive and precocious Beverly Hills types—and more comfortable socially on the fringe with those who didn't run with the in-crowd—it was more that I was, for years, the youngest and (until I shot up past six feet) the smallest in my grade.

Roger Corman as a boy in Detroit and on the set of *Frankenstein Unbound*

The notion of a career as a filmmaker in glamorous Hollywood was the furthest thing from my mind during my early childhood. I always figured I would become an engineer like my father, William Corman. He had grown up in St. Louis and was ranked at the top of his class at the Engineering School of Washington University there. After serving as a naval engineer during World War One, he took a job with a firm in Detroit. He met my mother, Ann, while playing tennis. Their courtship, as it were, was a close enough match for them to get married.

Both of my parents were first-generation Americans. Their families immigrated to the United States from Europe without much money but worked their way into the middle class as small shop owners and, later, in real estate.

I was born on April 5, 1926. My brother, Gene, was born about eighteen months later. We grew up in the Six Mile Road section of Detroit in a small brick house with a green lawn in front. Even during the Depression my father worked, designing bridges, roads, and dams for the McCray Steel Company. He helped Henry Ford on a project called Greenfield Village, a reconstruction of nineteenth-century Midwestern homes. He designed the dam that was needed to create a lake in the village.

I attended Post Junior High and did well academically, skipping a grade, and played all the usual sports with the neighborhood kids—tackle football, basketball, and ice hockey whenever the streets froze. I was tall and thin and an above-average athlete, so there was a fair amount of banging around and general abuse at the hands of the bigger and tougher kids. In football I always played end because I could reach up and catch, but these neighborhood kids were really tough on a big target like me. I did it just on nerve more than anything else. I was no muscle man.

My mother was Catholic and so my brother and I were baptized. That was about it for religion. My parents did believe in schoolwork and insisted that I do well. I generally did. My hobbies were reading and building model airplanes out of balsa wood and rice paper. These were the gas-powered kind with three- and four-foot wingspans. I'd spend an hour a day on them during the week, two hours or so on weekends. The room Gene and I shared looked like a miniature hangar, filled with the pungent aroma of glue. My brother and I also went to Sunday matinees and saw plenty of films like *Mutiny on the Bounty,* one of my favorites.

Like many boys of my day, I read *Popular Mechanics,* Tom Swift, Howard Pease adventure stories, and *Boy's Life.* A lot of it was just low-key propaganda, selling the American way of life. There was always an emphasis on being a good citizen, a team player. The sports stories were often about little guys who excelled on guts and determination alone, but when I tried it on the football field the main result was that I got hurt.

My father didn't push me to work as a kid. He talked me out of getting a paper route. "You'll have your whole life to work," he said. He preferred that I take an allowance and spend my time playing and excelling in school. My father was extremely intelligent and logical. To him, intellect was probably more important than emotion. If he didn't express as much feeling as some fathers, there was never any question that he loved us.

My formative years were spent in a Depression environment—I was three years old when the market crashed in 1929—and I have always assumed that somehow shaped my attitude toward money. My film budgets have always been notoriously lean, while the waste and excess built into the major studios' productions have tended to appall me.

We were comfortably middle class. But I overheard the apprehensive talk about money, about saving, about friends wiped out. They worried about the future. My dad took a salary cut and the firm laid off half of its employees. So at a time when he was approaching his middle years, with a wife and two children and becoming established in his field, he was making less money than when he was a single man in his twenties. But at least he had a job.

My father was organized and prudent enough so that by the time he was forty-three, he was able to retire from engineering. There were also health reasons. Though he was quiet and not a socially aggressive man, he developed heart problems. California seemed like the ideal place for him. It was the "Golden Land," just as it had been to millions of other settlers and dreamers before him. He didn't exactly retire—he took consulting jobs. He had had enough of staff routine and we had all had enough of the Michigan winters and snow. I was just starting high school and was in for quite a change.

We moved into a one-story bungalow on South Almont, below Wilshire, in the less fashionable section of Beverly Hills. Some of my classmates at Beverly Hills High had famous show business names like Goldwyn, Warner, Zukor, Factor, and Laemmle. So I always heard exciting stories about the film industry.

My studies focused on sciences and math, but I read a great deal of literature as well, including Edgar Allan Poe's "The Fall of the House of Usher," which undoubtedly made quite an impact. It was a class assignment, but I enjoyed it so much I asked my parents to buy the complete works of Poe for a birthday or Christmas gift. Who knew that twenty years later I would bring a half-dozen or so of those stories to the screen?

I took college preparatory courses in math, physics, and chemistry—feeling that I should follow in my father's field. But I also contemplated some sort of literary career as an alternative to engineering. I had written for a junior high paper in Detroit. I was first-page editor of the Beverly Hills *Highlights*. I was always writing, and I liked it.

And there were other activities. I joined the High-Y, which was like a fraternity. I shot up past six feet and was a natural for varsity basketball. I played forward. But I was mostly a reserve, clearly not one of the stars—being a year or two younger than the starters.

I read the papers and kept up with events of the world. I took Radio Speech class at school and acted in some plays. We produced a fifteen-minute radio show at 11:45 every Saturday morning on KMPC. I wrote one of the plays we put on—*Before the Dawn.* It was about a resistance movement in Eastern Europe during the war, involving Marshal Tito and another resistance leader in Yugoslavia.

I wouldn't say I was in the absolute "in" crowd but these activities did help get me closer to the center of things. Still, I got off to a rather slow start in dating because I frankly couldn't imagine a girl would really want to go out with me. I did get up the nerve to ask a girl for a date to the prom—and to my amazement she accepted. It turned out to be a very pleasant experience and my life began to be a little more interesting.

★ **JACK BOHRER**

Roger and I were classmates. He just breezed through with an incredible memory, great precision in his sciences, and tremendous concentration. I worked with Roger on a number of his early films as assistant director, and I'd have to get information from him to the rest of the crew between shots. I'd see him concentrating on the next scenes in the script and have to tap him on the shoulder four or five times—practically *shake* him—to get his attention. His mental focus was amazing. He was great at solving problems. It was a game to him, whether it was for physics or chemistry equations or reacting in a split second to a curve thrown his way about the lights or cameras on location.

Roger was also a pretty fair tennis player when we played with friends at the Beverly Hills Tennis Club. There was tremendous competition between Roger and his brother, Gene. I used to be Roger's doubles partner and we'd play opposite Gene and his partner. It was murder. "We're down two sets, Roger," I'd say. "Let's give it up." Out of the question. Roger hated to lose. He'd *never give up.*

★   ★   ★

My father's advice about college was quite sound: go to a good all-around university with a strong engineering department, rather than, say, CalTech. If I changed my mind about engineering, I'd still get a good education. So I went to Stanford. My father was right. I graduated from high school at seventeen in 1943 and went up north to Palo Alto thinking I'd go into aeronautical engineering; then I switched to electrical engineering. By the time I was halfway through college I had decided not to be an engineer at all.

But since it was wartime, I volunteered for a Navy officer training program called the V-12, which ensured my four-year engineering education and gave me more control over my assignment. You passed a rigorous academic test and the Navy sent you to college as an apprentice seaman for two and a half years. Then you were commissioned as an ensign.

Though there was no moral issue, as there was with Vietnam, I had conflicting images of war at seventeen: often I was scared of getting killed and at other times I saw myself living on a sub when the seas were swarming with Japanese and German ships firing torpedoes. Excitement and danger. Anything but a desk job.

I finished my first year at Stanford and then joined the V-12 program at the University of Colorado in Boulder. The V-12s had to walk around campus in regular Navy military uniforms and were housed in Bigelow Hall, a former women's dorm turned over to the V-12s. We attended classes with "civilians," but were taught to use Naval terminology, like having to refer to the dorm floors as "decks": I lived on "Third Deck Bigelow." There was roll call every morning on the drill field and marching for an hour every Saturday. Besides regular engineering courses with faculty members, I took one V-12 class taught by Naval officers each semester, like Naval Science or Naval Tactics.

By spring 1946, as I finished my second year at Boulder, which was my junior year, the war had ended, and I left the V-12 program a few months early. The Navy sent me back to where I enlisted, which they assumed was "home." So I came in on a train to San Francisco and ended up at a Naval installation on Treasure Island, assigned a bunk for the weekend of my discharge. I tossed my belongings in a foot locker and went to sleep.

When I woke up, I opened the locker and everything had been stolen. I went to the chief petty officer and told him what had happened.

"Well," he asked, "did they break the lock?"

"What lock?"

He shook his head. "How long have you been in the Navy?"

"Two years."

"You've been in the Navy *two years* and you're still so stupid you don't know enough to lock up everything you own?" They issued me spare, ill-fitting clothes from a lost-and-found locker.

I was really embarrassed, but he was right. I thought: Beverly Hills High, Stanford University, and an officer training program at Boulder. I have never been in the real world. Last night was the first night in my life that I was ever in the real world. And everything I owned was stolen.

That same weekend, I left Treasure Island and hitched to Berkeley because the University of California chapter of my fraternity was giving a party there. Afterward, I was hitching home from downtown Oakland. A four-door car with just a driver inside pulled up. "Where you heading?" he asked.

"Treasure Island."

"Fine," he said. "Going to San Francisco over the Bay Bridge. I'll take you there."

I got in, looked in the backseat, and spotted another man—collapsed on the floor. "Who's he?" I asked.

"Oh, he's just drunk," the driver said. "He's passed out."

It seemed believable, because of the way people were partying and carrying on after the war. We drove a few blocks and the driver pulled off the main downtown street and into a dark, deserted alley. Suddenly, the one in the back sprang up, slipped an arm around my neck and lightly scraped a sharp knife against my throat. I tried to stay cool.

"Okay," I said. "Don't anybody get nervous. I'll give you everything I've got." I knew I should be able to talk my way out of this situation. Fortunately, everything I owned had already been ripped off, except for my watch, a cigarette lighter, and my wallet, which had been under my pillow the night before. I calmly said they could help themselves to the lighter from my breast pocket. I told them to keep the wallet, the money, and my watch, which I assured them did not work and was worth absolutely nothing. But I wanted to keep my Navy ID card.

They said okay and took the wallet and the five-dollar lighter and let me keep the ID. And they left me with my watch, which, in fact, worked perfectly and was the only thing I had worth anything. Then they pushed the car door open, told me not to look, and drove away. I was really angry, but I couldn't get a good look at their plates in the dark.

Now I had to hitch home because I had no money. It's ironic, I thought. I got through the war safely, but my first night in the real world I got ripped off. My second night in the real world—mugged at knife point.

When I went for my discharge papers the clerk filling out the forms saw that my rank was Apprentice Seaman. Ordinarily, you are an apprentice only for ninety days at boot camp and then you become a Seaman Second Class. Had I finished the two and a half years I would have been an Ensign. Apprentice is the lowest rank. So he said: "Kid, you've been in the Navy *two years* and you're still an Apprentice Seaman?" I nodded. "Hey, that's the worst record I have ever heard of in my life. Look, kid, no one will ever know the difference. I'm going to put down Seaman Second, because if you apply for a job no one's *ever* going to hire somebody with such a rotten record."

"Well," I said, "it's a point of honor with me. I never made Seaman Second and I don't want to claim a rank I never had. Leave it as Apprentice Seaman. I'll take my chances."

★ **RICHARD SHUPE**

You just knew Roger would never work for anybody else. But he could get you to do almost anything for him. He was incredibly persuasive. I had a car and Roger could *always* talk me into borrowing it. We'd drive down for the UCLA game or go over the mountains to Santa Cruz, where Roger once talked me into driving along the beach, dodging the waves. And I remember saltwater wrecking my car because he had that great idea.

Every spring our fraternity ran a charity drive for a local hospital. There were still some huge estates up in the Burlingame area, about ten miles north toward San Francisco, and Roger wanted me to go to the biggest estate up there—with high walls, gates, and everything—and solicit a donation. You usually went with a partner but I still said to him, "No way, I'm no good at that stuff, going in and knocking on people's doors."

But there was this gorgeous blonde on campus, a Kappa named B. J. King, and so I told Roger the only way I'd go up there and solicit was if he'd get B. J. to be my partner. Because I'd go solicit anywhere with her. And within an hour, I was out there soliciting with B. J. King. That's the way Roger operated. He could talk anyone into *anything*.

★   ★   ★

I returned for my senior year at Stanford on the GI Bill and graduated in 1947 with a degree in Industrial Engineering, a specialty that focused on efficiency and management. But my interests had changed. I had worked on *The Chaparall*, a campus satirical review, and the yearbook. I had also been sports editor of the Stanford *Daily*. I had grown more interested in film, particularly the work of the great directors such as John Ford, Alfred Hitchcock, and Howard Hawks. I went home to L.A., determined to get into motion pictures. I assumed you would make money if you made motion pictures, but that wasn't my main goal. I knew even then that if you wanted to make a lot of money in Southern California you went into real estate. My interest in films was for the creative satisfaction and the excitement.

For several months I checked the job offices at the major studios but couldn't get a job because I wasn't in a union. My parents were living in Westwood by then and I was on unemployment. I was only twenty, younger than most other graduates, and I had no connections. There were almost no independents in those days and so the system of major studios—Metro-Goldwyn-Mayer, Twentieth Century–Fox, Paramount, Universal, Columbia, Warner Bros., United Artists—dominated the industry.

It was a time of great change in Hollywood. The late 1940s marked the end of the major studios' rule over the industry. In 1948 the Supreme Court's Paramount Consent decree broke the virtual monopoly in distribution that the studios had enjoyed for decades. It forced the majors to sell off their nationwide theater chains and get out of distribution. This opened the market to smaller independents who would eventually have a better chance to get their low-budget films shown. It was also the dawn of television. As another outlet for films, television further eroded the studios' hold on distribution.

I had almost six months of unemployment and frustration. I even tried an engineering job. I showed up at U.S. Electrical Motors on Slauson Avenue as a junior electrical/industrial engineer. I started on a Monday and by Wednesday my career in engineering was over. On Thursday I went in to my boss and said, "I've made a terrible mistake. I really have to quit. Today."

Later in 1948, my luck finally changed. The father of a friend of mine knew somebody at Fox and got me my first studio job. I became a messenger on the Fox lot down by Pico and Motor, not far from where my parents were living. The job paid $32.50 a week. It never occurred to me that $32.50 was a low salary. Quite the contrary, this was clearly a breakthrough. I was in.

Chapter 2

Before you can wheel and deal in Hollywood, you have to learn how films get made. What excited me was observing the machinery of filmmaking at work. I didn't just jump in so I could wheel and deal. I don't have the attention span for tedious deliberation. I like to wrap up the negotiations as fast as possible and focus on the creative work. A good negotiator enjoys dragging it out. Not me. In this business, I have always been a sprinter, not a long distance runner.

At Fox, messengers were quite competitive for the right beats. They fought to work on the producers' floors, not the production managers' floors. Maybe a producer would be impressed and hire them. I wasn't one to wait for that kind of chance encounter. For six months I rode a bike and delivered messages, letters, film cans, pack-

Top: Pamela Duncan in *The Undead*
Bottom: Papier-mâché beast from *Attack of the Crab Monsters*

ages, whatever. It was clear that in the days of Darryl Zanuck, who ran the studio, producers rather than directors were kings. The studios were on six-day production schedules, so I went to the studio manager and asked him to let me work Saturdays for nothing, just to be on the sets and soak up what I could. I also did some script reading in the story department over weekends.

The strategy paid off. When an opening came up there, I got the job. Incredibly, my salary *doubled* to $65 a week and I was now a story analyst at Fox. This was 1948, I was twenty-two, and $65 a week was good money. I had my own little office in the Old Writers' Building. It should have been called the Rich Writers' Building. Some of the top contract writers were highly paid slaves, making several thousand dollars a week. As low man, I generally got the worst assignments—"spec scripts" recommended by agents who were anything but impartial. It was extremely frustrating. I plowed through two scripts a day and recommended very few. It wasn't that I was unusually tough. Most of them were unusually bad.

There was one quite appealing perk—getting to know Debra Paget, who was about seventeen and without question the most beautiful girl I had ever seen. She was under contract to Fox and had to come to a small room near my office for a few hours of schooling a day. Since I was the youngest man in the Old Writers' Building, we became quite friendly. She played the female lead for me in two of the Poe films a decade later.

Like others in the department, I tried writing scripts but never finished one. I did help get someone else's script produced. I had heard in the department that Fox was looking for a classy, offbeat Western for Gregory Peck. I remembered hearing about "The Big Gun," a script "covered" by a friend of mine who found the script "good" but not exactly "right."

I quietly retrieved it from the files, read it over, rewrote the coverage, and then added notes as to how certain stretches that weren't "right" could be made to work. I handed it in to one of the top executives in charge of the department. He called me to say, "Thanks, good work. We may do something with this."

They did. Peck starred in *The Gunfighter,* a film that stood out as an important and popular Western, since it was more psychological study than simple shoot-'em-up. Some film historians have even noted that *The Gunfighter* helped change the genre.

It definitely changed the way I felt toward work as a story analyst. I learned a crucial, if disillusioning, lesson about how the system works. The executive who had praised me got a big bonus. I got nothing. I was angry, but there was nothing to do.

Actually, there *was* something to do: go to Europe and see the world. I couldn't imagine myself sitting all day before a stack of everyone else's scripts. I wanted to write on my own. I thought I'd go back to school overseas and see something of life on the Continent. The lure of Hemingway and the Left Bank was still very big at the time.

I applied to Oxford on the GI Bill. When I was accepted, I had to go down to the Veterans Center at Wilshire and Westwood and apply for GI Bill coverage. I was on line in this huge Quonset hut that has since been torn down. The vet in front of me was going to Santa Monica College. I filled out my papers and told the officer taking down the information, "I'm going to Oxford." He looked down a long list of schools and shook his head.

"Sorry, but I don't see Oxford on the accredited list here." I said, "Now wait a minute. The veteran in front of me is going to Santa Monica City College. Do you *really* think that Santa Monica College is accredited and Oxford is *not?*"

"I guess you're right," he said with a shrug as he wrote Oxford on the forms. Fortunately, I'd found a bureaucrat willing to waive certain rules when it was obvious that there was something really wrong with the rules themselves. I have always felt some contempt for blind bureaucratic adherence to pointless rules, especially when simple logic dictates a more feasible and attractive option. I don't go out of the way to challenge the system, but if I want to do something and the system prevents me, I will find any legal way to bend the rules and get it done.

My term in the tutorial system at Oxford under the GI Bill turned out to be quite a pleasant interlude. I wasn't working for a degree; I studied modern English literature—mostly E. M. Forster, D. H. Lawrence, and T. S. Eliot. I knew I was going to be a writer, producer, or director of motion pictures and I needed more background in the arts of the twentieth century. I had a great time while it lasted. I lived in Balliol, one of the men's colleges, bought a cream-colored MG convertible, and played tennis on the lawn at St. Hilda's, one of the women's colleges.

After a term it was time for a change of pace. I got a room in a small hotel just off the Boulevard St. Germain on the Left Bank of Paris for about $1.50 a night—breakfast included—and started hanging around all the great cafes like the Deux Magots and the Café Flore. I immediately fell in with a crowd of American students. Existentialism was the rage in postwar 1950s Paris. We were all major existentialists, and we belonged to hip jazz clubs like the Rose Rouge and the St.-Germain-des-Prés and swapped membership cards among us to get in.

But even brooding existentialists come to need structure and purpose, so I wrote treatments for motion pictures that never got made. I'd generally wake up and have my breakfast, write through the morning, go out for lunch, and spend the rest of the day wandering through the streets, meeting people, traveling, seeing Paris. So instead of saying to myself, what am I doing with my life? I'm sitting here sipping espresso and anisette at a Left Bank sidewalk cafe, I could say, I'm sitting here, writing film treatments and sipping espresso and anisette at a Left Bank cafe. Which was just enough structure. I wrote one Middle East adventure story involving oil. Then I wrote another story that I *almost* sold to United Artists after I got home. It was about a young man who works in a Chicago meat-packing plant. He robs the plant and escapes with a young woman hostage. It was a cross-country chase to the Coast, very much in the Raymond Chandler/James Cain mode.

As my money supply began to dwindle I had to come up with ways to make more. I had one offer (through a very lovely young French girl) to play semi-pro basketball with a French team I practiced with at the Stade Français. Recruiting tall Americans was a big thing there. They offered me $50 a month, room and board, plus travel through small towns around France for the winter of 1951–52. Somehow, that didn't seem to be the answer.

I moved to the Right Bank and while walking home from practice one night I had an offer from a different team of professionals. I was on the Champs-Elysées and two exceptionally good-looking French girls drove up in a Hudson convertible with the top down. They pulled over and asked me if I'd like to come with them to the Lido, and I said I'd be happy to. But I told them I had no money on me. They said, "That's all right, we'll pay."

I hopped in and off we rode to the Lido, the famous nightclub. We sat at the bar and they spoke English as we drank cognac and water, or *fine à l'eau,* as it was called. Pretty soon, one of the girls got up, walked over to a young man, talked to him a few minutes, and disappeared with him. And then the other girl got up, did the same thing with another man, a total stranger. I was stunned. And then it hit me: *I'm with two hookers.*

After the stage show the girls came back. I said, "You know, this is a great show but I sure don't need to sit through it *twice* tonight and, anyway, I can't drink all this cognac you two are buying me."

They told me the Lido had passed a new rule prohibiting unescorted women from entering the club. They needed me to get them in and I could just sit there. At the end of the evening, one said: "We've had a great time tonight. If you'd like, you can join us and we'll cut you in for a percentage of our earnings and you can come every night with us to the Lido."

I thought: You know, there's a word for this kind of job and it isn't what I went through Stanford to end up doing. But at least I was getting some practice in the art of negotiation, something I would need if I were to make it in Hollywood. So I turned that proposal down and made a counteroffer. Since I'd been with them all evening and allowed them to earn a certain income, I thought that maybe I could go to bed with one of them on the house, as it were. Seemed fair enough to me.

They didn't go for that one but quickly came up with a counter-proposal of their own: If I did join forces with them, I could, in fact, have everything I wanted for free, plus a cut of the gross earnings. And if I didn't, then all I got was the cognac and the stage show. That was their final offer. Pretty tough negotiators. I was impressed. Then they mentioned where they usually ate dinner and told me that if I ever changed my mind I should stop in. If they hadn't found some-one else to be their partner by then, I could have the job.

We never did close the deal. A few days later I met someone who told me he had smuggled a Leica camera in from Switzerland and sold it for a profit. So I tried that a few times. It worked. This was *really amazing.* You could buy a Leica in a little German town right across the Swiss border at Basel and resell it in Paris—usually to an American tourist—for about a $100 profit. I cleared about four or five hundred dollars. Back then you had to have a permit to enter Germany and mine had run out. But I had seen that there was abso-lutely nothing to crossing the border. I'd park my car in Basel, ride the streetcar to the stop before the border. I'd walk past a row of apartments parallel to the border, cut between the buildings, scale a barbed wire fence, get across an open field, and I was in West Ger-many. Just like that.

Logic, cunning, conning, a little daring. I was learning how to do whatever I had to do to get what I wanted—and having some adven-tures in the process. But a big part of learning is also how to rely on instinct, especially when it comes to staying away from a bad deal altogether. Another scheme with higher stakes was tempting but doomed. Possibly because I had a young student look, I had an offer to smuggle gold in my MG from Iran across the Continent into Paris. As the all-American courier, I was to be paid $10,000. The gold would be built into the chassis of the MG. This was my first step-deal: $5,000 before I left and the other $5,000 when I came back. A voice inside nearly talked me into it: You know, you've never had $10,000 in your life. You don't even have any idea what an Iranian looks like. Think of it as a lark.

I decided not to run the risk. I had had my year off in Europe. The winter was cold and dreary. I was running out of money and the work ethic was taking hold. I preferred not to go to jail. So, I decided to go home.

There were no openings at Fox, but my story editor there rec-ommended me for a job at the Jules Goldstone literary agency. In addition to writers, Goldstone handled some stars like Elizabeth Taylor; the big event for me there was once having to go to a studio to pick up a huge paycheck for her. I then got a job as a grip at KLAC-TV, which led to working on the stage for some of their low-budget productions. I got restless there and ended up reading more scripts for the Dick Highland Agency. But while at Highland, I finally hit.

I sold a script to Allied Artists for $3,500, which was not bad at all. The story was mine and I had cowritten it with a friend. It was called "The House in the Sea" and Richard Conte had the lead. The title was changed at the last minute to *Highway Dragnet*—a way to exploit the title of the hit *Dragnet* TV series to help sell tickets. I quit my job, worked for nothing on the set, and ended up credited as writer and associate producer.

The story was a chase across the desert with an outlaw and a woman—very much like the one I had written in Paris. It had been inspired by a vacation I took at the Salton Sea south of Palm Springs, where beach houses along the banks were being swallowed up as the sea gradually swelled. I saw it as a great location for a climactic shootout of a gangster film—in a half-flooded house whose second story is just above the water level. I thought: *Now this is going to be great.*

I was horrified by what they did to *my* movie: my half-flooded house obviously stood on a soundstage with a rim of galvanized metal around the set—filled with about two inches of water. They wrecked my whole vision. My date at the sneak preview tried to cheer me up by whispering, "You must be really proud to have your name on such a fine film." I was saying to myself: What little chance I may have had to make it in this town has just been *destroyed.* What prospects I *did* have are completely shot. I have no job. My breakthrough film is an obvious *turkey.* I'm through.

Highway Dragnet actually did all right. What I learned from this first hands-on experience in filmmaking was that there are very few great successes or total failures. I also saw that there had been a certain amount of time wasted during production. I felt it could have been shot more efficiently.

I must have really been intent on making a movie at sea because my next idea came from an L.A. *Times* article about an electricity-powered one-man submarine that had just been tested. Sitting at breakfast, the idea hit me: Why not use this weird contraption in a film? I was a little nervous, but it never occurred to me that it couldn't be done. I just called up the firm that developed the sub, Aerojet General. I was put through to some executive and told him I was an independent producer with an idea for a movie with underwater sequences; if he would let me use his one-man sub for free I'd give the firm publicity and a credit in the film. I arranged a meeting some days later with the brass. I put on a coat and tie and played the producer bit to the hilt. I got to see the sub, which was far less imposing in person. The diver was not enclosed but needed scuba gear. But so what? They agreed to let me use it for nothing. We signed an agreement and I wrote an outline for a science fiction story, "It Stalked the Ocean Floor."

My tiny $25-a-month "production office" was actually an empty reception room for a secretary outside a larger office just over the Cock 'n' Bull Restaurant on Sunset. I hired a writer to work from my outline—for almost no money and a piece of the profits. We were on our way!

Then I started looking for backers. First I went to my parents, but they turned me down flat. "We've already put you through Stanford" was their answer. But I got my arguments down and sold $500 and $1,000 shares to a few friends from school. I had the $3,500 from *Highway Dragnet* plus some money from agenting and stagehand work. I figured I needed $12,000 and I was still about $2,000 short. Then I met a young acting student named Wyott "Barney" Ordung, who also had sold a script and wanted to direct.

"Well," I said, "I can't pay you anything now, but how much did you get for your screenplay?" I asked. Four thousand, Barney said.

"Fine," I said. "You put up the remaining two thousand and I'll let you direct for a piece of the picture." He agreed. This was great. I was beginning to feel like a producer.

People treated me very well. I had nothing working for me at all and I was about to do the film for $12,000 cash. Sid Solo, who was president of Consolidated Lab, told me it would cost about $5,000 to develop the black-and-white film and create the "answer," or final, print. He offered a $5,000 deferment—or credit. "You'll pay when the picture comes out," he said. Sid's generosity was instrumental in helping me get started.

The film—eventually released as *The Monster from the Ocean Floor*—was set somewhere off the coast of Mexico and had to do with a man-eating mutant created after atomic testing. In the story, local fishermen are disappearing. A Marine biologist, conducting research in his Aerojet General mini-sub, becomes curious. A pretty female tourist becomes involved. When the scientist learns she is in danger under water, he goes after the monster—an octopus with one blinking eye. For the climax, he mans the mini-sub and saves her by ramming it right into the monster's eyeball.

I had always read science fiction as a kid, and most of the low-budget films of the day were Westerns and mysteries. It was the dawn of the nuclear age, so I thought doing science fiction would add some excitement and novelty.

To budget out the picture I calculated minimum scale for the

Screen Actors Guild, the International Alliance of Theatrical Stage Employees crew, the film, equipment rental, editing, music, and the rest. But to do it for $12,000, Barney would have to shoot efficiently. We counted on using about one third of all the exposed film in the final cut, a very high ratio.

I signed with SAG and IATSE and did a full union picture on a six-day schedule with a skeleton crew—the minimum allowed by the IA. We shot all natural locations around Malibu. I scouted those myself and rented a beach house for a day of interiors.

I was probably the only grip/driver/producer in town. I would get up before sunrise, drive the equipment truck to Malibu, and unpack the truck myself. Because the crew was paid by the hour, I didn't want to run into overtime. I unloaded everything except the heaviest equipment, then set it in the sand so the crew could get to work immediately upon arriving. At the end of the day, the crew would load up all the biggest units and then go home; I would stay past dark and load the rest alone, then drive home.

There was tremendous excitement during the whole week, culminating with the wrap. I hired an underwater cameraman to go to Catalina for the underwater shots. The monster was actually a puppet shot from behind a cloudy fishtank. I certainly had no money for process shots, where the action is rear-projected onto a screen and the actors play to it on a stage.

The actors—Anne Kimball, Stuart Wade, a newcomer named Jonathan Haze, who would soon become part of my "ensemble" of cast and crew—were reasonably skilled. Haze had been pumping gas on Santa Monica Boulevard at night; Barney was a regular customer. As I heard it, Barney told him he could play a Mexican deep-sea diver if he grew a mustache. He did, and the station fired him. But I gave him the job.

When you make a picture as quickly and as raggedly as we made this one, things always go wrong. For instance, I helped build a camera platform so we could shoot from out in the ocean—then lugged it out into the surf. My director didn't want to help me. "I can't carry that platform," he said, "because I'm the director." I couldn't believe this. "Barney," I said, "I'm *the producer*. Just grab the other side." Barney let me know how he felt. He dropped his side. It fell and hit me.

The opening sequence is a pan of the deserted coastline with a narration setting the story "deep along the Yucatan Peninsula, where the mark of the white man has never been seen" or something like that. But at least one mark of the white man could be seen—the automotive mark, a flash of traffic along Pacific Coast Highway way up in the corner of the frame.

During the filming, a Teamsters rep came to the set and told me I had to sign a Teamsters contract. I said I did my own driving. "Look," he said, "I can see you got no money here for Teamsters. I'll let it go this time. But you make money off this picture, you'll do a second one. Then you come see me and we'll sign a contract."

It did make money. *Monster* was quite a successful venture. It was now distributed through the Lippert Releasing Company. My brother, Gene, was an agent and he knew Bob Lippert. We went with Lippert because he was the only one we met who offered me an advance—about $60,000—against his distribution income. This enabled me to cover my negative costs for *Monster*, immediately pay back the money I had borrowed, cover the deferments for lab costs, prints, and the composer, *and* have enough profit to go right into production on my next picture.

Realart had also wanted to distribute *Monster* but didn't offer an advance. Right away, I saw the trap in low-budget production. You put your money up, make your film, release it, and possibly wait a year for your money to come back, if it ever does. You're out of business for a year unless you have another source of income. I didn't, so I needed an advance—in this case, Lippert's—to go on to make a second feature, which I thought would cost $50,000.

It was Lippert who decided to change the title. He felt "It Stalked the Ocean Floor" was a bit too literary. The change may have helped. The picture earned enough at the box office to more than double the advance. All my investors and I made a substantial profit.

I went to see it with a girlfriend on Hollywood Boulevard. The picture was obviously cheaper than most but it was rather audacious and funny. The audience enjoyed it and actually *gasped* at the horror scenes. The film worked on a more significant level too. While we were out there every day around Malibu, I had discovered something that gave me real excitement. I loved every minute of it. I was definitely in my element. And so with my cash from Lippert, I went into production on *The Fast and the Furious*. This too was a gamble, since I had no distribution deal set. And I had no idea just how fast and furious my career was about to get.

Chapter 3

My career took a dramatic turn and picked up velocity with *The Fast and the Furious*. First, this was a considerably bigger, more intricate production. Second, I used the film to get a three-picture deal with a new independent production and distribution company—eventually called American International Pictures. That deal marked the beginning of a long, quite prosperous relationship stretching over fifteen years and thirty-plus films. And, third, I made the decision after *Fast and Furious* to direct films, not only for greater overall control but for the creative challenge.

As a novice producer/director I was quick to get my films in the can. By the end of 1955 I had shot two Westerns and a postnuclear

Top: Jonathan Haze and Dorothy Malone in *Five Guns West*
Bottom: Lori Nelson gets carried away in *The Day the World Ended*

drama and backed a $30,000 horror film called *The Beast with 1,000,000 Eyes*. And although these were different genres, I was beginning to develop what you might call a personal style.

For *The Fast and the Furious*, a race car drama, I hired established actors—John Ireland and Dorothy Malone—for less than their regular prices. Ireland originally rejected my offer, but like Barney, he had other goals. "Let me direct the film," he said, "and I'll play the lead for your price." Of course, I replied.

Again, I made a deal to get my main props for free. This time, they were Jaguar racing cars. We shot around Malibu and Point Dume in Southern California and up north around Carmel. The racing footage was shot at the Monterey race track, where the Jaguar Open Sports Car race was held. I was a big race car fan. The story resembled *Highway Dragnet* in some respects, with Ireland playing a truck driver who has escaped from prison after being wrongly convicted of murder. He commandeers a car in a cross-country road race that happens to belong to a beautiful woman racer played by Dorothy. She is barred from the race because she is a woman. They team up and follow the racing circuit to elude the police. They fall in love, and he proves his worth and decides to go back to prove his innocence. It's a story about two outsiders. Even then, I was attracted to stories about outcasts, misfits, or antiheroes on the run or on the fringe of society. That theme would recur time and again throughout my directing career.

John did a fine job of directing on a nine-day shoot with a budget of $50,000. It was quite a jump from the $12,000 for *Monster*, but I wanted to get into another class of film. Perhaps the most important point of the shoot for me occurred when we needed two cameras rolling for the racing scenes. I decided to get behind the camera and direct myself. I knew immediately that this was what I wanted to do.

I also went behind the wheel of the lead heavy's car and raced in the key action sequence. Because I couldn't afford two stunt drivers, John, who directed the long master shot, put our one driver in his own white Jag. Coming around the final turn neck and neck, knowing the other driver was supposed to surge ahead and win—I got carried away and beat him, ruining the first take. John ran to the track and said, "What the hell are you *doing* out there?" I said, "He wasn't going fast enough. I wasn't exactly going to *hit the brakes* and let him pass. This is a race track, not a county road. If I slow down that much, it looks bad."

John reminded the other driver, "You're trying to *beat* Roger. Get up some speed."

We got it right the second time and the white car overtook me and won. The truth was, I really just wanted to floor it and win. I hated to lose.

As a producer, I was on the fast track and didn't have to slow down for anyone. It took about six weeks to get an answer print. I got offers from Republic, Columbia, and Allied Artists to distribute the film with guarantees to get back my costs and possibly earn a profit. But I wanted to use this picture to set up a multipicture deal. Jim Nicholson, the sales manager for Realart, was setting up his own business. He knew Lippert had done well with *Monster.* I had several meetings with Jim and his partner, Samuel Z. Arkoff. Their new company was called American Releasing Corporation. Sam was an entertainment attorney who wanted to get into the distribution business. I told them I'd finance my own films but wanted to get back my negative costs—what it costs to make the movies—as soon as I finished each one. Essentially, I was asking for an advance upon turning over the negative so I could keep going. "This way," I said, "I can stay in production and have the financing for a series of films and you can get your new company started."

We agreed to do three pictures, the first of which would be *The Fast and the Furious.* But Jim had to sell the picture to subdistributors, or franchise holders, who were willing to advance money for the other films. So Jim, Sam, and I then flew to New Orleans, Chicago, and New York to arrange the backing from franchise holders. The West Coast was handled out of Los Angeles. Jim and Sam had a great deal. I was providing the movies as producer/director and the franchise holders advanced the money—about $5,000 to $15,000 per distributor per picture depending on the size of his territory. My deal was that Jim and Sam had to raise all the money from the subdistributors or it was no deal. The presentation to the franchise holders was simple: I screened *The Fast and the Furious* for them and told them that the two other films for American Releasing would be action movies. One would be a Western and at least one would be in color. There was a quality clause built in—the films had to reflect production value comparable to *Monster* or *Fast.*

I wasn't even thirty yet but these men were aware of the success I had had for Lippert with *Monster.* Some of them had even been involved in releasing it and were eager to continue the relationship with me. Everyone said yes except one subdistributor from Philadelphia. He stated flatly that he never gave advances. There were long, frustrating silences, so I finally spoke up. "Tell me," I said to him, "do you have any competition in your city?" The question seemed to make the others uncomfortable. "That's an unfair question," he answered.

"Sure, he's got competition," another one blurted out, "but you still shouldn't bring that up in this sort of deal."

"Well," I said, "since everyone else wants in except him, let's invite his competition to come in on it."

If he was bluffing to get our film without paying the advance, it failed. He backed down and Jim and Sam were in business with my three-picture deal. Jim was president, Sam the vice president. They soon changed their name to American International Pictures, or AIP, and AIP would grow to become the largest and most influential independent company in Hollywood through the 1950s and 1960s.

★ **SAM ARKOFF**

The early 1950s was the worst time for cinemas because of TV, the breakup of chains after the Consent Decree, and the fact that many of the old studio chiefs were dying or retired. Lots of exhibitors said there was no market for small pictures because TV would buy them up and show them to fill programming needs. Thousands of theaters went under—a downtime for the industry. That's exactly when we moved in.

Jim and I had a relationship with Roger that we've never had with anyone else. We shook hands when we made a deal and sometimes never had a written contract until after the picture was finished. Roger always delivered his films and we always paid him promptly. We had several different kinds of deals with him: sometimes he would direct for us for a fee plus participation; sometimes he would direct and produce and we would put up some of the backing for a piece of the profits. Or we would go to him with a project, a title, or just a poster—Jim was great at titles and campaigns—and Roger would come up with the story and direct it for a straight fee. The relationship was highly successful for all of us.

★ ★ ★

Before going ahead with my Pathécolor Western, *Five Guns West*, I decided I should have just a little practice at this new game, directing. I shot a one-day short subject. Chuck Hanawalt, my key grip, had a 16-millimeter camera and some lighting equipment; he was my director of photography. A friend of mine wrote a five-page script, I called some actor friends, and we all went down to the beach to shoot an eight-minute short. I shot it, but never edited it. Chuck and I looked at the footage we got that first day. "It doesn't look that good to me," I said. "I don't think we should bother to spend the money and finish it. Let's just say we both learned something out there and let it go at that."

That was the extent of my directorial training. But I had been on the lot at Fox and seen how it was done in the big time. I had seen my two little pictures being made. And I *did* set up a few shots that one day at the beach. I felt, I can do this. If a young man came to me today with similar credentials there's no way I'd hire him. I'd tell him to go out and get more training.

The truth is I was extremely nervous when I went out to shoot my first picture. The story for *Five Guns West* was mine, but the structure and screenplay were Bob Campbell's. I met Bob through Jackie Haze. Our collaboration became a model for countless future films: We discussed my idea and built a story structure. He wrote, we honed it together, and then I directed from the screenplay. I gave myself a nine-day shooting schedule and a $60,000 budget for *Five Guns West.*

This was a Civil War–era Western about five violent criminals who are pardoned and sent on a dangerous mission for the Confederate Army: Sworn in as soldiers, they go through Indian Territory to intercept a stagecoach and capture a Confederate traitor naming spies while in Union custody.

It was an unusual idea for a Western and a variant of the "outsider" theme: hardened criminals given a chance to redeem themselves. The budget also dictated that I shoot a picture with only a few people in it. This kind of "contained situation" is a key to low-budget filmmaking. Films about, say, the opening of the Oklahoma Land Rush don't get made on $60,000 budgets.

I only had the five men plus a few minor speaking parts. I was signed with SAG and always paid scale, unless I could go a little higher or throw in a modest profit participation. I offered John Lund and Dorothy Malone as much as I could afford and hired a young, rugged newcomer named Touch Connors. He later changed his name to Mike and became a TV star on *Mannix.*

I went to a stock footage library and bought what I needed for the Indian scenes. An audience sees a shot of Indians riding on horseback through the dust—who knows what film that actually came from? A soldier looks through binoculars from a hilltop—then I cut to the stock shot of five hundred Indians racing by on horseback. "Okay, fellas," he says, "the Indians are over here. Let's head over *there!*" That was by far the cheapest way for them to travel through Indian territory.

Five Guns West was a breakthrough for me. With almost no training or preparation whatsoever, I was literally learning how to direct motion pictures on the job. It took me four or five of these "training films" to learn what a film school student knows when he graduates. But while the mistakes *they* make in student films are usually lost forever, *mine* were immortalized.

I also learned how much control a director has over his film. Clearly, it seemed, a producer is in charge during pre- and postproduction. But a producer surrenders control to the director during the actual shoot. The work by the directors on the two films I had produced was acceptable. But I thought: I can do better, more efficient work; I can make better films.

Perhaps because a producer/director is in charge of both the financial and artistic aspects of a project, I knew I had to prepare carefully and was quick to see the importance of sketching each shot. I worked with both my director of photography, Floyd Crosby, a brilliant, Oscar-winning cinematographer, and my art director Ben Hayne, a Western folklore buff. Ben helped enormously with sketching—an absolute must. Directors with an art background often storyboard their shots as if through the camera—like crude cartoon panels. Or they can sketch them like a football coach's diagrams from an overhead angle. Trained as an engineer, I felt more at home with the overhead angle. I used a V to mark camera placement and drew arrows for the actors and camera moves.

I was nervous, but I never doubted that I could pull it off. The film was almost all exteriors and I decided to shoot in the parched, rocky terrain at Iverson's Ranch, on the far edge of the San Fernando Valley near Chatsworth. It was a popular Western setting, open to the sun, with a big sky and dramatic cloud formations. I was also planning to shoot at Ingram's Ranch, owned by cowboy actor Jack Ingram, because he had built a Western town there.

I had planned everything. Then I awoke on the first day of shooting and drove to the location through an incredible torrent of rain. This wasn't *possible.* My *first day!* I hadn't even started and I was already *behind schedule!* I got so worked up and tense that I pulled off the road and threw up. Then I just leaned against my car in the rain and pulled myself together. I made it to Iverson's and after about an hour's wait the rain stopped.

Actually, the opening shot was quite beautiful. We had great dark rain clouds with the sun just starting to shine through as the criminals were gathering on a hillside to be sworn in. It was the kind of shot you wait for on a big-budget picture: black sky with a little blue showing up, the shafts of sunlight piercing the darkness. I started with a wide pan of the horizon, then tilted down slowly to Iverson's, where sunlight was hitting patches of the ranch. You seldom get that lucky on a nine-day shoot because you don't wait for light. A good omen, I hoped.

I used a Mitchell 35-millimeter camera, the industry standard then, and shot in Eastmancolor. We worked ten-hour days. I moved around the set quite rapidly from the very beginning and the crew seemed to enjoy the pace. I picked up the camera movements and placements very fast. I had been in the editing room for the two prior films and just had a feel for working with the camera. Because I didn't know much at all about acting, I was not as comfortable working with the actors.

I learned to react decisively when circumstances like weather imposed script or schedule changes. I tended to move the camera quite a lot right from the beginning. And I tried, whenever possible, to frame shots with an interesting depth of field—placing objects or staging action from the foreground through the middle distances and out to the background. The elements of an individual style were taking shape—thorough preparation, a quick, disciplined pace on the set, a moving camera, dense composition.

★ MIKE CONNORS

Roger was one of the few people around who gave inexperienced actors a chance. I got, I think, $400. But just working was a great thrill. Roger had real nervous energy and a very analytical mind. He didn't waste time going for extra coverage or needless takes. Even then, he was a great razzle-dazzle man in getting the most on the screen for the least amount of money. Roger knew exactly what he needed and what he could get away with. That put some pressure on us as actors because we always felt we'd like another chance to run through something. Roger did not sit around discussing characters and delving beneath their surface. This wasn't *Gone With the Wind*. With Roger, it was: "This is your character, here are your lines. He's the good guy and you're the heavy, so be a heavy."

After my fourth film for Roger, I decided I deserved a little raise. So I called him and we agreed to meet. I figured we'd have a nice lunch at the Cock 'n' Bull. But he took me instead across Sunset to a drugstore and we sat on stools at the counter and ordered sandwiches. I told him that I'd done a few pictures with him, that I was married, that $400 for a week and a half wasn't that much money and that I wanted a raise.

He paused and said, "Here's what I'll do. I'm going to give you twelve hundred dollars." This was too good to be true. Then he said, "For three pictures."

"But Roger," I said, "that's still four hundred a picture."

"I know," he answered, "but at least you're guaranteed three more pictures."

That was no raise. I never did the films. And yet the work with Roger was great preparation for the grueling pace and grind of TV work I did on *Mannix* and other shows. When people were going absolutely crazy with the speed and pressure of a hit series—not understanding how they could continue after five, six shows in a row—and were ready for nervous breakdowns, I did not see that anything was so unusual because my upbringing with Roger was: "Let's get it done, bang-bang-bang, move to the next shot."

★   ★   ★

Once I started making films for Jim and Sam, I was continually employed, working in preproduction, production, or postproduction on two or more films at once. The pace never let up. Before *Five Guns West* came out, for example, I was already involved with *Apache Woman*, a Western they created and asked me to produce and direct from a completed script. It cost a little under $80,000. Both pictures were shot in color in under two weeks and both went into profits.

I was always politically liberal and I tried, even on my earliest films, to work in some of my beliefs. *Apache Woman* was a good action script written by Lou Rusoff to which I added a subplot dealing with prejudice against another kind of outcast, the so-called half-breed trapped between white and Indian cultures. A government agent, played by Lloyd Bridges, goes to the Apache reservation to investigate a series of violent crimes the whites believe have been committed by usually peaceful Apaches. He falls in love with a half-breed woman. It turns out her alienated brother has been posing as an Apache and leading the crime wave.

★   DICK MILLER

I came West from New York to be a writer. I beached it for a year and a half before anything happened—sold short stories, did one-page outlines for a science fiction anthology, partied. Then my New York buddy Jonathan Haze told me he had just done his first picture—an undersea monster flick—with a guy named Corman. So he brought me to Roger's office over the Cock 'n' Bull. And the conversation went something like this:

"What do you do?"

"I'm a writer. Need any scripts?"

"No, I've got scripts. I need actors."

"Fine, I'm an actor." That's exactly how it went. "Okay," he said. "I'll put you in a picture and you'll play an Indian in *Apache Woman*."

I didn't even use nose plugs, which was how they usually made you up as an Indian, to spread the nostrils. I just had dark makeup. After a week, Roger asked, "You want to play a cowboy?"

"Sure, great. You doing another picture?"

"No," he said. "Same picture." So I played a cowboy and Indian in

the same movie and just about shot myself in the end because I was part of the posse that was sent out to shoot my Indian. Everybody doubled for Roger's pictures.

★   ★   ★

My next picture was a science fiction story, *The Day the World Ended*, which AIP released at the very end of 1955. Like *Five Guns* and *Beast*, this was an idea reworked to fit a low budget. Lou Rusoff again wrote the script. It's 1970, Total Destruction Day, and only seven human beings have survived a nuclear holocaust. They find refuge in an isolated house in a valley where the surrounding mountains and winds have shielded them from radiation. Every other living thing in the woods is a radioactive mutant. Again, I tried to make it something of a psychological study of a small group of people thrown together under unusual circumstances.

The "valley" was Bronson Canyon near Griffith Park, which became another favorite location because of the caves. The mountain lake in the film was actually the small lagoonlike pond behind the Sportsman's Lodge Restaurant on Ventura Boulevard in the Valley. It was surrounded by trees and stocked with fish. We were allowed to film there only because the restaurant didn't serve lunch, but I had to promise to clear out before dinner.

AIP released the film as the top half of a double feature with *The Phantom from 10,000 Leagues*. They had been getting rather modest rentals for their previous films. With this double bill experiment, exhibitors agreed to give them the same rental figure as they paid major studios. This pioneering strategy—two low-budget films from the same genre on a double bill—was designed in large part to lure teenagers and young adults to drive-ins. It became a standard AIP approach once it proved to be commercially profitable.

The Day the World Ended was a successful experiment for me as well. It established me as a director in the science fiction genre, and its success positioned me quite favorably as a major supplier of much-needed product for AIP when it began its growth as an independent power. The next couple of years promised to be rather busy.

Chapter 4

The beauty of mastering low-budget filmmaking techniques for the "exploitation" market of the 1950s was that the films cut across such a broad and amusing spectrum of themes. It was never dull, particularly when in a two-year period, 1956–57, I produced and directed a dozen films. The whole idea was to tell an interesting, visually entertaining story that would draw young people to the drive-ins and hardtop cinemas, and not take yourself too seriously along the way.

By any standards those years were quite successful. I not only saturated the exploitation market with pictures costing under $100,000; the variety of subjects they covered allowed me to

Top to bottom: Don Durant, Bill Cord, Lisa Montell, and
Jeanne Gerson (left to right) in *She Gods of Shark Reef*; Susan Cabot (standing)
and Barboura O'Neill in *Sorority Girl*; Beverly Garland and Beulah from
It Conquered the World; Paul Birch in *Not of This Earth*

expand and refine my filmmaking. I tried mixing humor with horror and found audiences were receptive; I began studying acting to sharpen my work with actors; and I opened up the look of my films when I began using special—if rather crude—effects and found exotic locations like Louisiana bayou and Hawaiian lava.

"Exploitation" films were so named because you made a film about something wild with a great deal of action, a little sex, and possibly some sort of strange gimmick; they often came out of the day's headlines. It's interesting how, decades later, when the majors saw they could have enormous commercial success with *big-budget* exploitation films, they gave them loftier terms—"genre" films or "high concept" films.

Several of those films had strong, assertive women leads. I do believe in the feminist movement, but I can take only partial credit for the themes here. Of the four Westerns I directed, two of the titles were suggested by AIP: *Apache Woman* and *Oklahoma Woman.* The two titles I picked myself were *Five Guns West* and *Gunslinger.* We obviously had different notions of what a Western should be about.

Oklahoma Woman ran seventy-one minutes in Superscope black and white and cost about $60,000. I tried to create a bigger look than the budget might indicate and save time and money in the process. I experimented, for example, with shooting consecutively all the components of multiple scenes that faced in one direction in the saloon, though they were, obviously, way out of sequence. I could light one time for many setups. Then I reversed the angle and shot the components of multiple scenes that faced in the opposite direction. I found that to be, perhaps, an *overly* efficient way to work. Matching backgrounds and wardrobe—which I did from memory in the pre-Polaroid days—is much easier than ripping down all your lighting and relighting. But it was too difficult for the actors and since then I've tended to shoot more in sequence.

★   CHUCK GRIFFITH

The first script Mark Hanna and I wrote for Roger was "Three Bright Banners." The second was "Hangtown." Neither got made, but at least a struggling, unsold writer could get his work to Roger when you couldn't get it to anyone else in town.

Finally, Roger suggested a Western in which a sheriff dies trying to clean up a town and his widow carries out his work. That became *Gunslinger,* the first of many pictures I wrote for Roger.

★   ★   ★

Gunslinger was made around February 1956, just as IATSE and the studios renegotiated for a five-day work week instead of six. So I decided to squeeze in one last low-budget, six-day Western before the new contract went into effect. My brother put up half the financing. It rained five days out of six and it was the only time I ever went over schedule—I took seven days. Trucks, heavy cameras, and lights sank in the knee-high mud. It was one of the worst experiences of my life. This picture should have been retitled *Mudslinger*. I stretched a tarp over a makeshift stand and shot the actors beneath it, with rain in the background. We had to park outside the ranch and hike in. We left the equipment in the trucks down at the locations and didn't even bother to hire a guard. "Forget it," I told the assistant director. "Anyone who'd come out here, steal the equipment, and carry it through this mud to get it out is welcome to it."

Whenever the sun broke through, I stopped whatever I was shooting and raced to set up some long shots from my list of priority exterior shots. The rain forced me to shoot almost everything in close-ups or medium close-ups. We rewrote exterior scenes for the interiors of the ranch's buildings. So much rain fell on the rooftops and tarps that I had to dub in music and effects on the sound track to cover it up.

The shoot was rough on everyone. Allison Hayes, a very witty, humorous actress, came up with the best line of all. "Tell me, Roger," she said, soaking wet and cold, "who do I have to fuck to get off this picture?" Allison actually found another way out. Her horse slipped in the mud and she fell off and broke her arm. While we waited for a car to get down through the mud and take her to a hospital, I shot a reel of close-ups of Allison looking left, looking right, and so on. Allison understood what I was doing and cooperated completely. I'd have to finish her scenes with a double and this was my only chance to get some close-ups of her. I'd figure out later how to cut them in. For once the cast party at the end of the film was just that: We all autographed Allison's cast.

★ **BEVERLY GARLAND**

I always wondered if Allison broke her arm just to get off the picture and out of the rain. It poured constantly. But what I adored about Roger was he never said, "This can't be done." Pouring rain, trudging through the mud and heat, getting ptomaine poisoning, sick as a dog—didn't matter. Never say die. Never say can't. Never say quit. I learned to be a trooper with Roger. I could kid him sarcastically about these conditions and laugh. That's why we got along so well.

On *Gunslinger*, I was supposed to run down the saloon stairs, jump on my horse and ride out of town. Now we never had stunt people in low-budget films. Riding, stunts, fights—we all did it ourselves and we all expected it, and we all just said it was marvelously grand. I told myself just to *think tall.* So my first take I thought tall and sailed right over the saddle and landed on the other side of the horse. The second take I twisted my ankle running down the stairs—a bad twist. I finished my scenes for the day and went home and soaked my ankle in hot water, which is the wrong thing to do.

The next day I had my big saloon brawl scene with Allison Hayes and my ankle was swollen as big as my head. So I told Roger, "I can't even get my boots and pants on, no way I can do the barroom brawl." He said, "Oh, sure there is." And I laughed and said, "I'm sure you will find a way." He did—a doctor with this huge needle loaded with four shots of Novocain. Gee, my leg started to feel great. They then ripped the pants up the calf and taped the back, ripped open the back of the boot, taped the back of the boot and I worked all day and did all the fights and it was great. It didn't feel so great that night, but I was better in the morning and we finished the picture right on time. With Roger, you never felt you couldn't do good work. You sensed there was a high-energy, restless, mad genius at work out there when he was making his movie.

★   ★   ★

My work in low-budget exploitation films would eventually earn me some notoriety as "The King of the B's," which is ironic, since, to my way of thinking, I never made a "B" movie in my life. The B movie dated from the Depression and was a phenomenon only up through the early 1950s. In the 1930s, when attendance began to drop, the studios lured audiences into theaters with two-for-one double bills. The "A" movies featured stars like Clark Gable; B's were made quite fast and inexpensively with either new contract players seeking to rise to the A's or fading older stars. The B's were also a minor league for untested writers, directors, and producers and there was no shame or stigma attached to B moviemaking.

Everyone knew which movies were which; the studio publicity and production lists openly distinguished A's from B's. Also, B movies earned only flat rentals on the second half of a double bill. Because of TV, the Consent Decree, and the public's preference for more expensive color films, the B's had died out by the time I began directing. The term was never used in connection with any of my films within the industry, where the precise meaning of the term was always known. And yet, it caught on through the media. I remember seeing a 1975 *New York Times Magazine* article on me. The writer went on about the B pictures I had made. I never finished reading it. The only thing worse than being pigeon-holed is being wrongly pigeon-holed.

After outlaws, I did two films about aliens—*Not of This Earth* and *It Conquered the World.* Both were shot in black and white in two weeks for well under $100,000 each. Most major studio productions in black and white were roughly in the $1 million to $2 million range. AIP wanted me to keep making these films so they could book their double bills from the same genre. Traditionally, the A and B features were from different genres to offer crossover appeal to a larger, blended audience. Jim Nicholson was coming up with statistics showing we could outgross major studios by luring audiences with, say, an ad or poster reading GIANT ALL SCIENCE FICTION DOUBLE BILL.

With *Not of This Earth* I tried for the first time to have some fun with a suspense film. It was written by Chuck Griffith and Mark Hanna. A humanoid has dropped down from the planet Davanna possessed not only of superior intelligence but a dark suit and dark glasses. Behind the glasses were blank white eyeballs that burn holes in humans. His name is Paul Johnson. His entire planet is getting wiped out by a blood disease and he has come here to send back, more or less telepathically, human blood samples. It was a wild story line and the film caught on right away. Throwing in some tongue-in-cheek humor paid off: the picture took in close to $1 million in rentals. It was a definite turning point because it proved that mixing in some offbeat humor only increased the appeal of science fiction.

★ **DICK MILLER**

I played Joe Piper, the vacuum cleaner salesman who talks his way into Johnson's house. Roger thought Piper would wear a suit and bow tie and have a pocket full of pencils and say politely, "Good afternoon, sir, may I see the man of the house?" So I show up in a black cashmere jacket and a black shirt and Roger is still unsure of the image. He says, "You're not dressed." I say, "Hey, look, this is the way I dressed when I sold pots and pans in the Bronx for two weeks, let me dress this way. You think a guy goes to college to sell vacuums? If it doesn't work I'll go home on my lunch break and get other clothes."

I did the scene as a real hippie-dippy street kid with lines I ad-libbed as I went. "Hey, man, you wanna purchase, you purchase, you don't wanna purchase, you don't purchase. Look, here she is, the sweetheart of the industry." Johnson asks me in and I say, "Crazy, man," and I'm setting up the vacuum and singing and doing a Jackie Gleason and I look up at the humanoid, I see him, I do a "skull"—a hard, terrified stare—and he burns me and I'm dead.

★ ★ ★

I approached *Conquered* with the same loose spirit as *Not of This Earth*. Lee Van Cleef is a scientist trying to communicate with intelligent forces from the planet Venus. Beverly Garland, as his wife, questions the entire project with some very funny dialogue written by Lou Rusoff and Chuck Griffith.

Before shooting, Beverly ad-libbed a few sharp lines of her own. From my engineering and physics background, I'd reasoned that a being from a planet with a powerful field of gravity would sit very low to the ground. So with my effects man, Paul Blaisdell, I'd designed a rather squat creature. But just before we were to shoot the climactic showdown with Beverly and the monster, she stood over it and stared it down, hands on her hips. "So," she said with a derisive snarl, making sure I heard her, "you've come to conquer the world, have you? Well, take *that!*" And she kicked the monster in the head.

I got the point immediately. By that afternoon the monster was rebuilt ten feet high. Lesson one: Always make the monster bigger than your leading lady.

From outer space, I went back underwater for *Attack of the Crab Monsters,* which I did for Allied Artists from a script by Chuck Griffith. A team of scientists goes to a remote island in the Pacific to search for a lost expedition of colleagues. Giant crabs—again the mutant result of nuclear-test radiation—have been devouring human researchers and absorbing their intelligence in the process. In previous movies I had killed monsters with a mini-sub, floods, and fire. This time, electricity.

The crab was built by a Hollywood special effects firm and looked quite realistic. It stretched about fifteen feet and was held together with wires. Ed Nelson, who went on to star in TV's *Peyton Place,* made his acting debut inside the monster. He also played a Naval officer. He operated the monster from inside while my key grip, Chuck Hanawalt, and other crew members held up support poles. We shot at the very picturesque Leo Carrillo State Beach, where the rocks come down right into the ocean.

★ **BEACH DICKERSON**

I got the part of a scientist who comes ashore and the crab eats me. I also played the crab along with Ed Nelson. You never played just one role in a Roger movie. They brought this big crab out there and I asked,"How's it going to work?" And no one knew how this crab was supposed to work. It was made of papier mâché. We got some piano wire to help move the claws. I said, "Well, someone's got to get inside the fucking thing and lift it up and you need two people in there." Ed and I figured out that if we got inside, bumped asses, and locked arms at the elbows, I could pull him north, he could pull me south, I could pull him east, he could pull me west.

★ CHUCK GRIFFITH

When Roger first told me he wanted this crab picture, he said, "I want suspense or action in every single scene. Audiences must feel something could happen at any time." So I put suspense and action in every scene. Usually, I'd do a draft in two, three weeks, with very little discussion with Roger. Then he'd take my first draft and say, "Let's tighten it up a little." So I'd make a few changes and type it over with wider margins. That gave me a lower page count and Roger was happy.

I had recently seen Jacques Cousteau's first picture and loved it. I went to Roger and said, "Hey, I'll direct the underwater stuff for a hundred dollars." He grabbed the bargain. It didn't occur to Roger that I didn't know anything about diving or directing. Weeks later—I think he went to Hawaii and shot two *other pictures*—he called and said the actors were going to my place to learn how to dive. Not from *me* they weren't.

So I immediately called Haze, who was bringing the gear. He knew how to dive. I said, "Get here first, before the others. Teach me to dive." We went to an Olympic pool in a downtown hotel and he taught me, then taught them. The shoot in Marineland, the first time I directed, was horrendous and chaotic. We used a papier mâché crab on an aluminum frame, with Styrofoam stuffing inside. The only problem was the crab wouldn't sink. It floated. As Roger watched, we had to keep loading rocks, cast-iron weights, and people on this crab just to get it to stay underwater.

★   ★   ★

That $70,000 picture took in over $1 million and confirmed again that humor and horror were a successful formula. I was making so many pictures—shooting, editing, planning, overlapping projects all at once—that vacations were out of the question. So I did the next best thing: I set up a pair of deals that got me to Hawaii for about a month, where I did a pair of two-week shoots. One was for a lawyer named Ludwig Gerber, who approached me with a script he wanted to produce. It was set in the South Pacific.

When I mentioned this project to Jim and Sam at AIP, they asked me to do another picture for them. "We'll divide the costs with the other people and everybody'll pay half," they said. "You'll be there four weeks, do both pictures, and the transportation and equipment and costs will be halved for each production."

"No problem," I said and off we went.

I started Ludwig's picture, *Shark Reef*, on a Monday and finished two Saturdays later. I took Sunday off and started *Thunder Over Hawaii* on Monday, wrapping that one two Saturdays later. The AIP shoot was distinguished mostly by the fact that Jim and Sam brought their families over for a vacation and I put Sam in the film as a wealthy, cigar-puffing plantation owner in a Hawaiian shirt who speaks one line.

Of the two, the AIP story was more of a conventional South Pacific adventure plot. Richard Denning plays the captain of a yacht that has, unknown to him, been chartered by a gang of thugs who have robbed local plantation owners and stuffed cash in hollowed-out pineapples. Beverly Garland is the assistant working for the gang boss and his two henchmen are played by Dick Miller and Jackie Haze. They did some very funny scenes together.

We all stayed at the Cocoa Palms Hotel on the island of Kauai, which is probably the most spectacular of the Hawaiian islands. I always had on hand an airline pilot's handbook for weather patterns in every area of the world and I never shot on location without first consulting it. This book has saved me many times. I knew the rainy season was still a month away so I gave myself a couple weeks leeway for protection. Just a month after production, another producer complained to me that the sets on Kauai for his much bigger United Artists production got washed away in torrential rains. "You sure were lucky," he told me. "We went $500,000 over budget and we heard you just finished in Kauai and had perfect weather." I didn't have the heart to tell him.

But two decades later I did have the heart to tell an old friend of mine, Francis Coppola, not to go to the Philippines to shoot *Apocalypse Now*. He called me in April. "I know you've been shooting your films in that area," he said. "I'm leaving in two weeks. What advice can you give me?"

"My advice, Francis, is don't go."

"We've been in preproduction for months."

"You're going straight into the rainy season—May through November. Nobody shoots there that time of year."

"It's too late to change. It'll be a rainy picture." He went and an entire set was washed out.

I did the two Hawaiian pictures for less than $100,000 each. Like Aerojet and Jaguar, the Cocoa Palms offered me a tremendous break on the room rates if I credited the hotel in the film. Naturally, I agreed.

The exotic settings—mountains, volcanoes, sugarcane fields, the ocean, expanses of tropical lushness—provided some great-looking backgrounds in Pathécolor. But not without some challenges.

We needed a big fire scene. Sugarcane growers regularly set fire to their fields to burn off the stalks and thorns and force the sap up into the cane. I scheduled my shoot around that fire and got some spectacular shots I'd never have gotten for a $100,000 film.

Also, I died on-screen in *Thunder*. I play a plantation administrator in a Hawaiian shirt who gets fatally stabbed behind his desk when Haze robs the office safe. On a distant location you can't afford to fly actors from Hollywood for every small part, so members of the crew and I often played the bit roles.

★ SAM ARKOFF

I remember thinking to myself: We could probably make this movie just as cheap or cheaper in Catalina. But shooting in Hawaii seemed intriguing. So Jim and I brought our wives and kids down. Then Roger invites us to the location so he can use us as extras. He says he has a line of dialogue for me and I say, "I can't do it. I've never been in a picture in my life." You don't argue with Roger. I still remember my one line: "It's been a good crop this year; the money is in the safe." Which is a key line because the villains later come in and rob the safe—and kill Roger in the process. And I was never asked to be in a scene by anybody ever again.

Roger was a handsome, affable bachelor in those days, and he was going with Beverly Garland. Filmmaking was his one interest but he obviously had other urges. Still, he seemed to always go out with girls he worked with. He had a head start that way—didn't have to waste time wooing and looking around. We flew to Kauai with Beverly—she was only in the second movie—and she was really looking forward to being with Roger in this idyllic setting. But once he was on a picture, especially as producer/director, he was all work, no play. Worked every night after the day's shoot, preparing and cleaning up problems. My recollection is that his time with Beverly was extremely limited. Roger, when he did a picture, was a man bewitched.

★ BEVERLY GARLAND

Roger was—is—very shy, intense, with a fascinating, computerized mind. I adored that in him. You had to be a very bright lady to be around Roger. And he was not comfortable around a lot of people. I was fascinated with him. He adored that I was mentally able to keep up, that I was fast and witty. Nothing ever came of that, though. We'd have dinner, go bicycling. I helped him look for an apartment. The reason that it never became a romance is that I also needed something else. There was a puritanical side to him, almost like a Boy Scout. I didn't want a

Boy Scout. Roger debonair? No. Not an Omar Sharif type. He was happiest when he was wheeling and dealing.

* * *

AIP started turning out films for teenagers with both escapist and topical themes. The spreading popularity of the drive-ins helped open a new film market for rebellious youth. For years the studios either didn't notice or didn't care that TV had altered moviegoing patterns. But Jim Nicholson saw the movie audience shifting to young people primarily from thirteen to about thirty years old with a heavy emphasis on teens and early twenties. I never knew why it took the majors at least fifteen years to capitalize on summer releases geared to the youth market. But Jim and Sam had that figured out.

In that vein, in 1957 I directed *Rock All Night* and *Sorority Girl* for AIP, *Carnival Rock* for Howco International, and *Teenage Doll* for Allied—all in black and white and running between sixty and seventy-five minutes. *Teenage Doll* was produced by Bernie Woolner, who owned a string of drive-ins throughout Louisiana, and released by Allied Artists. Bernie had the idea and Chuck Griffith wrote the script—a juvenile delinquent story about a girl-gang member who kills another girl during a rumble with a rival gang. She is then tracked by the dead girl's vengeful gang.

I had one of my first location hassles doing *Teenage Doll*. An older woman lived next door to the house where I was shooting for a night sequence in West Hollywood. To squeeze some money from us, she turned on her sprinklers. She demanded a payment to shut them off, plus an agreement to compensate her for any damage done to her lawn by *not* having them on.

My a.d. delivered my answer to her: I would be willing to pay for the water if she kept the sprinklers going *all night long*, since I now saw that it added a lovely visual effect in the background. But I would need the sprinklers running through the night to shoot coverage and get multiple cuts. She slammed the door on my a.d. and shut the water off, figuring I now wanted them *on*. So I got my shoot without the sprinklers.

Susan Cabot, a very talented, stunning brunette, became another fine actress in my ensemble of regular players. Having played the singer in the love triangle for *Carnival Rock*, I hired her for the lead in *Sorority Girl* when the company decided they wanted a campus exploitation picture. Susan had trained as a Method actress. There was one important scene at home with her mother. I got a fine long shot of the two women. But when I came in for a close-up, Susan's inner emotions were spent, she said. She had not paced herself correctly and fell flat when I needed a strong moment from her.

That shoot left me thinking that if I really wanted to improve as a director I would have to learn more about actors and their process. And so immediately after *Sorority Girl* I enrolled in classes with the great acting coach Jeff Corey. I had asked Jeff if I could just come in and observe. Jeff didn't go along with the concept of observing and welcomed me only if I participated. He was quite correct. I met and worked with some fine talents. I first met Jack Nicholson there and I would soon be using Jack in some of my films. I also met Robert Towne, before his screenwriter/director days. I went to weekly classes for a couple of years and the class proved to be invaluable training for me.

Just around the time of *Rock Around the Clock* AIP wanted to jump on a trend. And I had wanted to do a rock and roll picture. In fact, they wanted to jump so fast they gave me no time to develop a script. But I had recently been impressed by a half-hour TV drama set in a bar called *The Little Guy.* I thought we could change the bar to a rock and roll club and add music. So I bought the rights to the show and hired Chuck Griffith to rewrite and expand it, using the story, the structure, and some dialogue.

The result was *Rock All Night,* another contained drama set almost entirely in a rock club called Al's Place. It was a seven-day shoot but it became rather complicated. AIP had signed the Platters to sing as well as appear throughout the story. But because of a scheduling error, they were on tour and couldn't come to Hollywood. So we had to furiously rewrite without them, shoot the rest of the film, and wait until the Platters were available for one section of the story. I finally got them for a day in a studio and they lip-synched two of their songs.

Dick Miller was cast as Shorty, a wisecracking misfit who insults and disarms the killer who has taken the patrons at the club hostage. He also gets the girl in the end—an insecure young singer played by Abby Dalton—and takes her to see his favorite movie, *King Kong.* This was the typical "Little Guy" theme that recurs in many of my films. As with *Day the World Ended,* this was a chance to explore the psychological tensions among different kinds of people thrown together under peculiar circumstances.

To get the film shot within a week, I'd go all day with just the lunch break, then shoot till dinner time. Then after a bite to eat, I'd work on the next day's shots and production problems, get a few hours' sleep and begin again the next day. Paul Blaisdell once said I worked like a stevedore.

It's true that the David Leans of this world do make magnificent films when they spend eight or ten months shooting them. A fine young director friend of mine once related how he visited a Paramount set where Billy Wilder was shooting a big-budget film with Jack Lemmon. He wandered over to watch one of the masters at work. At lunch, back on his own set, someone asked what he had seen them doing. And he said, "They spent the morning lighting a close-up on Lemmon."

I worked quickly to capitalize on the public's brief fascination with reincarnation in the mid-1950s as exemplified in the best-seller titled *The Search for Bridey Murphy.* Chuck Griffith wrote a script entitled "The Trance of Diana Love" but the fad passed and we released it as *The Undead.* Pamela Duncan starred as a girl recruited by a psychologist for past-life research. Under hypnosis, Diana relived her life as the witch Helene, who was guillotined in the Middle Ages.

We were on a small soundstage built in an abandoned supermarket on Sunset. The film cost about $75,000 and it was a fun shoot. We achieved some nice period effects. I used one exterior, a wonderful 1930s house in Beverly Hills known as the Witch's Cottage, and carefully framed the shots to keep from getting neighboring homes in the movie. To bring off the medieval effects, we built the interiors on the stage, moved in lots of trees, shoveled dirt on the concrete floor, blew fog into the background, and rented our set dressings, props, and wardrobe from the rental houses that also equipped the major pictures. One of the actors showed me a label inside his shirt that read TYRONE POWER.

★ MEL WELLES

This was a medieval spook picture requiring lots of fog blowing. The fog was done with creosote oil, so we were always choking and being asphyxiated. The creosote fog caused an oil slick on the concrete floor and my gravedigger's horse would slip. So instead of moving me, they blew the fog past me.

Roger was amazing then. No one else was shooting that quickly or that often. In spite of the shortcomings and short tempers involved in trying to shoot a movie in a quarter of an hour, Roger was a driven, committed filmmaker. He was also very decisive whenever things fuzzed. He knew how to focus and forward the action when there wasn't time for subtleties, courtesy, politeness, and innuendo. And the funk that came from doing a lot in a very brief time is something that's never been repeated.

★   ★   ★

In the first half of 1957 I capitalized on the sensational headlines following the Russians' launch of their Sputnik satellite. Jack Rabin, a special effects expert who had his own firm, came to me with a Sputnik-inspired story idea for which he would develop the effects. This sounded good, so I promptly called the head of Allied Artists and told him I could do a ten-day picture about satellites, cut it in four weeks, and have it on screens in two or three months. He said fine, do it. He didn't even ask me what the story was; it was just as well, since I didn't *have* one yet.

I pieced one together from the idea by Jack and his partner, Irving "Fritz" Block: Hostile alien forces send dire warnings to earth to stop all space exploration. I commissioned a script and went into pre-production with the first draft, all within two weeks.

I shot *War of the Satellites* in a little under ten days. No one even knew what the satellite was supposed to look like. It was whatever I said it should look like.

From up-to-the-minute headlines I traveled back to the ninth century to direct *The Viking Women and the Sea Serpent,* which I shot and produced for AIP toward the end of that hectic year. This overly ambitious, Norse adventure story was shot before a title was set. AIP had been going with short catchy titles for its films, but no one could summarize the complicated plot in a few words so I went the other way. I came up with *The Saga of the Viking Women and Their Voyage to the Waters of the Great Sea Serpent.*

I did learn an important lesson from this movie: Don't fall for a sophisticated sales job about elaborate special effects. I was presented with the idea by the Rabin-Block team of effects and matte experts. They had acquired Louis Goldman's script and wanted to do the effects. The story told the wild adventures of some Viking women who set sail to find their long-lost men who have disappeared at sea while fighting the dread Monster of the Vortex.

The presentation, with the paintings prepared by these two men, was breathtaking. Their pictures were beautiful, absolutely wonderful. The script was not especially great, but they forged ahead. "Give us a piece of the profits," they said, "and a small amount of money to create the effects and we'll do magnificent work."

I told Jim and Sam that I was a little worried about putting my money into it, but I said I would make the film if they backed it. They saw the presentation, which made this look like a $2 million picture. Jim and Sam discussed a $70,000 or $80,000 budget. We should have known better.

I shot it in ten days, with most of the rugged Nordic exteriors done at Iverson's Ranch and Bronson Canyon. It turned into an insanely difficult shoot. At Iverson's I hit my all-time record for most camera setups in a day—seventy-seven. I was just going like crazy. Even so, the picture was too big for ten days. A contained story line—a *Five Guns West* or a *Rock All Night*—can be done in ten days, but not some Viking epic with a Monster of the Vortex.

My problems started on day one of our water location work. We lost our leading lady. She had been under contract to a studio and taken this job, her first independent work, with some reluctance. Abby Dalton was cast as the second lead.

★ JACK BOHRER

We were all supposed to meet on a corner at six A.M. and bus to Paradise Cove. The equipment was on its way. There were four girls in skimpy rawhide Viking outfits, one agent, and me. I was a.d. The agent wouldn't let the lead girl sign. He thought he had a real star there. The girl and her agent probably assumed they could pressure Roger into more money. Big mistake. So I called Roger at the location. He was always there an hour ahead of everyone. I told him the situation and asked what we should do. "Make Abby the lead," he said without hesitating. "Move all the other girls up one spot in the cast. Have the girls learn their lines on the bus ride to the beach. Tell the agent to get lost."

"What about the last part—the lead's sister?"

"Get Abby's sister. She's one of the extras anyway."

★   ★   ★

When it came time to shoot the effects, I realized I had been had. But if I could fault Jack and Fritz, who I knew were basically honest men, I had to fault myself more. It was clear they had simply promised us something they could not deliver. A great sales pitch had distorted my judgment and AIP's. As a result of that experience and others, I was no longer the recipient of any oral proposals. I no longer had people tell me stories. I told them to start typing, put it on paper, send me the treatment or script. But to line the room with huge paintings—no more.

I knew we were in trouble when we were to shoot the girls at sea in a storm with the process plates—the rear projection shots—of the monster. The mock-up of the boat was on rockers in a studio, with the translucent projection screen behind it. And on that screen was projected the process plate of the serpent rising out of the stormy seas to menace the boat.

First, I saw that they had shot the plates from the wrong angle and I couldn't possibly match them. Second, the serpent was too small. I thought: My God, I'm not going to fit this on a ten-day shoot. It was supposed to be thirty feet tall. I had rarely shot process myself because it is a specialized art, but I did the best I could. I put a couple of grips in front with hoses to try to match the water on the screen, and with the boat rocking and the girls moving to obscure as much of the process plate as possible, I shot the scene very low-key and fairly dark so you didn't see too much.

★ ABBY DALTON

Roger, on his way to setting his record, set up shots so quickly in the canyons that one of the Viking girls in the background raced through a shot with her sunglasses on. No one even noticed.

The process shots were hilarious. They were rocking the boat in this cavernous studio, squirting hoses and tossing buckets of water at us in our wet Viking buckskins. Between every shot the crew plied us with brandy to keep us from freezing to death. By the end of the day I was so out of it I could hardly walk.

We were shooting at Bronson Canyon and one of the actors was supposed to run up a steep, rocky hill. The guy told Roger it was impossible. "Don't be ridiculous," Roger snapped back at him, "nothing is impossible." Then Roger tossed his script down and ran up the hill himself. That's his tenacity. Those films cost $1.98 and made money, but they were hard work—and dirty.

Roger and I dated on and off for about a year. He was a fun, wonderful date, a tall, broad-shouldered, very handsome man with a wonderful smile and great sense of humor. We'd go for a drive, have dinner at the beach. He was quite attentive and sweet. I was impressed that he had his own home—a very nice contemporary house in the hills.

Sure, I had fantasies of ending up with him, but it never happened. I think we both realized it wasn't going to work out for either one of us— that neither of us was that emotional about the other. Maybe he needed a little more inspiration from me. I think Roger was dating half a dozen other actresses at the time and I dated others. Roger had a very clear picture in his mind of how he wanted not only his films but his life structured. I was not the woman he was looking for. I was too wild and flighty. He wanted a helpmate, a woman with both feet firmly planted. He didn't let passion get in the way of what he wanted. You always knew where you stood with him. You knew he was trying to make films and make money. Roger's background was Stanford, he wore a button-down collar, short hair, pretty straight-arrow kind of guy. He was extremely energetic and strong-willed. He was like the first yuppie I ever met.

★   ★   ★

It had been a frantic and exhausting stretch. By the end of those two years, I needed a break. I was setting up a ten-day shoot for *The Cry Baby Killer*, which I would finance. David Kramarsky was going to be in charge of production. The shoot was still five weeks off. Then

AIP called me and asked if I would fly to Australia to scout locations and meet a producer. I thought I could use a vacation.

AIP gave me a first-class round-trip ticket and I called a travel bureau. An agent computed the difference between a first-class round-trip ticket to Australia and a round-the-world coach ticket—to Fiji, Sydney, Tokyo, Manila, Bangkok, Rangoon, New Delhi, Cairo on to Europe and then home—to be only $30. I paid the $30 and was off on a monthlong trip around the world.

Chapter 5

My first stop was Suva, the capital of Fiji. I stayed at the Corolevu Beach Hotel. One day the skin-diving instructor and I swam out to a reef together and he asked me if I wanted to become a member of a headhunting tribe. He was a headhunter.

On his next afternoon off we hiked up into the hills to a cluster of thatched huts. By nightfall, we sat around a fire with other people with fuzzy black hair. They were Melanesians and they wore Levi's, sport shirts, and tennis shoes. But there was a gourd with a brownish liquid inside it and my friend said, "Drink this." As I did, people stared and murmured in the tribal dialect. I had completed my initiation into a tribe of headhunters, and I was sworn to return to the

Top: Charles Bronson as the notorious *Machine Gun Kelly*
Middle: Robert Vaughn in *Prehistoric World*
Bottom: Jack Nicholson and Carolyn Mitchell in *The Cry Baby Killer*

island and join my brothers in a revolt against the British and take back the island that was rightfully ours.

Singapore was far more refined. I met the famous Shaw brothers, two of the most influential producers in the Far East: Run Run, who was based in Hong Kong, and Run Me, who lived in Singapore. Run Me's home was an awesome vision of Oriental opulence, and I was treated to one of the greatest meals of my life.

On my first night in Tokyo, I checked into the Imperial Hotel and started wandering around, vaguely lost but confident I could find my way back. A car pulled up, and an American and a Japanese told me I was under arrest and ordered me to get in the car. They identified themselves as a Tokyo detective and an American MP. "I'm not getting into that car," I said. "I have no idea you're telling me the truth. You aren't in uniforms of any kind, you could very simply be intending to get me in the car to rob me and then kill me. No way."

The MP showed me his papers. "They could be forged," I snapped back. "I'm not getting in." He told me I looked exactly like a deserter they were after. "But you don't have a Southern accent and don't talk like a private," he said. "But you've walked into the most dangerous part of town, an area a guy like him'd come to. I suggest you walk straight back to the Imperial and stay away from here."

Bangkok was by far the most exotic, exciting, and unusual city I had ever seen, with American expatriates in the big hotels and bars, dreaming of Asia's emerald mines. A local producer took me to see one of his films and this proved to be a very strange experience. Because they still couldn't record sound there, they made silent films and hired men and women to stand in a booth inside the theater and lip-synch dialogue from the script. But they would change the dialogue from day to day, depending on the news, so the plot line was always shifting slightly. And these readers in the booths were the equivalents of movie stars themselves.

I was perversely drawn to Rangoon to check out its reputation as the "hellhole of Burma," assuming this was the arrogant opinion of spoiled and crass Americans who expect plumbing and running water everywhere they go. But it was all true—Rangoon was just about the worst city I had ever seen in my life, and I got out of there as fast as I could. It was a dirty place with bad accommodations and an extremely rigid, totalitarian form of military rule. There was nothing to do, nowhere to go; even the few Buddhist temples of interest paled next to those in Thailand. I thought Calcutta might be an improvement.

Calcutta was unbelievably poor, with families living and sleeping in the streets. I hired a guide and his idea of sightseeing was to visit a burning "ghat," where a body is cremated and the ashes thrown into the river. The guide showed me to a long concrete ramp leading down from an archway right into the river. We walked up to the arch. Along this ramp were raised concrete slabs roughly the dimensions of a human body. And he told me they placed the dead bodies on these slabs and burned them. I looked over to my left and saw a woman's corpse engulfed in a bluish flame. Evidently they had just lit her—her hair and face were still identifiable. I looked the other way and walked down to the river.

In New Delhi, a Sikh mind reader in a white turban and long beard came up to me on a street and, after a brief conversation, said, "Beware of D.K.," without elaborating.

"D.K.? I don't know a D.K.," I muttered.

"Just beware of D.K.," he repeated slowly. The whole thing seemed preposterous. Then, a couple weeks later in L.A., I was told that the *Cry Baby Killer* script had been "fixed"; this was peculiar, since the script had seemed fine to me when I left. It was my assistant, David Kramarsky—the only D.K. I knew—who had asked screenwriter Leo Gordon for the "fixes" while I was gone. Indeed, the film was the first I ever produced that didn't immediately make money—and I always felt the "fixes" weakened the plot. A Sikh with those powers of prophecy could do quite well running a large studio in Hollywood.

After visiting the Taj Mahal and the spectacular fortress city outside Agra, I flew to Cairo to see the pyramids and the Sphinx. I stayed in Shepherd's Hotel, the center of international intrigue and glamour, at least in the books I'd read. Cairo was wild then, truly one of the great cities of the world. Again, I hired a guide and, after a day of sightseeing, asked him where the best, most authentic belly dancing was. "I can tell you where to go if you want to go where the natives go," he said. "But I will not go there with you. It is in the roughest part of town."

He was right. I was having a fine time, drinking beers, watching the dancers gyrate atop the horseshoe-shaped bar, when a knife fight broke out between two men next to me. Blood started to flow and everybody cleared back. I threw some money down on the table and, wiping some blood from my sleeve, walked rather quickly to the door. I thought: Okay, I've seen the belly dancers and I've seen a knife fight. I've done downtown Cairo.

I returned to L.A. via Athens, Rome, and other European cities. *The Cry Baby Killer* was going into production with D.K.'s "fixed" script and a very youthful Jack Nicholson in the lead. I had met Jack in Jeff Corey's acting class and felt he was the best of several actors who read for the part. The film finally made a little profit, once money from TV and foreign sales came in. When AIP asked me to try my hand at a crime film again, I decided to take my story from the headlines again, as I had done with Sputnik. I thought back to the name Machine Gun Kelly. I researched the life of George R. Kelly, who in the 1930s was the FBI's Public Enemy Number One, the most feared bank robber in the nation. Kelly was eventually captured—giving up in an astonishingly meek fashion—after a kidnapping.

I was especially fascinated by the line he was reported to have uttered to an FBI man when he gave up. The FBI had him surrounded and called out, "Surrender, Kelly, or we'll kill you." And he called back, "I surrender." One of the agents who apprehended him said to Kelly, "We never thought you'd surrender. We thought you'd fight it out to the end. Why'd you give up?"

"I knew if I didn't surrender you'd kill me." Kelly died in 1954.

I hired a fine screenwriter, Bob Campbell, who had done *Five Guns West* and a few other films for me. Bob wrote a very good script with strong, well-sketched characters. He based the story to a large extent on the actual events of Kelly's life. The key to Kelly was that he was afraid of dying. So I built into his character a streak of cowardice and insecurity. I felt the picture was an intelligent psychological profile of a weak, self-loathing man who masked his fears and social and sexual inadequacy with gun-wielding bravado and acts of violence.

We had a strong story line and good action in *Kelly*, but the black-and-white film's real power and dramatic complexity came from the performance of the rugged character actor I hired for his first starring role, as Kelly—Charles Bronson. I had been out there a number of times with weak scripts and actors who weren't very good. This wasn't one of those cases. We were telling a legitimate story with excellent actors. Susan Cabot was terrific as Flo, the ruthless, manipulative power behind Kelly's machine gun. She hurls sexual taunts at Kelly, and even makes him break down and cry in the end. Reversing roles, she grabs a gun and tries to fend off the FBI once Kelly decides to surrender.

On the set, Bronson himself showed far more swagger than weakness, though I got on well with him. During one break Charlie and I started sparring off to the side. I thought, I have no idea how I ever got into something like this with a guy as massive as Charlie Bronson. I held up one hand and he pounded it with a left, knocked it right back. My hand went back up, he came in again and pounded it again. Then he punched at least twenty lefts and rights straight into my stomach—not hard shots, just strong enough to let me feel his power. I said to him, "Okay, Charlie, that's great, I think I'm going to go over there and work on the script now." That's when he mentioned that he had come out of the Pennsylvania coal mines and been a successful semipro boxer.

Kelly was a career breakthrough for Charlie as well as a major turning point in my career. The film got extremely favorable reviews in Europe, was shown at several festivals there, and became a hit in France. Suddenly, my work was being scrutinized and praised by critics and film scholars in journals like *Cahiers du Cinéma* and *Positif*. I was being treated as a major filmmaker and *Kelly* was seen as a serious American film. To the French critics, the film expressed *themes*, I was making a *statement*, there was *significance* in certain moments, and the film had a *visual style* expressed through the camera.

American criticism at that time was rather snobbish in regard to little films and confined itself to the major studio releases. The typical American review called it a "good little gangster film, better than the average low-budget job." *Variety* called it "first-rate," with a "remarkable" script. The film caught on and made a lot of money here as well as overseas.

All this was quite timely, since I, too, was beginning to take my filmmaking more seriously. I had never thought of myself as doing Great Art. I felt I was working as a craftsman, and if, out of some good, solid craftsmanship, something transcended, some portion of art emerged, that would be fine with me. But this was still low-budget stuff—fast schedules, five-figure productions, exploitation subjects. Art was not something I consciously aspired to create. My job was to be a good craftsman.

After *Kelly*, I did *I, Mobster* for an independent producer who distributed through Twentieth Century–Fox. He had acquired a script about a mob chief who "sings" to the Feds and then gets rubbed out by his ex-mentor. Steve Cochran did a very nice job as the kingpin, but this was simply not the film *Kelly* was. It was far more conventional and it lacked *Kelly*'s psychological subtlety and power.

Conventional was not the way to describe *The Wasp Woman* and *Prehistoric World,* two pictures in the mode for which I was best known. For *Wasp Woman,* I hired Susan Cabot to play a cosmetics executive who dreads losing her stunning beauty. Even her firm's revenue is sagging, so she hires a demented dermatologist to discover the perfect rejuvenation cream. There was a time when bee jelly was reputed to retard aging, so I thought, why not a wasp serum? That sounded more exciting. Leo Gordon built the story around that. No one but the executive is willing to test the magic formula. She overdoes it and has to face the fact that she's turning into a killer wasp. We used a gruesome-looking prosthetic mask that was, by today's standards, rather primitive. Small wonder: I shot the film for about $50,000 in less than two weeks.

This was the first film I financed and directed for my own production and distribution company, The Filmgroup. My career was expanding, I was investing more frequently in my own productions, and I was hiring staff. I saw the importance of controlling the distribution of my films, and the success of *Wasp Woman* got my new company off to a fast start.

Despite what most filmographies suggest, I never shot a picture called *Teenage Caveman* for AIP. I made one called *Prehistoric World*, but for one brief, insane moment, AIP had major hits with *I Was a Teenage Frankenstein* and *I Was a Teenage Werewolf.* So they released my film as *Teenage Caveman.* It featured Robert Vaughn in his first starring role. I can still remember the opening sentence in the first review, in the *Los Angeles Times*: "Despite its ten-cent title, *Teenage Caveman* is a surprisingly good picture." The next day Jim and Sam changed the title back to *Prehistoric World.*

Prehistoric World was shot in Bronson Canyon in ten days, on a $70,000 budget, sixty-five minutes in black and white. Actually, the idea was so intriguing to me that I have at times considered a remake on a slightly bigger budget. The Boy's tribe forbids members to venture beyond its own dry, desolate terrain into the more lush land beyond, where the God that Gives Death with Its Touch lives. This area is believed haunted by the spirits of the tribe. Violators who cross the river are put to death. The independent-minded Boy crosses the river, only to learn that the dreaded beast is in fact a mutilated human victim of a nuclear holocaust who carries with him a postcard from Manhattan.

Beach Dickerson and Jackie Haze were tribesmen. I asked Beach to double as a bear that stalks the tribe. I had him come down a steep path, stop, look over the valley below, then continue down. That's all I told him. How much direction or rehearsal can you give a bear? So Beach came padding down to his spot, stopped, lifted his paw to his forehead, and shielded his eyes with it as he scanned the valley below.

I yelled, "CUT! Beach, a bear doesn't pick up his front paw and hold it over his eyes against the sun. This time, just look. You don't need your paw."

★ BEACH DICKERSON

I must be the only person who ever played three death scenes and attended his own funeral in the same movie. I had to be the guy who drowns in the Sucking Sands, as the tribe called them. It was actually a rather scummy junglelike part of an arboretum in Pasadena. Then we go to Bronson and we're filming the funeral and Roger says, "What are you doing here?" and I say, "Roger, this is my funeral. The tribe is grieving over me." He says, "No one will recognize you. Play a tom-tom at the funeral." Then he asks me to be the Man from the Burning Plains

who rides into the tribe's land, drops off the horse, and dies. "What about the stuntman?" I ask. "Put Beach in the stranger's outfit," he yells, and they drape me up looking like General Grant with a bearskin rug and a big black wig.

Then we go to the big bear hunt scene. "Who do you have for the bear?" I ask Roger. "You," he says and they bring me this huge bearskin suit. "How the hell am I going to play a bear?" I ask him.

"How do I know?" he says.

"But Roger, this is insane. I'm no stuntman. I'm just a fucking half-assed little actor."

"Don't make problems. Just do it." The true Roger Corman speaks up. So after a couple of these takes where I come down this hill with my head hanging down between my legs it's 150 degrees inside this fucking bearsuit and I'm *dying*. I get down the hill, he yells, "BEAR, STAND UP!" I stand up. "BEAR, GROWL!" So I growl. He goes, "MEAN, BEAR, MEAN!" I growl louder, scratch the air violently with my deadly paws. "MEANER, BEAR, I WANT YOU MEANER!" he yells.

I'm going nuts inside this suit, growling and flailing, and then he yells to the rest of the extras, "Okay, tribesmen, KILL THAT FUCKING BEAR!" and thirty guys jump on me, take me down, and beat the shit out of me.

★　★　★

Unbearable was the word to describe the dead of winter in the Black Hills of South Dakota, where I took a small cast and crew to shoot *Ski Troop Attack.* This was another Filmgroup release—a World War Two ski patrol story written by Chuck Griffith. To save money I looked for a location allowing me to work with an IA crew out of its Chicago jurisdiction, which sets lower pay scales than in L.A. and allows much smaller crews.

The answer was Deadwood in the Black Hills. We were booked into the Ben Franklin, a picturesque, well-preserved hundred-year-old mining hotel, a relic from past boom times. The town had become slightly run-down over the years but was on the way back with the growing ski-resort business.

My brother, Gene, came out to produce a second movie, *Beast from Haunted Cave,* so that we could amortize transportation and other costs over two pictures. In *Ski Troop Attack*, an American ski patrol seeking to destroy a bridge used to transport Nazi munitions gets trapped behind German lines in a snowy forest. They try to make it to a mountain pass on skis but encounter a German ski patrol. It's a running battle from there. I cast a few major leads from L.A., seeking actors who could ski. For the troops, I hired the rival ski teams from Deadwood and Lead High Schools. We shot on weekends and after school. The Deadwood skiers played the Americans. For

the German ski troop leader, I thought I had landed a casting coup—
a German-born ski instructor from Sun Valley. I sent him the script,
he signed the deal, we were all set.

Two days before shooting began, he called and broke the news
that he had broken his leg in Sun Valley. There was no time to get
anyone else. So I decided to play the role myself. Aside from the fact
that I neither skied nor spoke German, I was totally prepared for the
part. I had skied once or twice in college. I took a lesson the Sunday
before the first day. What I did was simply ski into and out of frame.
For the long approach shots we used a skier on the Lead team about
my height with dark hair and put the biggest goggles I could find
over his face. I wore a duplicate pair.

With the possible exception of my performance, the picture had
an authentic look to it and did well at the box office.

This was my first snow shoot and it was a very tough challenge. It
was unbelievably cold and it snowed all the time. At the top of
Mount Terry, the highest peak in the state, it hit 38 below during a
storm and the film froze while I tried to get the title shot. But the
hills looked great.

I had to shoot through virgin snow because this was a chase/attack
movie. If the skiers ruined a shot, their tracks would mark the snow
and we'd have to find another location. That happened a few times.
But what I did was cut to a close-up at the point where someone fell
and pick up from there and that would be the end of the long shot
on virgin powder.

★ **PAUL RAPP**

You never played just one position on Roger's team. For the ski movie,
I was location scout, assistant director, propman, wardrobe, the works.
I played a young radio operator trapped behind the lines. Plus, I drove
Roger from L.A. to Deadwood so he could save on airfare and have an
extra car on location. We carried the props in the back of the car.

Roger wanted one shot real badly, up in a bowl at the top of a virgin
hill. We climbed waist-deep for over an hour and a half to the peak and
we were exhausted. Then, we were supposed to ski down, making great
wide S-curves in the powder, chasing each other with our machine
guns. So Roger, down at the bottom, screams directions into the bullhorn and calls for "ACTION!"

The sound waves from the bullhorn started a small avalanche that
ruined the pristine powder. It was incredible. I was scared to death, but
I knew it was a great shot as we came down, and Roger keeps screaming into the bullhorn, "STAY AHEAD OF THE AVALANCHE!"

★ **KINTA ZABEL**

I had been a Phi Beta Kappa at USC and was in a doctoral program and teaching English there when I answered a job listing at the student employment bureau. It was to work as Roger's assistant. This was one of my first locations, and I worked as Roger's script clerk as well.

Another function was to find ways to keep the film warm enough so it wouldn't get brittle and crack. Beach Dickerson was the soundman and he had the only car on the set, so we stored the film in his car. The camera froze. Everyone in South Dakota thought we were crazy. There weren't even Forestry Service people out there.

Roger's work often left him drained and needing long periods of time to recoup his energy. He was—is—capable of withstanding tremendous physical discomfort and that shoot proved it.

★   ★   ★

I only had one real problem on the skis. I shot the Americans side-stepping up a very steep cliff. I wasn't thrilled. They were going too slowly. "You guys are running for your lives here," I yelled through my bullhorn. "You didn't come up that hill fast enough!"

Then I went down to the base with my "Germans." I tried to spur them on by exploiting the rivalry between the two school teams. "We're going to make them look like idiots!" I shouted like a coach.

Unfortunately, I had to be the first guy up because I was their leader. Halfway up I started losing my breath. I was weak. I thought: First, I'm going to wreck this shot—and it's a major shot to set up— by looking this weak. Second, I'm going to lose face with both teams because I told Deadwood they were too slow and they'll be laughing at me and I told Lead that we were going to make Deadwood look bad. So I kept going.

I barely made it through the shot. I knew exactly where the marks were set and the *instant* I moved out of frame I just collapsed in the deep powder. I couldn't move. I had never been so exhausted in my entire life. For the first time in my directing career, we actually had to *stop shooting* for ten minutes because the director couldn't continue.

Chapter 6

Of all the films I ever directed, the one that has survived the longest as a genuine "cult classic" is the one I did the fastest and the cheapest. It only took me two days on a leftover soundstage to shoot principal photography for *The Little Shop of Horrors*, but it has lived on for nearly thirty years now in midnight shows on campuses, revival cinemas, videocassette outlets, and remakes for stage and screen.

One reason for its astonishing durability is that when I made the film, I was, as I believed at the time, virtually creating a new genre—the black-comedy horror film. Whereas I had mixed a little humor and science fiction in films like *Not of This Earth*, now I was out to create a different kind of film—more cynical, darker, more wickedly funny.

Top: Jack Nicholson (left) and Jonathan Haze in *The Little Shop of Horrors*
Bottom: Dick Miller admires his new creation in *A Bucket of Blood*

The new mix worked and I ended up with a "trilogy" of black comedies: *A Bucket of Blood,* then *Little Shop,* and finally *Creature from the Haunted Sea,* a six-day wonder shot in Puerto Rico almost as an afterthought. The credit for all three screenplays went to my main writer, Chuck Griffith. Taken together, these remarkably modest black-and-white films—with their loose, raw energy—were a major departure in my career. They added a sharper, more satirical edge to my films and brought a new level of awareness to my work. Film scholars may disagree and find some title I've never heard of, but I believe I was the first and only filmmaker working in the black-comedy "genre" for some time.

With these pictures I put together some of the definitive elements of my style: quirky plots built on somewhat gruesome premises; fast-cutting and fluid camera moves; composition in depth; unconventional, well-sketched characters; and solid performances from the ensemble of "Corman players." And the shoots themselves—three films done in a total span of about two weeks—demanded an unprecedented kind of sprinting intensity from the director that provided its own loose, crazy highs just to keep it all flowing together.

If *Bucket* and *Little Shop,* two of the cheapest films I ever directed myself, look like they were made on a bet, they pretty much were. In the middle of 1959, when AIP wanted me to make a horror film but had only $50,000 available, I felt it was time to take a risk, do something fairly outrageous. I shot *Bucket* on only a few sets in five days. When the film worked well, I did *Little Shop* in two days on a leftover set just to beat my speed record.

My fastest shoot until *Bucket* had been six days. I accepted AIP's challenge, but I was tired of horror. I wanted to have some fun and change the equation. I decided to do a horror-type film with a hip, cutting edge. I called Chuck and we decided to create a comedy-horror-satire about the trendy beat coffeehouse scene. For research, we spent a long evening drifting in and out of coffeehouses along Sunset Strip. We kicked around story ideas as we wandered and, by evening's end, had a plot structure.

A young, mildly demented busboy at the Yellow Door coffeehouse named Walter Paisley wants to be a sculptor and gain acceptance by the cafe's cool but pretentious art crowd, which only teases him. In his gloomy apartment, while molding a face from clay, he tries to cut into a wall because his landlady's screeching cat is trapped behind it. But his knife fatally stabs the cat. The landlady comes knocking for her cat. Paisley panics and covers the cat's dead body—knife and all—with clay. She notices this new "sculpture" and he boasts that it's his latest work, "Dead Cat."

When Walter shows off "Dead Cat" at the coffeehouse, Carla, the beautiful woman he wants to win over, promptly calls it a master-piece. Another new fan offers him some dope, though the naive Walter doesn't know what it is. The club owner displays "Dead Cat" and soon Paisley's the darling of the Yellow Door.

Paisley delivers to the club two more masterpieces, and his price soars to $25,000 per piece. He now struts around the Yellow Door as a parody of beatnik cool—in a beret, ascot, and cigarette holder. One sculpture, "Murdered Man," is the cop who had come by to bust Walter for the dope; the other is a naked model in a chair, clutching her throat. She had insulted him at the club but Walter had lured her over for a sitting.

When the police and Walter's new friends learn that he is, liter-ally, a "killer sculptor," they chase him to his shabby apartment and find his ultimate creation—his own corpse covered in clay, hanging from the ceiling.

This was truly a fast-paced romp from the start, almost like a party. It didn't feel like work; we were all laughing throughout the shoot. The spirit on the set was very loose among my "family" of players: Dick Miller as Paisley, Barboura Morris as Carla, the art groupie, and Julian Burton as the way-out beat poet who first belit-tles Paisley, then celebrates him. Everyone was coming up with ideas as we went and we just tossed them in.

Julian, for example, had been wearing sandals through the shoot. The last day we shot Paisley's big opening to show off his work, and Julian had to wear a dinner jacket. But he told me his feet had swelled and he couldn't get his shoes on. There was no time to buy bigger shoes. So I told him to wear sandals and no socks with the tux. I convinced him it would look great. The minute he walked into the scene that way, tux and sandals, the sneak preview audience started laughing. The improvisation hit the mark.

The audience at the sneak laughed throughout the film and applauded at the end. I had made a successful comedy that also com-mented on the ambitions and pretensions of the art world. When a critic wrote that the art world was a metaphor for the movie world, I didn't deny it.

After *Bucket* I wanted to do another film in a similar tone, this time distributed by my own Filmgroup company. When the manager of Producers Studio, where I had an office, mentioned that a film with a fairly big office set was wrapping and he had nothing coming in, I had an idea. "Leave the set standing," I told him. "I'll rent it for two days and I'll shoot a picture there. My set construction budget will be zero. I also want it for three rehearsal days." Two days' shooting after three days' rehearsal was one week's salary for the actors.

I called Chuck and told him I wanted a variation on the *Bucket*

story line. There was one constraint: It had to be written for a standing set and able to be filmed in two days.

★ CHUCK GRIFFITH

**Roger and I went bar-hopping again on the Strip and started brainstorm-
ing. I got drunk and ended up in a fight at Chez Paulette. I hardly remember getting hit. In our more lucid moments, I came up with gluttony: the
salad chef in a restaurant feeding, stuffing people. Then cannibalism.
But the censors wouldn't have allowed it. So I came up with a man-
eating plant. And that was it. I followed the structure of *Bucket* almost
exactly, but where *Bucket* was more of a satire, this would be a flat-
out farce with no social commentary.**

★   ★   ★

I always liked the idea of the guy who killed and sculpted in *Bucket*,
and we reprised elements from *Bucket* for this new picture. Now, the
Little Guy/Outcast is Seymour Krelboin, a dimwitted apprentice at
Gravis Mushnik's failing skid row florist shop. Mushnik is an irasci-
ble, demanding boss who speaks broken English with a heavy Eastern European accent. Seymour crosses some seeds he's found and
creates an exotic plant that seems to be dying. When he cuts his fin-
ger and blood drips into the plant, the leaves come to life. The plant
moans, "Feed me, feeeeed me."

Seymour drips more blood inside the plant and is astonished to see
it grow. He names the blood-hungry plant Audrey Jr., after his girlfriend. Just as Paisley murdered to keep his artistic fame going, Seymour has to go out on skid row at night and kill to keep his creation
alive. Ultimately the face of every victim is reflected on one of
Audrey's broad leaves.

The man-eating plant becomes a popular neighborhood attraction.
Mushnik's business takes off—he now calls Seymour "son"—and
Seymour, like Paisley, becomes a local celebrity. The police tracking
the local murders suspect Seymour. By the time they get to Mushnik's, Seymour, like Paisley, has killed himself with his own creation—by jumping inside Audrey.

The Krelboin lead was written with Dick Miller in mind. But he
decided not to do it; he doubted I could pull it off in two days. Dick
offered to stay on in a supporting role and we promoted Jonathan
Haze, who had had a small role in *Bucket*, to the lead. He was just
right for the part. Mel Welles was the only actor Chuck or I had in
mind for Mushnik, the comic center of the film. Mel's delivery was
perfect, with his thick accent, immigrant inflections, and malaprops.
Jackie Joseph, a singer and comedienne who had done some work in

musicals, played Audrey, the sweet, simple girl Seymour wants to marry.

Dick added his own deadpan style of humor as a customer who sprinkles salt and pepper on Mushnik's carnations and grazes his way around the shop. It was an ironic twist—a man eating plants in a story of a man-eating plant. "You know," he says in the opening sequence, "those big places, they're full of pretty flowers, expensive flowers, and when you raise them for looks that's when you're bound to lose some food value." Chuck Griffith's grandmother, Myrtle Vail, a onetime radio star, played Seymour's mother.

One sequence that greatly helped turn the film into a cult favorite featured an utterly inspired bit of black humor by an actor I would begin using more regularly—Jack Nicholson. Seymour gets into a duel with his dentist—scalpel versus drill—and kills him for more plant food. But then a wild-eyed masochistic undertaker in a black suit and bow tie shows up for his first appointment with the dentist. He grins madly as he sits in the waiting room reading *PAIN* magazine. That's Jack. Seymour emerges from the office, posing as the dead Dr. Farb, and the unsuspecting undertaker, Wilbur Force, takes the chair, refusing Novocain because it "dulls the senses."

When Seymour tries to get him to leave and come back the next day, Wilbur just grins and says, "Oh, I couldn't do that. I have three or four abscesses, a touch of pyorrhea, nine or ten cavities, I lost my pivot tooth, and I'm in terrible pain." Once inside the office, he smiles happily and says, "You know, most people don't like going to the dentist, but I rather enjoy it myself. Don't you? There's a real feeling of growth, of progress when that old drill goes in."

The payoff moment comes when Seymour, posing as the dead dentist, grabs the drill and Wilbur lies back, saying, "Oh, goody, goody, here it comes." As he drills, Wilbur howls with delight and yells. "Oh, my God, DON'T STOP NOW!"

Again, it was an ensemble of Corman "regulars" that kept the mood informal and spirited. I simply called people I knew and cast actors I had used before and could rely on. They all came through. Nobody took it, or themselves, too seriously, and they gave sharp, animated performances. No one tensed in front of the camera. There wasn't enough *time* for that.

The assistant director, Dick Dixon, set the tone early on the first day. We started shooting at eight A.M., and at nine he announced between setups, "Let's get going. We're falling hopelessly behind schedule."

I shot between Christmas and New Year's 1959, using the plant shop set for about 80 to 90 percent of the movie. I had to shoot so tight in there I couldn't show the street outside. But by then I was

getting fairly skilled with camera movements, so even in the opening
scenes I was moving from over-the-shoulder, panning back and
across, and dollying more fluidly as the actors crossed the store in
long scenes. I tried to get a fair amount of movement in the background—people wandering outside the doorway, busy customers
inside—to open up the look as much as possible. That is why this
became such an easy film to adapt to the stage.

We adhered quite closely to the script, and despite a loose, impro-
visational feel to the witty exchanges, this film was in no way created
on the set as we went—as some people assume. Any changes made
were worked out in the three days of rehearsals before rolling.
Everyone just came in very well prepared.

The plant was primitive as special effects go and was worked by
monofilaments. But it was effective. In fact, this was one of the sim-
plest, least expensive films in history, and yet we got perfectly
acceptable performances—in some cases, their best work—from
everybody.

To break up the flow of interior scenes in the florist shop I needed
a few exteriors, but I was signed with the union and didn't have the
money to take a union crew on location, so I gave Chuck the chance
to make his debut as a second unit director shooting some footage on
skid row with a pickup crew.

★ CHUCK GRIFFITH

I was going to shoot the skid row stuff from a bread van using a long
lens. But Roger wouldn't pay for the long lens so we had to get out of
the van and shoot on the sidewalk. As soon as the bums saw what was
going on, they started acting all over the place—staggering, falling over,
showing off. I needed some guys to lurk and brawl in a doorway so I
found some old winos. I gave them the change out of my pocket and we
were off to the races. They shot craps, brawled, acted out knifing each
other, staggered around.

Mel produced the second unit and he lined up the world's largest
used-tire yard and the world's largest used-toilet yard. We got to the
Santa Fe train yards and lined up a train, two switchmen, the engineer,
and everything else for two bottles of scotch. We shot all night down
there, with our own little generator towed behind my Volkswagen. We
had one rent-a-cop watching our headquarters, which was a vacant lot.

My soundman couldn't believe I had winos all over the place handling
cables and stuff. The bums didn't have speaking parts; they had mumbling parts with a lot of special business to do. It was wonderful.

I brought in all my relatives just for the fun of it to put them into crowd scenes. My dad was the hobo in the dentist's chair. My grand-mother Myrt was in it. It flowed right along and worked very well. The script was tight, there wasn't time for improv, but a few words did get changed. I played a robber who breaks into Mushnik's at night and gets eaten by the plant. When he and I forgot my lines, I improvised a little, but then I was the writer. I was allowed to.

★ JACK NICHOLSON

The part in *Little Shop* was written for a man of forty. I asked to read for it, but Roger didn't see this as my kind of part. I was only twenty-something and I had done little except the lead in *Cry Baby Killer*, which was an insane film, a couple years earlier. I was learning, though: you get a chance to see what you're doing that is horrible and then you elim-inate it. I didn't have any other consistent work. But I wasn't exactly Roger's favorite leading man because other guys were doing movies that—how do I put this?—came out better. So Roger thought of me for the wilder things. But I knew this was very funny. He knew I wanted it and he said, "Well, I can't keep you from reading for it."

I read for it and he immediately gave me the part. Roger took the script apart and gave me only the pages for my scenes. That way he could give the rest of the script to another actor, or actors. That's what low budget was like.

I went in to the shoot knowing I had to be very quirky because Roger originally hadn't wanted me. In other words, I couldn't play it straight. So I just did a lot of weird shit that I thought would make it funny. Roger shot this stuff in one take but at more than one angle. In fact, we never did shoot the end of the scene. This movie was pre-lit. You'd go in, plug in the lights, roll the camera, and shoot. We did the take outside the office and went inside the office, plugged in, lit, and rolled. Jonathan Haze was up on my chest pulling my teeth out. And in the take, he leaned back and hit the rented dental machinery with the back of his leg and it started to tip over. Roger didn't even call cut. He leapt onto the set, grabbed the tilting machine, and said, "Next set, that's a wrap."

I went to the opening of *Little Shop* at the Pix, at Sunset and Gower. It was, oddly, a full theater. I had had a horrible experience at the open-ing of *Cry Baby Killer* because the audience just went absolutely ber-serk. So I was a bit nervous going in there. I took a date. And when my sequence came up, the audience went absolutely berserk again. They laughed so hard I could barely hear the dialogue. I didn't quite register it right. It was as if I had forgotten it was a comedy since the shoot. I got all embarrassed because I'd never really had such a positive response before.

★ DAN HALLER

The crew and staff went to a sneak preview in Glendale and the whole theater saw what we were up to. Then, as Roger often asked us to do, we all went back to the office and everybody had to write a review as if we were working for the *Saturday Review* or *The New York Times*. And these were hard reviews, man. Nothing was held back. You could take shots at the art direction, sound, acting, story—whatever. There were no excuses, like, "Sure, but they only had two days" or "The art director only had three thousand dollars to play with." Uh-uh. We spent an hour writing them up and if you weren't finished you talked it through. Roger, I must say, had a thick skin for this, but he used the notes both to make changes in the current picture and to learn for the next. He could take it all, any of it. The notices we wrote on *Little Shop* were great ones, better than anything the *Saturday Review* critics could come up with.

★   ★   ★

By the time I finished the movie, I felt I had learned much in the way of technique. There was some rather intricate work in the film—the composition, blocking the camera movements, the pace—that could not possibly have been done by a beginning director in two days. I had to have a certain level of skill to do it. The script breaks you out of the shop just enough to not get overly bored; we cut away and cut back to vary things, a technique I used in all of my studio films. I actually charted scenes to know exactly how long a scene could play in a specific set. I always tried to redesign the script to get people out of a room and into another room or down a hallway before a scene became too static.

We shot the film under a different title, "The Passionate People Eater," and then I changed it to *The Little Shop of Horrors*. The sneak audiences loved the picture and caught on to the weird humor right away. The plant's "Feed me" became a hip line that kids picked up on.

Nevertheless, in its initial release, the film was only a moderate success, which was a sort of anticlimax. A movie that wild and strange shouldn't be only a moderate success. It should have either been a hit or a flat-out failure. It was a letdown to make back the $30,000 negative cost with just a modest profit.

But over the years, *The Little Shop of Horrors* caught on as a cult item and just kept going and going and going, generating rentals on campuses and at midnight shows in art houses through the years. It became a phenomenon much like *The Rocky Horror Picture Show*, where people who have seen it dozens of times and memorized the entire film shout lines in the theater.

The cult status of the film expanded my reputation in Europe. Long before the off-Broadway musical production, a producer wanted to option the rights to do it as a play in Paris and I gave him a verbal commitment, but he never got full financing. Years later, I learned of a group of young German filmmakers in Munich who had formed a cooperative and named it Mushnik Productions after the owner of the florist shop.

Then, long after I had quit directing and formed New World, I negotiated a very casual contract for a musical through my attorney, Barbara Boyle. We didn't really get as strong a royalty deal as we could have because I thought of the film, quite frankly, as more of a joke than anything else.

But the 1982 stage adaptation was an immediate triumph off-off-Broadway. Howard Ashman, the artistic director of the WPA Theater, wrote the book and lyrics and Alan Menken created the music for the WPA production. After several weeks there, the show moved to off-Broadway, running at the Orpheum Theater between July 1982 and November 1987. In 1983 *Little Shop* won, incredibly, the New York Drama Critics Circle Award for Best Musical and several other awards. There was a touring company and productions throughout Europe. It remains one of the longest-running off-Broadway musicals of all time.

When Geffen Films wanted to buy the musical for the movies, we had to renegotiate our original contract because it was drawn so loosely. We got a cash payment plus a percentage of the movie's profits for Chuck and me. The film cost somewhere around $30 million, and it never made its negative cost back even though it was rather successful. There were no profits. This is common in Hollywood with big-budget films. It grossed a great deal of money, but the cost was so huge they never broke even.

I thought the stage version was wonderful. It caught the spirit and youthful energy of the film. Running off-Broadway helped, since I always believed both my film and the musical would have been diminished with more expensive, slicker productions. It was reminiscent of a college humor show.

The Geffen film looked very good and the special effects for the plant were excellent, but the picture didn't seem to get as many laughs as the play or my original film. Maybe my theory was right and the very bigness of the production worked against the comedy.

Bigness, though, was never an issue when I took a cast and crew to Puerto Rico to direct *The Last Woman on Earth* and produce a World War Two film, *Battle of Blood Island,* soon after we finished *Little Shop.* I had discovered that tax incentives were available if you "manufactured" in Puerto Rico. That included making movies.

But before leaving, I also set in motion another film in Northern California that I would merely finance, *The Wild Ride,* to be directed by a graduate from UCLA's Theater Arts Department, Harvey Berman. Harvey taught a high school drama class and ran a film course in Walnut Creek. He approached me with the idea that he could shoot one of our juvenile delinquent films with his students for very little money. That sounded good to me. Harvey started shooting, but when I saw the first day's rushes I told him to stop because it was clear we were on our way to making a truly amateurish film.

"Wait for summer vacation," I told him. "I'll send up a cameraman, a leading man, leading lady, art director, and my assistant." So we held off. Then, I got Jack Nicholson and Georgianna Carter to play the male and female leads. I sent my art director, Danny Haller, and my assistant, Kinta Zabel. I prepared to leave for San Juan and gave Kinta a check for $30,000. "You write the checks," I instructed her, "coproduce the film, keep track of everything, pay the bills. When the picture wraps draw out whatever is left of the money and fly to San Juan, because I may well be running out of funds."

Meanwhile, for my own project, I had come to depend on Bob Towne, whom I had known from Jeff Corey's acting class. He was also trying to break in as a screenwriter, so I asked him to write *The Last Woman on Earth.* Bob has since become one of the very finest screenwriters in the business with scripts like *The Last Detail; Shampoo; Chinatown,* for which he won the Best Screenplay Oscar for 1974; and *Tequila Sunrise,* which he wrote and directed. But back then he worked slowly, an unfortunate fact that would cause me some problems.

I was ready to go to San Juan but Bob's script wasn't finished. "The only possible way," I said, "for me to afford to take you down there so you can finish is to hire you as one of the actors. You have to play the second lead." Bob agreed and did some nice work in the film, using the pseudonym Edward Wain.

I rented a large Mediterranean-style house on the beach in the Condado district and hired a cook and housekeeper. Some of the cast and crew stayed in the Caribe Hilton Hotel, which we also used as one of our locations, but most of us stayed in the beach house. It made the trip feel more like a vacation, except for Bob, who was closeted inside, racing the deadline so we could begin shooting.

Starting with an idea of mine, Bob created a very sensitive script for a postnuclear story: A wealthy industrialist has taken his stylish wife and handsome younger assistant on his yacht for a Caribbean cruise. After going skin diving, they surface to find their crew and everyone else ashore dead. They learn that only people who were lucky enough to be skin diving, trapped in mines, or otherwise beneath the earth's surface have survived. Then the story turns into a love triangle. I gave Bob the role of the assistant who eventually gets killed by his jealous boss.

Last Woman was a two-week shoot. It was going so well and we were having such a good time that I decided to do another movie. I called Chuck Griffith in L.A. and woke him up. "Chuck, I need another comedy-horror film and you've got a week to write it," I said. "There's no time for rewrites. I've got a small cast so write for them. If you need more actors write small roles for Beach Dickerson and me as well." He was very sleepy and I wasn't certain he understood completely the story line we discussed, but he agreed. I would use the same three main leads from the first movie, plus pick up some local Puerto Rican actors. I thought: Kinta will come and put the rest of the *Wild Ride* money in the account, everyone else is already here, I'm shooting a third movie with leftovers. We called it *Creature from the Haunted Sea.*

The story was truly insane: We are in the closing days of Batista's Cuba in the 1950s and some of his generals are absconding with a chest full of his gold and must get a boat to sail from Cuba in the middle of the night. The only man they can trust is an American gambler and gangster. He and his assistant then plot to kill off the generals one by one during the trip, blaming a sea monster for the killings. The plan is to end up with all the gold. The trouble is there actually *is* a sea monster and it looks *exactly* like the one the gangster has invented.

I dictated the ending to Chuck: there are no good guys who destroy the monster. The monster wins.

★ **KINTA ZABEL**

The night I flew in was incredibly hot and humid. I got a taxi to the house and the lights downstairs were on. There was Bob Towne. "I've been up all night," Bob said. "Roger is screaming. He wants me to get this damned script written. I'm doing the best I can."

I held Bob's hand while he finished over the next few days and dealt with all kinds of other details. Roger rented one production vehicle—a

little VW. So I'd drive him around to locations and leave him there and
the production manager and I would argue over who would get the car.

In Deadwood I had to keep the film from freezing. In San Juan I had
to keep it from melting. It was scorching hot. We had to refrigerate the
cans until shipping them.

★   ★   ★

Blood Island finished on a Saturday and I started *Last Woman* on
Monday. Two Saturdays later we wrapped *Last Woman* and were
ready to start *Creature* the following Monday—one day of preproduction per picture. Chuck's script came in on the Thursday night
before we finished *Last Woman.* It was clear he hadn't remembered
the story line we discussed completely so I did a fast rewrite that
night. Kinta made copies of the draft while I was shooting Friday.
We cast some local actors Friday night and gave them their pages. I
had already told Chuck which locations to write for, so Kinta went
out and locked everything in Saturday. On Sunday I worked out the
production in the morning and planned my shots in the afternoon.
There was just enough money for a one-week shoot.

I had mentioned to Chuck that he could write a minor part for me
and he deliberately came up with Happy Jack Monahan, without
question the most complex acting role Chuck ever created. In every
scene Happy Jack had to express a different, powerful emotion. In
one scene he "fights like a brave tiger." In another, he "runs away
with cowardice." He "laughs with hysterical joy," then "cries
uncontrollably." He falls in love with a girl, then ends up hating her.
I read the part and realized Happy Jack practically became the lead.

I know Chuck did this to drive me crazy. It was too big a role, and
required an actor. I gave the part to Bobby Bean, a young performer
who had been in *The Wild Ride* and had come to Puerto Rico on his
own on the chance that we might have something for him either as
an actor or on the crew. I hired him for both.

★   BEACH DICKERSON

I'm doing sound and Roger says to me, "We have to make the monster,"
and I say, "Yeah, I've heard this 'we' shit before, Roger. I don't know
this monster shit. I didn't have toys as a child. I had a pony."

"The monster's got to run on land and swim underwater."

"Okay, I was half your *Crab Monster* but I have no expertise here.
I'm an idiot. I can't change a bicycle tire."

"We have to make it."

I said to Bobby, "What the fuck do we do? The man is *serious*!" We go to Roger. "Okay, Roger," I say, "what kind of budget are we talking about?"

"You tell me, Beach."

"Roger, I'll tell you right now, we are discussing one hundred and fifty dollars' worth of monster."

"You got it."

Well, with Roger when the chips are down you do what you gotta do. So Bobby and I have a challenge. Bobby's the one who's getting inside this monster. Now we have to build it. They'd just wrapped the war picture, so I decide to get five helmets and make this *giant* head. Then we get a wetsuit, some moss, lots of Brillo pads. Then we get tennis balls for the eyes, Ping-Pong balls for the pupils, and pipecleaners for the claws. Then we cover him with black oilcloth to make him slimy. I mean, we decked him out and he was absolutely *glorious.* And I must say, that son of a bitch, he ran on land and swam underwater for the whole shoot and when it was all over he went to heaven.

★ ★ ★

We had a great deal of fun making *Creature.* The film turned out to be very funny. Beach, as the gambler's goon, kills the first soldier, the one standing guard over the chest of gold. Beach goes back to bed. The monster crawls on board and kills another guard. At breakfast the Cuban general says to the gangster, played by Tony Carbone, "Two of my men were killed last night."

Tony explains about the sea monster, but complains to Beach privately, "I told you to kill *one.* What'd ya kill two for?"

"I only *did* kill one, Boss," Beach says. "I don't remember killing that second guy."

I was trying to get more movement into long dialogue scenes. Chuck had one scene in the script that especially bothered me because I couldn't figure out how to give it some action. We were shooting in a palm grove and I had these Americans playing touch football with a coconut. I lined everyone up on two sides and gave them a coconut and they started running and lobbing passes back and forth as they played a game and said the lines. If nothing else, there was a lot of movement in that scene.

Another time, I gave Tony the business of loading his gun during a scene—a real gun. As we were rolling, the whole gun fell apart unexpectedly. We shot another take that worked perfectly, but the first was funnier. We had some voice-over narration in this sequence, so I decided to use the first take and rewrite the narration so you hear something like, "This Mafia leader is one of the world's experts on firearms"—and BAM, you see the gun fall apart in Tony's hands. I was using anything that worked, planned or not.

We had all the remaining Cuban generals—the Puerto Rican actors—get into a little rowboat for a scene where they have to come ashore. But we overloaded the boat in the harbor and it accidentally started to sink. The cameraman, Jack Marquette, said, "Shall I cut it? The boat's sinking." And I said, "No, it's shallow water. Don't cut, keep shooting. As soon as their heads go underwater, cut and we'll pull 'em out." So Jack kept shooting.

It was phenomenal. These Puerto Rican actors were *cooperative*. Their boat was sinking and they were all standing straight up, just as they had been directed to do. Didn't flinch. Talk about trusting your director! It was a great shot. Every one of them sank right into the water. Then we pulled them out and saved them.

The craziness of the shoot showed in the finished film. The audience at the sneak preview laughed and applauded just as they had with *Little Shop*. Nobody was making movies like these.

EDGAR ALLAN POE'S

THE PIT AND THE PENDULUM

IN PANAVISION AND COLOR

"It was designed to
cross the region
of the heart.
It would return
again and again
...Down and
still down
it came..."
—POE

STARRING
VINCENT PRICE · JOHN KERR · BARBARA STEELE · LUANA ANDERS
SCREENPLAY BY RICHARD MATHESON · PRODUCED AND DIRECTED BY ROGER CORMAN
RELEASED BY LEE BAXTER · AN AMERICAN INTERNATIONAL PICTURE

Chapter 7

T he three comedies proved that I could make movies cheaper and faster in a new genre, but I was ready to move on to bigger, better movies on longer schedules and to direct more experienced actors from better scripts.

The chance to do all those things came in the visually and thematically rich gothic horror genre. I directed a "cycle" of eight films shot between 1960 and 1964. These films were adapted from the often macabre, psychologically unsettling imagination of Edgar Allan Poe, whose poems and stories I had enjoyed immensely as a youth.

I had begun reading a lot about Freudian psychoanalysis and the

Top: Vincent Price strangles Basil Rathbone in *Tales of Terror*
Middle: Vincent Price displays duplicate of Peter Lorre's head used for *Tales of Terror*
Bottom: Poster for *The Pit and the Pendulum*

inner workings of the psyche. I had also been intrigued by a book by a Beverly Hills psychiatrist that analyzed the connection between humor and horror. I actually scheduled an hourlong appointment and Bob Towne and I went over to his office to discuss the subject for $100. I had also begun seeing my own analyst—classical Freudian work, couch and all—to better explore my own emotional and psychological makeup.

The Poe cycle started when Jim and Sam asked me at lunch one day to make two more black-and-white horror films for $100,000 each. I said no. "What I'd really like to do," I told them, "is *one* horror film in color, maybe even CinemaScope, double the budget to $200,000, and go to a three-week schedule. I'd like to do a classic, Poe's 'The Fall of the House of Usher.' Poe has a built-in audience. He's read in every high school. One quality film in color is better than two cheap films in black and white."

Jim wondered if the youth market was there for a film based on required reading in school. I said kids loved Poe. I had.

"But where's the monster?" Sam asked.

"The house is the monster."

I got the go-ahead for a fifteen-day schedule and a production budget of around $270,000, a large portion of which went to the actor I wanted for the part of Roderick Usher: Vincent Price. It was the most money AIP had ever gambled on a film.

I felt that Poe and Freud had been working in different ways toward a concept of the unconscious mind, so I tried to use Freud's theories to interpret the work of Poe. *Usher* had many of the elements that became standard fare for the Poe films. We created a story about the last insane days of Roderick and Madeline Usher, living in seclusion in the family home, with its deeply fissured, creaking walls. Her fiancé, Philip Winthrop, comes to visit, but Usher won't let them marry for fear of spreading their dreaded hereditary madness.

Usher then insists that Madeline has died from a heart attack, but actually her brother has buried her alive during a cataleptic seizure that makes her appear dead. Madeline awakens and claws her way out of the coffin. A colossal electrical storm rages over the house as it starts to burn and crumble. She tries to kill Winthrop but he escapes, and in the climactic sequence, the blazing walls collapse upon the Ushers.

In Vincent, I found a man of cultural refinement for Usher. He was a first-rate actor and handsome leading man who had a distinguished career. I felt audiences had to fear the leading man but not on a conscious, physical level based on strength. I wanted a man whose intelligent but tormented mind works beyond the minds of others and who thus inspires a deeper fear.

Dick Matheson, an accomplished science fiction fantasy writer, gave me a well-crafted, literate script, and Vincent's performance was brilliant. The real star of the show may have been my art director Dan Haller. He went over to Universal and for $2,500 bought stock sets and scenery—large, well-built units we couldn't otherwise afford. Dan would have a trailer right on the set and be there around the clock while the crew built the sets for *Usher*. He'd sketch things on the back of the script or even on napkins as we'd sit at night and have a drink to discuss the look of the film. We were working with standing units and we designed big sets. All studios gave you free access to their scene docks and we put together some great, big-looking sets from columns, arches, windows, and furniture from all over the place. Then we saved everything from each picture and stored it in the scene dock. So if anyone looks at these Poe films back to back, they'll see some sets and specific units reappearing. If we had the same art department budget for the second picture, we had, say, $20,000 of sets stored from the first, so it became a $40,000 design. For the third set, we had, say, $40,000 in stock and spent another $20,000 on new design. It wasn't quite that mathematical, because there is money spent to strike sets and store them and you do rebuild each time. But it explains how the Poe films looked increasingly more elaborate without stretching the production budgets or shooting schedules.

I used matte shots for the houses and castles that may not seem convincing today but were state of the art then. For flashbacks and dream sequences in red and blue, I used either gel over the lights or a colored filter over the lens. We even blew in some fog. Danny, all told, did an incredible job of creating the dark, claustrophobic, haunted atmosphere within the castles.

As I had promised Jim and Sam, the *Usher* house really did become a monster. In one scene, Vincent had to utter the line "The house lives, the house breathes." "What does that mean?" he asked me.

"That's the line that allowed us to make this movie."

"Well, fine," he said reasonably. "I suppose I can breathe some life into it then."

Vincent breathed plenty of life and gothic horror into all the lines and action. This was a case where the audiences were truly frightened. I was seeing that my theories worked. I set up sequences to demonstrate how laughter and horror worked together through the creation and sustaining of tension. One classic Poe sequence went like this. A character with whom the audience empathizes—Roderick, Madeline, Philip, anyone—must walk down a long, dark hallway while thunder is crashing, lightning is flashing. The hallway is filled with cobwebs, spiders, possibly rats running along the dimly lit wall. The protagonist must find, or find out, something at the end of the hallway.

What he is going for is both incredibly enticing and incredibly horrible. So he must—and he must not—go. If the audience is with you, they are saying, "Go down the hallway and see what it is." And at the same time they are saying, "No, don't take another step. Turn. Get out of the house."

And so you build the tension as he moves. Invariably, a cobweb will get caught in Vincent's face; a rat screeches in the silence and runs over his foot. He might miss a step going down the dark creaking stairs with his torch; a step might collapse. A creaking door might open on its own behind or beside him. Out of the musty, subterranean darkness, a loud blast of thunder, a brilliant bolt of lightning. The torch might suddenly go out.

My own bias was for a moving camera. I always liked camera movements to lead people into and through scenes. The point-of-view (POV) shot was always a key in heightening tension. The critical shots then are with the camera in front of the actor, tracking back as he moves forward and then the POV reverse shot along the same dolly track, as the camera "sees" what he sees. And I would mix up the angles and distances, keeping the camera in motion.

I was also using what I knew of Freud's dream interpretations and my own analysis to make the picture work on an unconscious, symbolic plane as well. Horror can be a reenactment of some long-suppressed fear that has seized a child, even a baby. A dream. A taboo. A fear gets locked in the subconscious. In dealing with suspense at a later stage of development the house can be seen as a woman's body with its openings—windows, doors, arches. The corridor becomes a woman's vagina. The deeper you go into the dark hallways, then, the deeper you are delving into, say, an adolescent boy's first sexual stirrings. These are contradictory urges—an irresistible attraction and desire for sex and the fear of the unknown and illicit. The very ambivalence builds tension.

Put together correctly, the classic horror sequence is the equivalent of the sexual act. The sharp, shocking event at the end that releases the tension is the equivalent of the orgasmic climax. A comedian building tension successfully to a punch line gets a laugh at the climax. A director in a horror genre does the same but gets a scream. Either way, there is growing tension and release—all analogous to the rhythms of a sexual act.

The Poe films did earn me quite a bit of critical attention, first in

Europe and then in the States. I believe it was partially because of the integration of the symbolism into the development of the story; it was also because of the way the gliding, swooping camera and jarring angles helped sharpen the edge of tension and fear. In horror, where you try to present an interior dream or psychological state, you are free to use any cinematic technique. You are limited only by your creativity, the schedule, and the budget.

Usher was a projection of Roderick Usher's fevered and deranged mind, or more precisely, it was an emanation of the unconscious mind of Poe himself. There are no eyes in the unconscious and so I thought the films should be all interiors or, if exteriors were necessary, they should be set at night. I told my cast and crew: I never wanted to see "reality" in any of these scenes. If I did go exterior, there should be something out of the ordinary. I shot the exteriors of the house on a soundstage and it, indeed, looked unreal, just a little bit off.

Beyond matte shots, filters and colored gels, and optical camera work—shooting two images one over another and recompositing them through a special camera in a lab to create a third image—we capitalized on luck. Or rather, on others' misfortunes. Directing sometimes means taking advantage of that kind of unforeseen occurrence. The one exterior at the outset of *Usher*—when Philip Winthrop rides his horse through woods to the castle—had to have a stark fantasy look. As "luck" would have it, there was a forest fire in the Hollywood Hills just as we were going into production. I heard about it on the car radio, turned my car around, and drove to the scene. I watched the firemen put out the tail end of the fire.

The next day I went out to the hills with a skeleton crew, the second male lead, Mark Damon, and a horse. It was great. The ground was gray with ash; the trees were charred and black. And we threw a little fog in to add some effect. I got exactly what I wanted: to not show green grass, leafy trees, or any other organic signs of life. The film was about decay and madness. This was a great instance of being fast on your feet—a forest fire that had wrecked peoples' homes and the hills had provided a wonderful opening sequence.

A similar stroke of luck gave me the spectacular fire sequence at the film's climax, when the House of Usher burns down to the ground. Just by chance, we located an old barn out in Orange County that was going to be demolished by developers. We asked the owner: "Instead of demolishing it, how would you like to burn it down? But burn it down at night and I'll be out there with fifty dollars and two cameras rolling."

He agreed. That's how we got the incredible long shots of the Usher house burning. I think we tossed some gasoline on the damned thing to get it going out in the middle of a field. I covered this with two cameras, which seemed like a major production back then. Today, you cover something like that with five. We got some really strong stuff—the burning rafters coming down, the flames shooting higher and higher. That sequence would stand up to almost anything done today. In fact, fire destroyed castles in other Poe films, and since one roaring blaze looks as good as another in a long shot, I cut the *Usher* sequence into the other films. It certainly never occurred to me back in 1960 that people someday would *rent* these films on cassettes, watch them at home *back-to-back*, and notice the same flaming rafters crashing down in different movies. But I tried not to do it too often.

Shooting interior fire scenes always inspired a lot of fun on the set. The trick was not to burn the actual flats—or sets—but burn off the flammable plastic gunk that gets spread along the walls. This stuff burns with great light and flare but spares the walls. If walls got scorched and we needed a second take, two special effects men would put out the fire and then I'd reshoot something else while the crew repainted sections of the wall. I'd come back when the paint was almost dry, the gunk would be spread over the clean walls again, and then I could reshoot.

Everybody got excited on Fire Day, the last day of a shoot when we'd burn down the castle. On one of the later Poe sets, the crew got a little *too* excited and set fire to the roof of the soundstage. Those were major flames. A couple of effects men had to race up ladders and catwalks and extinguish them.

That first Poe film was pretty hot itself in its initial release during the summer of 1960, with well over $1 million in rentals. There was no question we would do another.

I was initially interested in adapting *The Masque of the Red Death* and I commissioned a treatment. But by then I was involved in a project that became very important for me, *The Intruder*, a film about desegregation in a small Southern town. And I went to Greece to direct *Atlas* for Filmgroup. But AIP was eager to move ahead with a Poe project and I decided to shoot *The Pit and the Pendulum* on a fifteen-day schedule and a similar budget.

Vincent was cast again, this time as Nicholas Medina, the son of an Inquisition executioner whose torture chamber is still downstairs by the crypt. After Medina's wife awakens from *her* premature burial, she plots with the family doctor to drive Medina insane. He locks her up in an iron maiden, but he falls into the pit at the end.

The climactic sequence stands out as a technically complex and visually stunning payoff. Dressed in the executioner's hooded robe, Medina mistakenly subjects his brother-in-law, not the doctor, to the pit and the pendulum torture. John Kerr is strapped down on a table, staring up at a giant razor-sharp pendulum. The blade swings with increasing force and begins to descend toward the table as Medina stands behind, controlling its noisy, grinding motion. Danny Haller built immense sets all the way up to the trusses and ceilings of the soundstage to create an aura of depth and menace. In places the film looked even more elaborate than *Usher*.

The contraption was actually operated from above, a very large mechanical system that didn't work as quickly as I liked. So I skip-framed it with an optical printer later, taking every other frame out optically to make the blade appear to move twice as fast. For the long shots I used a wooden blade but for close-ups I used metal sharp enough to do some harm. John had a pad on his chest and a device that looked like skin. His shirt would open up under the scraping blade and he would bleed from this device.

We did that sequence in a day. The end was fun. I used a crane and just started to make up shots as we got to the last hour or so, knowing I'd cut it all together in editing. We got a shot off every two or three minutes, or thirty or forty shots in the last two hours. I got shots of the blade from above it and below it; I had the camera panning and swooping. Danny had murals painted along the walls and so I had the camera zoom along the walls. These cutaway montage shots would give the sequence color, vitality, and a dynamic tension. They worked. I was always quite satisfied that these two films really looked much bigger than their budgets and schedules suggested.

The profits looked quite impressive as well. *Pit* did, I believe, just a bit better than *Usher*, with close to $2 million in rentals on a negative cost of some $200,000. AIP and I had a dispute over my piece of the profits after *Pit*. In negotiating my fee, Sam and I had had an informal tradition of flipping a coin to settle, say, a $10,000 difference. I won the first time, he won the next three times, and I quit flipping. This time we settled our differences but I still decided to do my own Poe film based on an essay, *Premature Burial*. I arranged financing through Pathé Lab, which helped back some AIP productions and did their print work. I hired Chuck Beaumont and Ray Russell to create a story out of Poe's work.

I was planning to hire Vincent again, but AIP, aware of my intentions, locked Vincent into an exclusive contract. I went with Ray Milland, the best available actor for the part—a sophisticated, debonair native Welshman who still had a cultured trace of a "mid-Atlantic" accent.

On the first morning, Jim Nicholson and Sam Arkoff came on the set. I thought: They have *never* shown up like this before. And why are they smiling? "Roger," Sam said, shaking my hand, "we just wanted to wish you luck. We're partners again."

AIP, then the largest independent studio in town, had gone to Pathé, which did not have a distributor lined up yet, and *bought out* their position as producer. They had some leverage, as I had heard it: "In case you don't want to play ball," AIP told Pathé, "we're pulling all our lab work with you." So *Burial* became an AIP picture.

Ray played Guy Carrell, a med student in nineteenth-century London who dreads falling into a comalike trance and being entombed alive, as he believes his father was. When he finds out his father *was* buried alive, he faints "dead" away—and gets buried alive. Obviously, that wasn't the end of the story. Nor was it the end of the cycle. *Burial* generated more than $1 million in rentals but did not do as well as the first two. It was clear the formula had to be varied. Some reviews pointed out the similarities of the sets and design. *The New York Times* called it, "static, slack, and starchily written."

With *Tales of Terror* I went back with Richard Matheson and Vincent but tried something different. I directed three short films based on Poe stories, each in one week: "Morella," "The Black Cat," and "Facts in the Case of M. Valdemar." The middle one was actually based on "The Black Cat" and "The Cask of Amontillado" and, while all were quite well-acted, "Cat" was the most interesting because it blended humor with the macabre. It also matched Vincent with Peter Lorre. Vincent and Peter proved to be two truly classy and versatile actors, especially in their delightfully humorous wine-tasting contest.

The success of the trilogy, with close to $1.5 million in rentals, encouraged Matheson and me to transform Poe's classic poem *The Raven* into a lighter comedy-horror project and use those two again. It was the biggest-looking Poe film to date because we were using sets from previous films.

The cast was superb and these films gave me the rare pleasure of working with some distinguished veteran actors. Vincent and Boris Karloff played rival sixteenth-century sorcerers, the kindly Craven and the sinister Scarabus, respectively. Peter was the magician Bedlo, who has been turned into a raven by Scarabus and who goes to Craven to be changed back. Jack Nicholson played Bedlo's son, Rexford.

Scarabus wants the reclusive Craven's secrets. But Craven has withdrawn from sorcery, still mourning the death of his wife, Lenore. Craven makes a friend when he changes Bedlo back, using his recipe of jellied spiders, rabbit's lard, dried bat's blood, vulture dung, and a dead man's hair. Bedlo tells Craven he believes Lenore is alive and, worse, is Scarabus's mistress. So they all visit Scarabus and learn that it's true. In the end, Scarabus and Craven square off on an immense and ornate gothic set for a dazzling duel of sorcery tricks. Craven wins and brings the flaming, crumbling castle— actually, the House of Usher again—down on his foe and adulterous wife. They somehow survive but Lenore wants to go back to Craven. Boris's last line is a great one. As they climb from the rubble, he says to Lenore, "I guess I just don't have it anymore."

The climax was rather intricate. There were some interesting optical effects used for the shafts of light shooting from their fingertips. I put Vincent in a crane, which I seldom used, and had him floating all over the room when he was supposed to be levitating. We set off a small cannon beside Boris. All these exchanges were sketched and planned carefully in advance.

I have always felt *The Raven*, for a three-week shoot, is one of the more accomplished films I directed. Danny Haller again created lavish-looking, stylized sets that gave the film great-looking production value for the money.

Working with three master actors was fascinating. They all brought very distinct styles to the scenes. Peter was the loosest, a truly extemporaneous actor who could improvise beautifully. He didn't spend much time learning his lines but he knew his great strength was the vitality and humor and energy he brought to his scenes.

Vincent had more classical training, along with Method, and did scenes exactly as scripted. But he could remain open to change. Boris, nearing the end of his career, knew his lines and expected to do his scenes exactly as written and no other way. Vincent was a balance between the others, adjusting to Peter's looseness and shooting a scene out as written, as Boris would have it.

With Boris and Peter, there was tension and an incredible clash of acting methods. Boris frankly did not like Peter's way of doing things. It made him nuts and threw off his memorized reading of the lines. He told me a couple times he was not happy with his scenes with Peter.

Peter was a little bit weird but a very funny, intelligent, and fine artist who was endlessly inventive. He was always coming up with new bits of business. I thought Jack and Peter managed to turn their scenes into some amusing little pieces. This idea wasn't scripted but it was a Method-type subtext worked out on the set, a tactic I learned at Corey's acting class.

It was this: Jack wants nothing in the world more than the love and approval of his father and Peter wants nothing more than to get rid of his idiot son. So Jack is constantly playing up to Peter, and

Peter is constantly pushing him away. For instance, Jack keeps playing with the top of Peter's cloak, distracting him. Peter just goes with
this and slaps Jack's hand twice, screaming, "Don't *do* that, Rexford!" Then, when they are all tied up at the end, a remorseful Bedlo
says, "I'm a disgrace." Jack's eyes glaze over in disgust—a look that
has become one of his trademarks—and says, "I had a stronger word
in mind."

★ JACK NICHOLSON

Roger gave me one direction on that picture: "Try to be as funny as
Lorre, Karloff, and Price." I loved those guys. I sat around with Peter all
the time. I was mad about him. They were wonderful. It was a comedy,
and Roger gave us a little more time to improvise on the set.

The business with Peter's cloak was just actors' devices. I grabbed
his cloak—actually I grabbed a lot of other things that aren't visible in
the frame—just to keep him alive to the fact that I was trying to get
him out of there. Of course, the good actor that he is, he just reacted
to it spontaneously, slapped me and lashed out.

One other thing I remember about *The Raven* was that the raven we
used shit endlessly over everybody and everything. It just shit endlessly.
My whole right shoulder was constantly covered with raven shit.

★ VINCENT PRICE

Boris, Peter, and I wrote some additional jokes and brought them to
Roger. He approved almost everything we'd done, added business to
match, and integrated the result into the script. This was one instance
where the actors and the director made a funny script into an even funnier picture.

Roger had a quiet authority and a definite psychological approach to
the Poe films and we talked about it at great length. Then after the
analysis, he left the rest up to us to flesh out the roles. Roger's intensity
on the set made up for the fact that these were low-budget, short
schedules. He asked us very coyly to visit the sets before shooting, discussing the film in situ to get us acquainted with each other and the
sets.

His energy was mystifying. We would go over to his house for con-
ferences and I'd go to the refrigerator to get a bite to eat. It was so
strange: Roger never seemed to eat solid food, but rather contained
himself to a can of some high-protein diet called Metrecal. My God, I

would think to myself, what does this man live on? He had a truly Spartan lifestyle and so I always joked about sending him CARE packages.

★ ★ ★

AIP wanted more Poe. And though I felt the formula was starting to get stretched, I eventually decided to make two more. So in November 1963 I flew to London for *The Masque of Red Death*, starring Vincent and Jane Asher and written by Chuck Beaumont.

One reason I had waited to do *Masque* was Bergman's *The Seventh Seal*, in which Death, in a black-hooded robe, stalks the medieval Swedish countryside as a plague destroys the land. That setup resembled *Masque*. I figured Bergman must have read *Masque* as well and been somehow influenced by it. And *The Seventh Seal* remains one of the great pictures of all time. I was concerned that someone might say I copied Bergman, so I stayed away from the story for a few years. *Masque* was a surreal, philosophical tale set in medieval Italy with Vincent playing Prince Prospero, a sadistic, debauched Satan-worshipper who retreats into his castle and hosts a lavishly decadent ball as his land is ravaged by the Red Death.

Masque was the most lavish of the Poe films. I used terrific sets left in the scene docks from *Beckett* and other historical epics and used some fabulous costumes. Also, my cinematographer was Nicholas Roeg, whose work on the film won him a Best Cinematography award at a major European festival. I had a five-week schedule, though with the slightly slower U.K. crews, it was actually closer to four U.S. weeks. And I still regret my decision not to pay extra mandated union fees for going over a day at Christmastime. I still feel that would have made the large-scale ball sequence—with dozens of extras, plenty of fire, and lots of action—a true tour de force instead of a merely good sequence.

Actually, two of the most memorable things I remember about the *Masque* shoot had nothing to do with the actual film. The first was the assassination of John F. Kennedy. It was a great shock to us and we felt strange being so far from home. The day of his funeral we shut down production for a few minutes.

The second involved another kind of historic moment. I had started going out with my *Masque* leading lady, Jane Asher, and we were having coffee on a Friday. But Jane showed up with a young companion. "Roger," she said, "I'd like you to meet a friend of mine from Liverpool, Paul McCartney. Paul's never been on a movie set and he'd just like to see what's happening."

"Fine. Let him hang around."

"Paul," she said, "is with this singing group from Liverpool and they're making their debut in London tonight."

"Well, Paul," I said, "good luck on your big debut. Stick around and have lunch." I was in an expansive mood, I guess. I had no idea the Beatles were already the number-one group around England. They had played everywhere but London. Indeed, the next day I saw the headlines all over town: BEATLES CONQUER LONDON. Jane had been dating Paul but because he was constantly away on tour, she was seeing me in London.

The Poe films brought my directing up a few notches in budgets and schedules and I have several very good-looking, psychologically effective horror pictures to show for it. But I was repeating myself, taking ideas, images, themes, and techniques from my own earlier work.

And yet no recounting of my Poe cycle would be complete without mentioning *The Terror*. I was getting so familiar with the standard elements of Poe's material—or at least our adaptations—that I tried to out-Poe Poe himself and create a gothic tale from scratch. In fact *The Terror* began as a challenge: to shoot most of a gothic horror film in two days, using leftover sets from *The Raven*. It turned into the longest production of my career—an ordeal that required five directors and nine months to complete. But, like *Little Shop*, it's a classic story of how to make a film out of nothing.

A week before wrapping *The Raven*, I remarked to Danny Haller, "This set looks wonderful. It's a shame we'll have to tear it all down next Friday." He said, "Yeah, it's almost the culmination of all the Poe work."

It was a rainy Sunday. I was scheduled to play tennis. As I sat in my house I decided I could shoot enough footage in two days on the *Raven* sets to make another film. All I'd need was a script. I called Leo Gordon, who had written *Cry Baby Killer* and *Wasp Woman.* "Do you have anything with a castle in it?" I asked.

He said no but I invited him over for a brainstorming session. "And," I noted, "I want to shoot the week after next. I have to shoot sixty pages in two days. That means writing about twelve pages a day for the next work week, which is not impossible."

I was sure only of the ending. "I just can't burn another castle down," I said. I looked out at the rain. "That's it," I said. "The opposite of fire—water! This castle will be destroyed by a flood." While Leo wrote, I wrapped *The Raven*.

Vincent was unavailable to play the lead—the Baron von Leppe. Boris agreed to the two days of work—and no more. He was close to eighty, in failing health, and he wanted to get home to England. I called his agent and we worked out a salary—AIP had paid Boris around $30,000 for *The Raven*—plus a percentage.

I asked Jack Nicholson to play the young French Army officer who shows up at the Baron's castle, and he suggested his wife, Sandra Knight, as the leading lady, Helene. "We shoot the Baron-Lieutenant scenes, sixty pages, in the castle," I explained. "When we get the whole script and other sets we'll shoot the rest of the picture."

★ **SAM ARKOFF**

In those days we used to have a little wrap party after each picture. My wife and sister-in-law would make up some Jewish delicatessen, etc., and bring it down to the set. Roger had these actors he always used and they were always hungry. I think they never ate between his pictures. Anyway, I came down to the *Raven* set and was a little surprised to see the cemetery flats still standing. Normally, by then, the set would have been taken down and put in the back lot. Knowing Roger, I got a little suspicious. So I came down Monday morning and sure enough there was the clapboard—American International Pictures, *The Raven.* Which had wrapped. He was shooting a different fornicating picture on us. And Karloff was still there, getting his $30,000 for two days' work.

I greeted Roger. The wonderful thing about Roger is that he looked startled for a moment and then he smiled. He has great poise. Incredible poise. And I asked him what he was doing. And he just kind of passed it off. Because eventually I knew he'd put that film in his vault, finish, and come to us for the distribution deal. So it turned out to be our picture anyway.

★   ★   ★

Dick Miller played Stefan, the Baron's servant, and Jackie Haze was a mute named Gustav. We did those two days on the *Raven* stages with the four principals. This wasn't easy. We had a roughed-out story line, but no one really knew what their characters' motivations were because we didn't exactly know what was supposed to happen to them. But I kept shooting. Pressed for time and with an hour or so left the second day, I told my d.p., "Don't slate the shots. We'll worry later what to do with this film. We'll just start and stop the camera for now. When I'm ready to roll, I'll say 'ROLL, ACTION' and you have one second to see if anything's wrong. If you say nothing, I'll say 'ACTION' a second later and you get it going. I'm going to print the whole thing. I'll remember what I shot."

"I've never heard of anything like this in my entire career," he said. Of course he hadn't. No one had. Everybody got into the spirit and laughed.

Though I made good use of the sets, I still had only half a movie. And the twisted plot kept changing over the months it took to complete the shoot. Jack's Lieutenant Duvalier gets lost from Napoleon's army along the Baltic seacoast. He falls in love with a mysterious young woman by the sea named Helene. She vanishes. He ends up at the Baron's castle. She may or may not live at the castle and may or may not be the spirit of the grieving Baron's long-dead wife, Ilsa. Gustav the mute may or may not be mute. He works for an old witch, whose son, Eric, had had an affair twenty years earlier with the Baron's wife and died in a fight with Stefan. In fact, we later learn that the Baron may or not may not even be the Baron. It was that kind of movie. Duvalier sticks around to unravel the mysteries.

It was all played very loose. When the Baron assures Duvalier that Helene is a mirage, the skeptical Duvalier answers, "With all due respect, Baron, for a ghost she's a very active young woman." Boris was playing the Baron with an amusing light touch, almost like an in-joke. He smiles at one point and mutters, "You think I'm mad, don't you?" and Duvalier grins. "Right now, Baron," he says, "I'm not sure just what I think."

Before leaving for Europe to start work on a couple of other films, I realized I needed some exteriors shot up in Big Sur, which was *The Terror*'s Baltic coastline. Since I was a DGA member, I needed a non-union director. So I went to my ace assistant, a young man I had hired months earlier just out of the UCLA film school. His name was Francis Coppola.

Francis's background was largely in theater production at UCLA but he had also won the $2,500 Samuel Goldwyn prize for screenwriting.

His first assignment involved a Russian science fiction space picture I had acquired rather inexpensively. I asked him to edit, write, and loop English dialogue so it made sense to an American audience and then shoot postproduction inserts with special effects. That movie came out as *Battle Beyond the Sun*.

Francis eventually did go to Europe as my soundman on *Young Racers*. From there, he went to Ireland to direct his first feature, *Dementia 13*, which I backed with $22,000. But before this trip, I made him an offer he couldn't refuse.

"Francis," I said, "this is your chance. Go on up to Big Sur with Jack and Sandra and shoot this stuff."

"Great," he said. So Francis put together a small crew from UCLA and went up. Once there, he decided he could change and improve the script.

He came back about a week later and edited that footage. It didn't exactly *mesh* with what I had shot. But it still looked pretty good and he shot some very beautiful scenes around Big Sur. The guy clearly had talent.

★ FRANCIS COPPOLA

Roger, having heard about my theater experience and good work with actors, which was rare for a cinema type, took me on as his assistant for $90 a week. He was very proud that the winner of the Goldwyn prize was in his employ. He also made sure to tell me he once worked for $45 a week. Of course, I'd have worked for him for nothing, except that I needed a meal once in a while.

The Russian sci-fi film was very ideological and symbolic in its conflicts. Roger's thinking was that there was a fortune in special effects and he could jazz it up for American audiences. I had to translate the images into an English story line that fit the mouth movements. He told me to put in a scene where an astronaut has a vision of two moon monsters, one vaguely male, the other female, battling it out. I shot that for him and cut it into the film. Meanwhile, I was also given the job of dialogue supervisor on *Haunted Palace* during the day. I ran lines for Vincent and the others. Then I'd stay up most of the night to do the sci-fi work. I don't think I ever saw the final version of *Battle Beyond the Sun.*

Roger was always straight—he never gave you any false hope. He was always very precise about what you were going to get and do. It was a fabulous opportunity for someone like me—it was better than money.

★   ★   ★

One of Francis's UCLA friends proved that. For the flood sequences, we did close-ups of the castle on a set with hoses. But I wanted major flooding to match in scope the *Usher* fire. Before Francis left for 7-Arts several months later to begin a career as writer/director, he recommended the friend, Dennis Jakob, who was just out of UCLA film school, to be my next assistant. I gave Dennis a lightweight Arriflex and some film and sent him to the Hoover Dam for a day.

"I want you to keep photographing water pouring down at you," I explained before he left, "from thirty, forty angles, coming in real tight with hundred, two-hundred millimeter lenses and we'll cut it all together."

Dennis was gone three days. "Why were you gone so long?" I asked. "What were you *doing* up there? You were only shooting water."

"It was cloudy," he said. "Didn't look right. Thought I'd wait for better weather." I didn't care.

A little later I went out to the van we were using and in the back were all these Confederate Army uniforms. Jack was a lieutenant in Napoleon's army, not Robert E. Lee's. I went to Dennis. "Okay, what's the story?" I knew his thesis film at UCLA had to do with the Civil War. "You shot the flooding in ten minutes and spent three days with *my* camera, *my* film, and *my* equipment out in the middle of nowhere shooting your thesis film. Didn't you, Dennis?"

"Hey, it'll be a great piece of film," he said. "Tell you what. I'll dedicate it to you."

"Sure, Dennis." How could I get angry? He was doing to a certain extent what I had done with AIP and other companies—he was finding a way to beat the system and do his movie. He had been the driver, cameraman, and director and probably grabbed some pals to play soldiers. "I'll learn from you," he said.

I still needed another director to carry on after Francis. I called up Monte Hellman, a promising young talent. "I directed these two days," I explained, "and Francis directed a week up north and we need some more stuff on the cliffs in Palos Verdes. Would you like to direct a little while?"

"Sure, happy to," he said.

So Monte took Jack and Dick down to Palos Verdes and did some more exteriors on the cliffs. We cut that together. Monte decided to rewrite some of the script and changed things around some. But it looked all right. Then he got another job.

So I called Jack Hill, who had done some work for me and was making a name for himself. Jack just about pulled the rest of the film together but was unavailable for the wrap. We needed one more day of shooting.

Finally, Jack Nicholson came to me. "Look," he said, "everybody in this whole damned town's directed this picture. It's simple shooting. Let me direct the last day."

"Sure, why not?" I said.

I cut the five directors' work together into a complete film. We all had interpreted the story differently and it showed. I saw two things working against it. There were some genuine gaps in logic; and frankly, it struck me as a little dull. Leo and I had made up a story in one afternoon that *made sense* but it had no spark. It all seemed so predictable. And the lighting from those first two days was a little flat. You just don't get super lighting when you're shooting thirty pages a day.

I worked out a twist: The Baron was not the Baron. After catching his wife in an affair with Eric, there was a fight but Stefan mistakenly killed the Baron—not Eric—and for twenty years Eric posed as the Baron. "In his mind," Stefan explains to the astonished witch and Duvalier, "Eric *is* the Baron von Leppe."

This is good news for the witch: Her son Eric has been alive all these years. The bad news is that, believing he was the Baron, she has been trying to drive *her own son* to a guilt-stricken suicide by using Helene to evoke the Baroness's spirit. Now, it's too late to stop the flooding of the crypt, which was designed to free Ilsa's spirit and lead the Baron—actually, Eric—to kill himself. Or something to that effect. This was a long time ago.

★ JACK NICHOLSON

I believe the funniest hour I have ever spent in a projection room was watching the dailies for *The Terror.* You first saw Boris coming down this long hallway in the Baron's blue coat. Then he'd move out of the shot. Then I'd come down the hallway and after I'd cleared the frame— Roger didn't even bother to cut the camera and slate the shots—Sandra would come down the hallway. Then it was Dick's turn looking weird in his black servant suit. And then Boris would come down AGAIN, this time in his *red* coat. All of this shot as if in one take with no cut.

Then we went up to Big Sur with Francis for the stuff along the beach and the rocks with Jackie Haze, the horse, Helene, the young woman, and the witch's raven. Sandra got pregnant up in Big Sur with our daughter, Jennifer. I think Roger went wild with Francis because no one ever went over budget and he was supposed to be up there for three days and we stayed eleven or something like that. We all thought we'd be machine-gunned or fired forever out of the business.

I almost drowned out there in the ocean. I was supposed to go out into the water to find Helene. This was Francis's idea. I went out into that big fucking arch up there in Big Sur. This is wintertime and there's no stunt doubling. I had been a lifeguard so I wasn't that afraid but that arch is quite a ways out.

The water never gets deep. So in order to look disappeared—I made this up as I was going out there—I sort of crouched down to my knees so that when the first white water waves hit me, it did not hit me in the dick but all over. 'Cause that water was freezing. And the water knocked me under. When I went under with Lieutenant Duvalier's huge Fifth Chasseur uniform on, I felt I couldn't stand up. I was pinned to the ground from the weight of this uniform. I had that split second of panic because I was out a ways already. I came flying out of there and just threw that fucking costume off while I ran, freezing to death.

When we got back to town, Francis tried to blame me for going over budget, I might add, and, of course, he didn't know that I was pretty close with Roger, from having worked with him and being in Jeff Corey's classes. Roger didn't believe I was to blame. Neither was Francis, really. It had more to do with shooting in Big Sur—and trying something you never do on a Corman picture, which was run cables up from the rocks into the mountains. Roger's way would be to just shoot from up on the road. But Francis hadn't worked with Roger that much so he hadn't had that disdain for any kind of production expense burned into him yet. So he went ahead and just did whatever he wanted.

Then, moving south down the coast, Monte came on board and we shot in Santa Barbara and Palos Verdes, more raven stuff, more scenes with Jackie Haze. When we did the flood scenes, I had to dive from the stairs leading to the crypt into two and a half feet of water, which is why that dive looks a little funny. And by then, Sandra was like seven, eight months pregnant and her body was obviously quite different. And there I was, carrying her upstairs, soaking wet, with her very pregnant.

I remember standing behind Roger when I wasn't in the shot, because he was holding one of the big fire hose nozzles over his head, squirting the actors as the crypt filled up. I grabbed the hose without him knowing it, being almost hysterical with laughter as I pulled the hose and jerked him around while he sprayed these people, making it seem like tremendous water pressure. I mean, this was my fucking wife and it looked so hysterically goofy. Roger always had that grin on his face. He knew something was up. I had a great time. Paid the rent. They don't make movies like *The Terror* anymore.

* * *

Chapter 8

While those first Poe films in CinemaScope carried me into filmmaking on a larger scale, *The Intruder* was the first film I directed from a deep political and social conviction. It was, by far, the biggest artistic and commercial risk of my career—a mostly self-financed, $80,000 black-and-white film about small-town racial prejudice that was shot entirely on location in Missouri. Critical praise was nearly unanimous; the film was shown at the Venice Film Festival. And it was my first commercial failure after thirty successes.

The time was 1961 and the civil rights movement was a major priority of John Kennedy's New Frontier. I wanted to move toward socially committed filmmaking. I acquired the rights to a book called *The Intruder* written in 1958 by Charles Beaumont, as well as the

William Shatner in *The Intruder*

rights to his screenplay. Beaumont's story was based on an actual incident in which a Northern bigot went into a Tennessee town to create a semi-Fascist party and inflamed the populace so intensely the National Guard had to come in.

To my great surprise, the project was turned down by several companies. United Artists backed out; AIP wouldn't touch it. Allied Artists thought the topic was simply too controversial. I decided to make the film for my own Filmgroup company. Pathé Labs wanted to get into production and distribution and agreed to put up a portion of the cost. My brother, Gene, went in with me as a coproducer and together we came up with the rest of the negative cost out of our own pockets.

I decided it had to be shot entirely on location to be thoroughly credible. I was looking for just the right trees, architecture, road signs, and storefronts. I decided that only the leads would come in from L.A. I would hire the other actors locally so the accents and inflections would be genuine.

The main location was the town of Sikeston in the Southern "boot heel" area of Missouri. The proximity to Little Rock, scene of the school segregation crisis, made this site seem historically appropriate. This was still the mid-South and I didn't want to be subject to the extreme prejudices and outright opposition I might encounter in Mississippi or Alabama.

The film addresses two socially explosive issues in the news at the time—busing and racial hatred. A rabble-rousing white supremacist named Cramer arrives from Washington and insinuates himself into the town's drowsy life: he flirts with the newspaper editor's daughter, Ella; seduces the lonely wife of a salesman named Sam Griffin; makes bigoted speeches and incites violent acts against town blacks and liberals. A black minister dies in a church bomb blast. The local editor, a staunch integrationist, is half-blinded by racist thugs. Cramer tells Ella that her father will be killed unless she falsely accuses a black high school student of raping her. She does and soon a lynch mob strings the helpless student to a swing outside the school. But Griffin shows up in time to humiliate Cramer and save the student, having persuaded Ella to expose Cramer's tactics. The town abandons Cramer, leaving him powerless.

Sikeston had just the right feel. Once I had my permits, a local student on summer vacation from college became our main liaison with the townsfolk. A white teacher in the black section led Gene to a black minister, who, in turn, helped bridge relations in his community. I signed on local electricians and a beauty parlor stylist to handle makeup and hair. We went to a little theater in town and to the high school for extras. To play the student attacked by the mob, we found a high school honors graduate and athlete named Charlie Barnes. He was working on a road gang.

For Cramer, we were lucky enough to discover William Shatner, who had done *The World of Suzie Wong* and *A Shot in the Dark* on Broadway. Leo Gordon, an actor who had also written *Wasp Woman*, *Cry Baby Killer*, and *The Terror* for me, played Sam Griffin. Chuck Beaumont ended up on-screen as the liberal principal. Everybody was pulling for us on this project because we all very much believed in it.

And yet, we felt a sense of menace and danger the whole time. Only Bill Shatner and I had copies of the complete scripts. Other versions of the dialogue were watered-down for local consumption. Then, on the days of the shoots, I'd run the real lines for the actors on the spot, explaining that some rewriting had taken place. I didn't want to inflame the townspeople because we needed their cooperation.

But there *was* opposition. The town school had been integrated only a year earlier. One of the crew members was openly—and violently—opposed to blacks. Charlie Barnes, in fact, had been the school football star on the same team with this white kid—and they were *friends*. It was so weird. This was August and Charlie was on his way to the University of Missouri while the white kid was headed to Ole Miss. I asked him why and he snapped, "I ain't goin' to school where they got blacks." I said, "But Charlie's your friend, you played football together." "I don't care," he said, "I'm goin' to an all-white campus."

We practically took over the motel in town, and, as things got underway, talk spread about what we were up to. We received threatening phone calls and letters. People tried to find Chuck's novel, which was more inflammatory in tone than our script. Gene remembers that the library had a different book titled *The Intruder* that was a mystery-adventure story. But they began to get suspicious. One resourceful man sent away to a St. Louis bookstore for a copy of our *Intruder*. The book arrived, and things soon turned uglier.

Even when we went out to relax, tensions were high. One of the pretty girls who had been hanging around the set came up to Bill and me; we talked and ate lunch together. The next day she showed up with a girlfriend. Bill and I took them out Saturday night to one of the redneck country and western bars.

Then on Monday, one of the locals said to me, "Do you have any idea who you went out with Saturday night or what could happen to you? They're both married and their husbands are convicts in state prison for pulling armed robberies and bank jobs together. Do you

have any idea what would happen to you if and when they get out?"
So much for location romance.

I needed hundreds of extras for the scene where Cramer gives a
rabble-rousing speech from the courthouse steps. Gene and I got on
the local radio station and invited the whole county to come Friday
night and watch a motion picture being shot. Sure enough, a couple
hundred people showed and the shot looked very good on film. They
all knew Bill was an actor, but, in his white linen suit, they assumed
he was the *good* guy. I used a cheerleader's bullhorn to spur on the
crowd, though they were already quite responsive to Bill's dema-
goguery. He'd yell, "Keep your schools WHITE! The Commies
know the quickest way to cripple a country is to mongrelize it," and
they'd yell back "Yeah, RIGHT!"

My priority shot, done first, was an establishing shot of Bill over
his shoulder with all the people in front of him. People who show up
on a movie set tend to get bored after an hour. Sure enough, they
started drifting away. I then got the medium shots of Bill, shooting
through the dwindling crowd, with my regular extras in front of the
camera. When I did the close-ups on him, the place was deserted.
But it looked fine.

One scene was a meeting with Cramer in an old cafe. I got some
truly great faces on camera—old, toothless, lined, weary rural American faces, with their worn-out overalls and the whirring overhead
fans in the stifling heat. It looked authentic—Bill rattling off racist
idiocies about "niggers ruining the human race" and these old men
mumbling and nodding sleepily in agreement."Yeah, yeah, right, get
those niggers." They knew it was a movie, they were paid extras, but
they *believed* in Bill Shatner. They loved him as Cramer the racist.

The sheriff and local cops seemed to be shadowing us everywhere,
trying to intimidate us. The only sequences in which I felt we got
some tacit cooperation was the night we shot the Ku Klux Klan
parade, the cross-burning, and the church bombing in the black section of town—or Niggertown, as they called it. For Klansmen we
used some of the local boys who were hanging out at the bar; these
guys needed almost no preparation or direction to get into character.

But when it came time to shoot the lynch mob sequence, we got
nothing but trouble. I had decided to shoot in an East Prairie schoolyard ten miles away because that school was *exactly* what I needed.
I got permission to film for two days. The second morning I was
greeted by the sheriff. He was tougher than Rod Steiger in *In the
Heat of the Night* and he wasn't impressed by the permit papers I
waved in his face. "Get outta town," he growled. I explained we had
to shoot that day or fall hopelessly behind. He didn't budge. "Y'all a
bunch a communists and we know what you're doin'. You're trying

to start a revolution. I don't care about those papers. Get outta town or go to jail."

Sounded like a wrap to me, so we moved to Sikeston for the shot of a schoolyard swing, which was necessary for when Cramer strings up Joey Green. All I needed was the swing and a lawn. I assumed I'd get the establishing shot of the school anytime. We went to a public park and set up. But then the Sikeston police showed up and ordered us out.

Gene was always great in tight diplomatic situations. I told him to talk to the cops—out of frame—and stall. I worked as fast as I possibly could, while Gene double-talked about anything that came into his head. When I had gotten my last medium shot and it was time for lunch—an hour had gone by—I waved to Gene and he knew it was over. He assured the officer we would in fact be leaving after lunch and the officer said okay.

The instant we broke for lunch I jumped in my car and raced to a country school I had remembered from location scouting. I came back as lunch was finishing and said, "Okay, Gene, everybody, get in the trucks and follow me." And we went out there with no permits and shot all afternoon in the middle of nowhere. The gamble paid off; we got in the whole day's shooting.

It's a very dramatic and powerful climax. And the only clue that the sequence was shot with three different sets of swings—at the park, the country school, and town school—is that the swings are actually different heights and each swing has a different background.

Still, I needed the establishing shot of the school in East Prairie. I asked my cameraman, Taylor Byars, to come with me on Sunday morning with the Arriflex. "Roger," he said, "I'm with you all the way, but anyone from this company who goes out there is ending up in jail. I heard the guy and I believe him." No one else would come with me.

He had a point. The letter threats against us were getting scarier. Some equipment had been mysteriously damaged. We had to hire a night watchman. "I need that shot," I insisted. "I am not a cameraman. Do this for me. Put the camera on the tripod, give me a 25-millimeter lens and tape down the distance for infinity. The school is ten miles in that direction," I said, looking off. "Check the sky, the wind, the weather. Set the stop for the light you think I'll have in exactly one hour in East Prairie."

I drove out, got the camera and tripod set up, aimed the lens, connected the battery. Then, at the far end of the schoolyard I spotted the sheriff's car. I stayed calm, kept at it, walked the camera a few yards from the car, moving very quickly without looking frantic. The camera was rolling as he approached. I unhooked the battery, heaved the camera into the car, got in, and beat him out of there. We had the film complete.

★ WILLIAM SHATNER

We were surrounded by some very emotional people down there. Our lives were threatened. The only integration in the area seemed to be a gang of ex-convicts who had formed what the police called a wolf pack. They were the wolves of society and they had said they would kill us in our motel. One time Roger and I were elbowed off the curb as we walked through town by three guys we were no match for.

There was another very big and bigoted man who was fascinated by filmmaking. Roger hired him as a grip. Slowly he came around to a more thinking point of view and we became well acquainted. He lent me his car, told me about his lucky chaps when he rode horses, and let me ride his champion horse.

Then the night I borrowed his car, the fastest car in the area, it caught fire while I was in it. I went to put the fire out with his lucky chaps and burnt his chaps. The next day when I rode his champion horse I crippled the horse. He went from being even-minded about racial integration to hating us again.

We shot a white supremacy parade through the black part of town and a cross-burning scene at night and while this was being shot someone watching in the crowd was knifed. The whites thought we were with the blacks and they hated us. It was murder. Those three weeks seemed interminable.

Despite that setting, Roger was as dedicated as any director I have ever seen, particularly when he was threatened outside the schoolyard by the officer. He got that shot under duress, though he could really have been hurt.

Roger knew exactly what he wanted and I knew he loved this project. The reviews were quite wonderful, but everybody felt it wasn't sold right. Still, for many years people said to me, "This is the best thing we have ever seen you do and you're just going to be so famous."

★   ★   ★

This was one of the toughest films I ever shot. It was, thematically, the most serious. The reviews were absolutely stunning. The *Herald Tribune* in New York said,"This film is a major credit to the entire motion picture industry."

We took *The Intruder* to the Venice Film Festival and won a prize. The film was also to be shown at the Cannes Film Festival that spring and it got invited to the Los Alamos International Peace Film Festival; I went along.

At a cocktail party before the final vote—with the judges in attendance—someone asked me what my favorite film was. Trying to seem modest, I said *Fires on the Plain* by Kon Ichikawa was a good film. And it was. Damned if Ichikawa didn't walk away with the grand prize. I got second prize for *The Intruder* and Bill won Best Actor.

One of the judges told me afterward, "You know, if you hadn't given us such convincing praise of Ichikawa's work, we'd have voted for you."

The real jury—movie audiences—handed down a far more depressing verdict with the film's theatrical release. There were dark omens. First, the Motion Picture Association of America refused to give the film its Seal of Approval because we used the word "nigger." I was enraged. I spoke out in the press and charged the MPAA with its own form of discrimination—against smaller independents. The word had been used in studio films for years.

We finally got the MPAA seal, but when racial rioting broke out over James Meredith's registration at the University of Mississippi, the picture was withdrawn from Cannes. The project was dealt another crushing blow when Pathé Labs decided to pull out of the distribution business altogether. This left *The Intruder* with virtually no means of getting released. We eventually put it out through Filmgroup, but the picture died. At first I felt anger, then shock and deep discouragement. This was—and remains to this day—the greatest disappointment in my career.

Ironically, the recent film *Mississippi Burning*, set in 1964, grossed well over $50 million in its first two months; as it was produced two decades after the events portrayed, that film wasn't as big a threat to audiences. People can say, "That wasn't me." My film was contemporary and audiences thought, "This is a slam at us."

In the year after *The Intruder*, I took a long, hard look at what had gone wrong. I had been in analysis around that time and I had learned that the fifty-minute sessions were not unlike my work: in low-budget filmmaking you've maybe sixty, sixty-five minutes to tell the truth and make it work.

My mind had probably been channeled, if that's the right word, in a certain direction by the fact that my father had been an engineer and I was trained as an engineer. But then I started writing, producing, studying acting in Hollywood, and I became enthralled in a world that was foreign to me. And I raced to enter this world.

Analysis increased my awareness of some of my motivations and those of people around me. I was in my mid-thirties. Most of my friends were married. I wondered why I had not made that kind of full commitment.

There were deeper issues in my life as well. I had been raised early as a Catholic and fallen away—not really from a state of grace but certainly a state of belief in a divine system. I had a spiritual void to deal with.

I began examining a sense I had that I was not totally aware of my emotions. Despite the fact that I had directed more than thirty films in less than eight years in the business, I felt I was not functioning artistically and personally to my fullest potential.

For example, despite knowing plenty of young writers, actors and actresses, and directors working in Hollywood at the time, it was evident that I was not part of the mainstream. This was, in a sense, a pattern through childhood all the way into college. I had never been an outright loner. I had had friends all my life; I belonged to High Y in school, a fraternity at Stanford. But deeper down, I never felt part of the "in group." Today, the independent field is wide open but back then there were far fewer successful independents. I was building a reputation as a sort of Hollywood rebel or maverick because I was outside the majors.

I also felt that I could be making better movies and working on a higher, more sophisticated artistic level. People have said for years that I should have gone on and done the big movies for the big studios as a pure director. I was continually offered directing jobs with the majors, but every time I worked with a major, I stepped back and returned to independent filmmaking on much lower budgets and on probably inferior projects.

Maybe I steered clear of the mainstream because of a fear of getting lost as an artist. I was successful, comfortable, and in total control as an outlaw producer/director. Perhaps I needed to prove my ability to make it outside the system; perhaps I equated the risk of entering the mainstream with losing my artistic or financial autonomy. Worse, it may have exposed me to failure, critical or commercial. That was not necessarily a conscious, rational notion at the time. But after *The Intruder* I was obviously not particularly eager to take risks and set myself up for another beating.

In a sense, earning money became more than just a means to satisfy material desires. I had played a lot of poker at Stanford and it was like seeing the chips piling up before my eyes. I had a long unbeaten streak until *The Intruder*; even then, my won-lost record stood at something like thirty and one. There weren't too many other players in the game with numbers like that.

Chapter 9

f I had spent the entire first half of the 1960s doing nothing but those Poe films on dimly lit gothic interior sets, I might well have ended up as nutty as Roderick Usher. Whether it was a conscious motive or not, I avoided any such possibility by varying the look and themes of the other films I made during the Poe cycle—*The Intruder*, for example—and traveling to some out-of-the-way places to shoot them. That is one of the perks of a career in directing: You pick the place you'd love to visit and explore and you figure out a way to use it as a location. Then, you prepare yourself for the unexpected.

Atlas took me to Athens and turned into one of the strangest pro-

Top: Ray Milland in *X—The Man with the X-Ray Eyes*
Bottom: Advertisement for *The Secret Invasion*

ductions of my career—an epic about ancient Greece on a $70,000 budget. I combined work, my passion for fast cars, and a need for a vacation to do *The Young Racers* along the Grand Prix circuit. And when I saw Dubrovnik—in the pages of *National Geographic* while waiting in a dentist's office—I had a vision of sorts: to shoot *The Secret Invasion*, a World War Two action story, on the Adriatic coast. That film marked a turning point for me: my first movie for a major studio, United Artists. Also, the $500,000-plus budget was by far my largest, and it quickly opened *my* eyes to the way films were made within the major studio system.

The story behind *Atlas* shows why you have to be fast on your feet if you make your own movies. I was in Europe to develop a film called "I Flew a Spy Plane Over Russia," a story directly inspired by the Francis Gary Powers U-2 incident over the Soviet Union. Bob Towne worked out a story line with me. He had some imaginative ideas for the tale of a pilot who gets shot down over Russia and is used as a pawn by rival political factions within the Soviet Union. Bob was a slow writer. His scripts, though, were—and still are— excellent and worth the wait. This time, he gave me an outline and the first twenty pages and I went to Europe, where the old-world architecture and exteriors were appropriate to the script. On the strength of those pages I lined up a coproduction deal with Anglo-Amalgamated, an English company that had distributed my films in Europe.

I phoned Bob and broke the good news. "Send me the rest of the pages and I can make a deal." I waited. And waited. Bob was always a friend; give him enough time and he'll give you a *Chinatown* or a *Shampoo*. But I was never famous for my patience. Whether he got blocked, or weighed down—he just never finished. Summer was fading and I finally gave up.

So, it was on to Greece. I was introduced to an independent producer in Athens named Vion Papamichelis who agreed to put up half the money—about $40,000—and make *Atlas* with me. I tracked down Chuck Griffith in Tel Aviv and told him he'd have to write *Atlas* in three or four weeks. I sent him a plane ticket, and when he showed up a day later he had on sandals and a knapsack. Chuck ended up being production manager, assistant director, writer, and a Greek soldier on-screen.

He started writing as we went into preproduction. A week before shooting, as I was about to fly in three American actors, Papamichelis invited me to lunch and in the middle of the meal broke down and cried. His backing had fallen through. "I have no money," Vion said, sobbing. "We cannot make this film."

I was really stuck. Then the solution came to me. What are these Greek and Roman sword and sandal epics but Westerns in disguise?

I've done low-budget Westerns in *ten days*. I'll just make *Atlas* for my half of the budget.

Atlas's plot went like this: Praximedes, the tyrant of Seronikos, is trying to conquer the Walled City of Thenis. The weary armies agree to pick one man to fight a battle to the finish to determine the winner of the war. Praximedes enlists his seductive mistress Candia to persuade Atlas, an Olympian athlete, to fight for Seronikos. Atlas defeats his adversary and Praximedes gets Thenis; Atlas gets the girl. But then he learns he has been duped. He flees Thenis and joins the rebels outside the city. He kills Praximedes in a final showdown and retakes Thenis for its own people.

With half the backing gone, major script changes were in order. For one thing, I had no sets. So I thought: What are ruins if not sets? We'll shoot those for free. To explain the absence of interesting interiors, we put in an exchange between Atlas and Praximedes as they trek toward Thenis. "Tell me, Praximedes," Atlas says, "all the buildings in your part of Greece seem to be in ruins. Why is that?"

"We've had constant civil war for the past two hundred years," Praximedes explains, "and everything has been partially destroyed." Another problem, which I mentioned earlier in the introduction, was how the mighty Praximedes was going to storm the walls of Thenis and overwhelm its armies—when I had about fifty extras. That very question obviously had occurred to our curious Olympian—played by Michael Forest—who was relatively scrawny by the Herculean standards set by Steve Reeves. "Tell me, Praximedes," he asks, "how do you plan to attack such a large city with such a small band of men?"

"My theory of warfare," he explains, "is that a small, highly trained, mobile group of elite fighting men can defeat any number of rabble."

Sure, except I didn't exactly end up with a small, highly trained, mobile group of elite fighting men. I made a contribution to some Old Soldier fund and ended up with a hundred restless, rebellious itching members of the real Greek Army who had a lot of trouble dealing with the late summer Athens sun. We put them in their papier mâché helmets and scratchy period costumes, ready for the big battle scenes. And they started tearing away the papier mâché noseguards from their helmets because they were too hot and because they wanted their families to recognize them in the movie. I yelled at them and the officer in charge of the soldiers yelled at me for yelling at them. "I'm going to yell at them again," I screamed, "if they don't stop tearing up their helmets."

I did shoot at the Agora, a rebuilt ancient city, to show the architecture of the time. But I had to shoot long rows of columns very carefully and at sharp angles to block the spaces between columns and obscure any view of downtown Athens.

The permit we got to shoot at the Acropolis was for stills only and with no people in them. Since this wasn't my doctoral thesis in architecture, we had to find another site for the Walled City of Thenis. I drove around and discovered a monastery outside Athens. The only problem was that the monastery was just off a major freeway and my crew could barely back up twenty feet from the Walled City of Thenis without having freeway traffic whipping by. So the battle for Thenis was the military equivalent of a half-court basketball game— with *very* shallow views of Thenis.

I had a battle of my own to fight outside the walls of Thenis. My crew struck in the middle of the three-week production. The budget was moving up toward $70,000. "There's no way you guys can strike," I said angrily. "We're behind schedule and you've got to work. Look, work today, and tonight I'll buy everyone rounds of ouzo and retsina at a tavern and we'll work out your problems."

We did. Their real problem was that no Greek producers would recognize them as a legitimate union and give them any power. So I signed a document that, in effect, made me the first union producer in Greece. I also ratified a fractional raise—five dollars a week. The Greek film industry union was born that day. Whether that contract gave them real clout or merely a psychological validity I don't know. But when we wrapped they threw a party for me and offered me a number of gifts. And more than a quarter of a century later, I was discussing a joint production deal in Athens when a Greek producer told me, "You know, your name is still known around here. Producers do not think very highly of you." I asked why. "Because," he said, "you were the first producer to do a union film in the country."

Atlas was cut down pretty brutally by critics and barely made back the total negative cost. It was the fifth and last release by Filmgroup. The company made a few thousand dollars each year on those small pictures but it wasn't worth the trouble.

In the summer of 1962 I was supposed to do an AIP film. But at the time they were cash-short and didn't want to spend another quarter-million dollars. I had always thought a Grand Prix film would be fun to shoot with the races and the crowds. Getting people to come along on token salaries would be no problem; I had done this in Hawaii and Puerto Rico.

This was late March, early April. The races started in early summer. AIP gave me the green light on a budget of $150,000 for *The Young Racers*. All I needed was a screenplay. I called Bob Campbell, who had written *Five Guns* and *Kelly* for me. He had been the youngest screenwriter to get an Academy Award nomination—for *The Man of a Thousand Faces,* a film about Lon Chaney made in

1957. I had seen a fine screenplay he had almost sold to Fox about a young American who gets involved with a great bullfighter and his wife in Spain. I thought Bob might be open to some minor script revisions. "Can you make this bullfighter a young race car driver who gets involved with a great Grand Prix racer and his girlfriend? Race car driving, bullfighting—same thing. Danger. Action on the weekends. Intrigue during the weeks."

"Sure," he said. I told him I needed the rewrite when I left for Monte Carlo in two weeks. "I'll pay your way to Europe. You can polish the rewrites as we move through the circuit."

I called on all my old friends and put together one of the all-time great crews, offering them low money but round-trip airfare and room and board along the circuit—Monaco, Rouen, Spa in Belgium, Holland, and England. The plan was to shoot the dramatic scenes and the races every other weekend—the qualifying Saturday and the actual race Sunday. Then, we'd all get a week's vacation, showing up Monday a week at the next city.

Everyone I called accepted immediately. Francis Coppola was my first assistant, grip mechanic, and soundman. Bob Towne flew in for part of the trip as my third assistant. Chuck Griffith came on to be another a.d. Menachem Golan, who later became president of Cannon Films, was a USC film school student, and I hired him to be my second assistant. Menachem was looking for a way to return to his home in Israel for the summer. "If you want a job," I said, "meet us in Monte Carlo." I figured, why pay his way back if he's going anyway? He said he was planning on buying a car in Europe and driving it to the Middle East. "Would you pay part of the cost of the car?" he asked. "If you do, you can use the car on the picture."

I said sure and gave him the job. His wife, Rachel, came along and did makeup and wardrobe.

Menachem turned out to be probably the hardest-working guy in the company, an intellectually bright, very shrewd guy you knew would go far. He worked half the night to prepare the next day's work. He was production assistant, assistant director, production manager. There was great spirit on the crew.

★ **FRANCIS COPPOLA**

We all knew that when Roger went to Europe or Hawaii or Puerto Rico for a picture that he always made a second picture with his own money. He asked me if I knew a good soundman for the European shoot and I said, "Gee, yeah, I do. I'll do the sound." So I immediately got the Nagra out of the closet at the office and went home to read the manual.

★　★　★

Campbell redid the bullfighting story and ended up with a love triangle involving a roguish Lotus team champion named Joe Machin,
a former driver named Stephen Children, now a writer who wants to
profile the champ, and his fiancée, Monique, who has had an affair
with Machin.

This was bound to be a complex shoot but I was convinced that
nothing could go wrong. I went out with no permits whatsoever.
However, I sent out an assistant who was just out of college, Mary
Anne Wood, and she did a remarkably efficient job of advancing each
race town—locations, hotels, local hands.

To get the critical racing shots we enlisted the help of the world-
class Grand Prix racers like Jimmy Clark and Bruce McClaren and
their Formula 1 teams, Lotus and Cooper. For instance, Bill Campbell, as Joe Machin, would wear Jimmy's Team Lotus helmet for the
close-ups and then we could shoot Jimmy's car in the race and cut it
all together.

I made a deal with the race organizers that after a practice run
before the race, Jimmy would come once around the final turn, drive
up, stop, I'd come in for a close-up of Bill with Jimmy's helmet, and
he would run out of the "winning" car. Then in one shot the girl
would run out and put a wreath around him and kiss Bill. He then
drives off in front of a hundred thousand people. Clark was the
world's premier racer then, so it figured his car would be in the lead
at *some* point, and who could tell what lap he was on at any given
time?

I was all set for my special shot of Clark's car—I was shooting
races with three cameras—when suddenly a Shell Oil truck pulled
onto the track. I couldn't believe it. I had ten minutes to get this
carefully rehearsed sequence. Who wins a Grand Prix race with a
huge Shell Oil truck on the track behind him?

I was so mad I started waving and screaming. I ran down from my
position, about a quarter of a mile away. I kept screaming, "Get out,
get out," and he finally backed away. I looked at my watch and we
only had a few minutes. I'll never forget the feeling. The crowd
understood that I was the director and had been cheated. They knew
the shot was blown and they knew I wasn't kidding around. A
hundred thousand people yelled and cheered me as I ran across the
track. And we did indeed get the shot and it was a great one.

Another problem developed with a famous tight turn that I absolutely had to shoot. The trouble was, so did every other person in
Europe who owned a still, newsreel, or movie camera, because they
were all crammed in on the outside of the track. And there was one
insane rule that you couldn't run from the outside of the track to the
inside until after the race had begun. They were lined up so tightly
there was no room to squeeze in. I told my d.p. Floyd Crosby and

Chuck that we had to be in the *first row* of the inside track. "There is no question," I insisted, "we are going to be there. I didn't come all the way out here from L.A. to put my camera behind the pack."

I decided to run forward on my own. The horde of photographers was on that track before the last car sped by, assuming it wouldn't slow down or stop and kill a few dozen people. "You bring the camera and the batteries," I yelled to them. It was clear the other photographers were experienced on the circuit. This was our first race. I got to my spot and guys were fighting me for it but I kept my elbows up and established *position,* as if I were jockeying for a rebound in basketball. We set the camera up and got our shot.

There was one car crash during the shoot but it wasn't in a race. It was, in fact, a Team Corman driver who wiped out. After we wrapped in Monte Carlo everyone had a week off before resuming up north in Rouen or Spa. We were promoting cars for the picture in exchange for using them. Joe Machin's personal car in the film was a fast little Sunbeam. Chuck Griffith decided to get into the spirit of the shoot. "Let me drive the Sunbeam north," Chuck asked. His girlfriend was in from Israel, he had a hot European sports car and a week off on the Continent. "Okay, Chuck," I said, "but just be careful. This is the lead's car."

I headed off to Nice.

★ CHUCK GRIFFITH

My girlfriend, Irena, and I had just left Monaco heading north and hit a bad rainstorm. An English van camper kept tailgating us until we got to this huge hill, where the gendarmes had to stop traffic to let people proceed with caution because it was slippery. Everyone slowed going downhill—except the camper. It just plowed into us and knocked us all to hell. We flipped over five times. The ambulance got us to the hospital. I got hold of Roger at the Nice airport and broke the news.

"Well," he said calmly, "tell 'em to patch you up and get here as quickly as possible."

We escaped from the hospital. The Sunbeam was history. Roger had to write it out of the picture. Whenever Machin was supposed to drive into frame, now he *walked* into frame instead.

★   ★   ★

We managed to smuggle equipment into England for the final race. By then, a different sort of competition was going on behind the scenes as we wrapped up north near Liverpool. I had decided to finance a second movie, and Francis and Menachem both wanted to do it. We had the minibus with the cameras, lights, dollies, and tracks. What we didn't have was a work permit. The most logical place to shoot the other film was Dublin, because we could just ferry the minibus from Liverpool. Plus, Ireland was much looser with labor permits.

I wanted to keep the budget to $30,000. I told Francis about my intention; if he could come up with an idea for a film in Ireland he could direct it. Menachem heard about this and came to me. "What if I come up with an idea to shoot in Tel Aviv? Instead of sending the minibus to Dublin send it to Tel Aviv."

I said fine. So Francis and Menachem both came up with ideas. I liked Francis's idea better—it became *Dementia 13*—and it turned out to be a solid success for a first feature. Besides, it made better sense to send the equipment across the channel to Ireland than to Tel Aviv. Menachem still will not let me forget that I chose Francis over him.

Francis was a highly intelligent, talented man who knew what he was doing. He was also trying to get something going with the very pretty French leading lady, Marie Versini, but he couldn't get anywhere with her. But as soon as she found out that Francis was going from assistant director to director of his own movie, she became *very* friendly. And to Francis's great credit, he wouldn't have anything to do with her then.

★ **FRANCIS COPPOLA**

Working as a team for the races was quite exhilarating for me. I was soundman and second unit director and I was in Europe and I bought an Alfa Romeo with my money over there. When Roger decided not to direct a second film himself, I went to him and said, "I'll do the other film. Let me take the camera and some of the equipment and staff and make a low-budget psychological thriller." So I immediately went home that night after the shoot and wrote the big horror scene—a Hitchcock-type ax murder sequence—and showed it to him. He came back with some changes and said, "All right, if you can do the rest of the script like that you can do it for $20,000."

★ ★ ★

After *Racers* Francis went on to Dublin to shoot *Dementia 13*. I had been invited—all expenses paid—to a Yugoslav film festival on the Adriatic coast. First, though, I visited Francis on location and saw he was in control. It was going so smoothly I decided to take a vacation after the festival. I had been all over Europe so I made arrangements to travel to the Soviet Union, a country I had always wanted to visit.

I remember going to the Soviet Embassy in London to apply for a visa and they said, "It will take a month." I laughed and said, "You know, in the United States, I could get this kind of thing done *in a day!*" The guy said, "All right, come back tomorrow and you'll have it here."

I came in through Kiev on a blistering summer day. Passengers were led to a corrugated metal shed with one little window. It must have been 110 degrees. We just sat there, sweating. No one knew when anything would happen. A sign outside said NO ENTRY and beyond that was a civilian airport. On the other side of the field were rows of Air Force bombers. This heat was unbearable, so I walked out there. No one stopped me. I wandered around freely in the middle of the Soviet Air Force, checking out their sleek bombers. Guys were gassing up the planes, loading up, the full activity of an air base. I went right up to the jets and felt myself becoming more nervy as I went. I looked at a pilot as he tanked up his plane and gave him a friendly nod. He nodded back, smiling, and I moved on, inspecting Soviet bombers two feet from the cockpits.

When I had seen enough fighters I walked back inside. At that point it occurred to me: This notion of super-tight security is a myth. Their country was like any other. It's a big bureaucracy and they're all inefficient. They don't know what they're doing. I knew it when I walked back inside that shed and that attitude stayed with me the whole trip.

My first night in town I began dating a girl named Nina Zapok, who told me she was the Secretary of the Young Communists League in Kiev. I met her at a party, when I heard her tell someone her boyfriend was in Siberia. "Voluntarily, I assume," I said with a smile.

I hired a guide for daytime touring around Kiev and saw Nina all five nights in Kiev. I tried to portray myself to her as a working man, someone who had simply made some films. Once, we came back to my hotel and I found a message to call Francis in Ireland. Nina helped me place the call. So she was sitting there next to me as Francis told me that an English producer wanted to put up another $20,000 for *Dementia* in exchange for the European rights.

"I will NOT sell the European rights for twenty thousand," I said emphatically. "You tell your man I will not take less than twenty-five." I got off the phone and Nina knew this was no ordinary proletarian deal. "It is clear," she said, "that you are a different kind of person from what you have told me."

One night, when Nina and I went to the Dynamo restaurant in Kiev, I instinctively waited by the door after we entered. "Why are we standing here?" she asked.

"We're waiting for the headwaiter to seat us."

"In the Soviet," she said proudly, "we have no headwaiters, but soon we will have."

"Nina," I assured her, "having headwaiters is not one of the criteria of high culture or economic superiority."

That was symptomatic of the Khrushchev Cold War mentality. The Soviets wanted to compete with the U.S. in anything—moon landings, headwaiters—and if they were behind, they would catch up.

At the Pula Festival in Yugoslavia the screenings were in an ancient Roman amphitheater, the most spectacular movie theater I was ever in. I met an executive from one of the state-run studios. His name was Georgi. "I hear you can make a deal faster than anybody else," he said to me. I smiled.

"We've got a crime story script to shoot in English," he went on. "If you can give us a leading man, the lead heavy, and someone to handle the English dialogue, we will shoot it and give you the English rights for twenty thousand."

"Let me read the script tonight and I'll meet you in two hours," I said. I read the script, called "Operation Titian" because it was about the theft of a Titian work. I closed the deal with Georgi around midnight with a few shots of slivovitz. The studio would house and feed my people; I would fly them in and pay them. I then called Francis in Dublin. He was wrapping his three-week *Dementia* shoot.

"Francis," I said, "come to Zagreb next week. Get Bill Campbell and Pat Magee." They had been in *Racers*. Pat would be the heavy, Bill the lead, and Francis the dialogue supervisor. He'd coach the Yugoslav actors through their English lines.

The three showed up a week later. I was already gone. I distributed it and actually made a little profit. It wasn't that good, even with a different title. I did speak with Georgi afterward. "You know," he said, "those actors were good but I don't think that guy Coppola knows what he's doing."

"Well," I told the fastest dealmaker in the Eastern bloc, "I think he's pretty good and, you never know, he's just a young guy and he's still learning."

Back in Moscow, I bought a science fiction film from Mosfilm and met with their top executives. They showed me around their impressive studios and made me an offer that really intrigued me. I would stay in Moscow for a year on salary, whether I made a film or not, and get an apartment, car, use of a summer cabin on the Black Sea or wherever the filmmakers' encampment was, and a percentage of the profits. The film would be made in both languages and I'd retain English rights.

I had no idea there was a profit motive in the Soviet Union, but they boasted that all their movies made money, that all directors shared in the profits, and that films were shown in every theater throughout the Soviet Union. I had never even contemplated a studio contract in Burbank, let alone Moscow. But this was unique. "I'd like to make a futuristic science fiction film," I told them. I'd seen their sci-fi films and thought, I could come back and make a really giant picture here, a major film.

They wanted to give me the go-ahead and put me in an office. I was supposed to create an outline while there. Then I met the official censor who evaluated all projects. I laid out my idea to this educated and gentle man. It was set far in the future, beyond Cold War issues, a very technically oriented film. To this day, I find his response startling. "Very interesting idea," he said. "Science fiction is very popular here in the Soviet Union. I must caution you on one point. Many Soviet filmmakers come to me with science fiction ideas about the future. I must turn many of them down because their stories do not portray the future five hundred or a thousand years from now the way it is going to be. Even though I know you are working here in good faith with your capitalist education, it might even be more difficult for you to predict the future."

Having failed the ideological test, I headed back to more familiar capitalist terrain. I returned to the U.S. to make a picture for AIP about a daring scientist who can't see the future but *can* see through all physical reality. Jim Nicholson told me, as he often did over lunch, that he had a title in search of a movie. The title was *X—The Man with the X-Ray Eyes*. We threw ideas around over the next day or two—a jazz musician on weird drugs, a criminal who uses X-ray vision for robberies. They seemed like dead-end stories. Then it hit me that the most logical direction was a medical researcher. Maybe it was my own training in science and engineering, but I decided it shouldn't be by accident. He's a scientist deliberately trying to develop X-ray or expanded vision. The X-ray vision should progress deeper and deeper until at the end there is a mystical, religious experience of seeing to the center of the universe, or the equivalent of God.

Ray Russell wrote the script with Robert Dillon from Ray's story. I had a three-week schedule with a budget between $200,000 and $300,000, with Ray Milland getting a big portion of the budget to play Dr. James Xavier.

Xavier injects himself with an experimental serum he has developed to expand human eyesight and he goes insane because he soon sees *everything*. Obsessed with the God-like possibilities, he pushes a colleague out a window when he tries to inject X with a tranquilizer. He is now a mad genius on the run from the law.

Lead-reinforced goggles shield him from overpowering light but his life becomes a pathetic, tormented odyssey. Aided by a con artist played by Don Rickles, he works as a sideshow mind reader and healer before winning $20,000 in Vegas so he can develop an antidote. In a tussle with security guards, his goggles fall off and he panics, tossing the money in the air. When patrons riot, he flees to the desert.

Driving toward the desert, he sees through buildings and describes "a city unborn, flesh dissolved in an acid of light, a city of the dead." The car crashes and X staggers, blind, into a desert tent revival. The preacher, offended by X's claim to see at the center of the universe the light of God, quotes Matthew: "If thy right eye offend thee, pluck it out." Tortured by voices in his head, he bends down and gouges out his own eyes.

I had almost no money for the special optical effects. The trip through Vegas, which we shot on a soundstage and at locations in L.A., was the toughest challenge. To create the effect of X seeing through buildings, I decided to shoot a building at varying stages of construction and to show it backwards. I picked a five- or six-story building site and went out a few times with a cameraman. First I photographed the steel girders, then went back a month or two later after principal photography, when the site was three-quarters finished. For the completed building I matched another one with the same dimensions because the first one wasn't finished in time. Then I cut, going backwards, so that his first view of the building is the finished one, then as the "X Effect" takes hold, he blinks and sees a little deeper into the building until all he sees are the girders. The movie was filled with tricks like that, including use of an optical effect known as "Spectarama."

Reviews of *X-Ray Eyes* were positive. In fact it won the Trieste Science Fiction Film Festival award for Best Film of 1963. It was seen as an *important* film. Later, I realized it was the concept that was important: a researcher moving through science toward a religious mystical experience. The theme of *X-Ray Eyes* was rather similar to *2001: A Space Odyssey*, made five or six years later, in that there is at the end of the odyssey an hallucinogenic, mystical vision of light and motion. Kubrick's trip was through space; X's was interior.

Characters in many of my movies wear sunglasses—Paul Birch in *Not of This Earth* and Xavier, Peter Fonda, and Bruce Dern in *The Wild Angels* are a few. Sight, eyes, vision—is this a theme that threads these films together or is it pure coincidence? Or that *Prehistoric World* was similar to *X-Ray Eyes* and *The Trip* in that it was about a man's willingness to break laws and risk being ostracized in order to explore what lies beyond one's normal, limiting world?

These stories may all be linked by a reference to myself. I had numerous opportunities to join the Establishment, and from time to time I did. But I have always stepped away. Perhaps that is why X has been called in some circles a serious Corman film—because of an identification with a scientist who is cursed by his vision and cast out by his community.

And yet, despite the "outlaw" stance toward the studio system, it was, perhaps, inevitable that I would make a film for a major. The head of production at UA, David Picker, had approached me to work on a project in the past but I had no ideas for him then. However, Bob Campbell, who had just done *Racers* for me, had finished a script titled "The Dubious Patriots." British intelligence frees five convicts whose mission is to spring a top-ranking Italian general from a Dubrovnik prison in order for him to turn his own men against their Nazi allies. Once again, the theme was one I liked very much: bad men sent to do good as a way to redeem themselves and win their freedom. In New York—on the way back from *Racers*—I gave Picker the script on a Friday and he said, "We'll look at it. But we're backed up with scripts and it might be a few weeks before I can get to it."

I said, Sure. Fine. I understand. This was one reason I never rushed to work for the majors. On Monday, I wasn't back in my L.A. office five minutes when the phone rang. It was Picker. "I read the script and we want to make the picture," he said.

It went that fast. Right place at the right time.

The title was changed to *The Secret Invasion,* which was believed to be more commercial. UA budgeted the production at $600,000, which was *double* my bigger Poe pictures. The film was shot in the summer of 1963.

Initially, the prisoner being held was an atomic scientist, the only man knowing the missing key ingredient in the equations to make an atomic bomb. So by freeing him, the five criminals help unleash atomic warfare. And UA said they liked the idea but not that man. So I changed him to an Italian general who would lead the resistance against the Nazis and thereby facilitate an Allied invasion of Italy. UA wanted them to be full-out heroes with less subtlety than I might have sought. I had wanted them to unwittingly and *ironically* do something bad on their way to being heroes. But this was the majors and with a half-million of their dollars at stake, I had a feeling these characters might lack nuance. I knew this was one of the drawbacks to working with the studios—story by committee.

My brother produced the film and we did some preproduction work out of UA's London office. I already knew the rules would be slightly different. UA told us that they were sending an auditor to Yugoslavia. Right away we realized the cost of sending the auditor— airfare, room, board, expenses, transportation—would be a considerable part of the half-million-dollar budget. Gene asked the executives why they needed to do that. "Don't you trust us?" he wondered.

"Of course we do," was the answer, "but he's going there to check the books and authorize each payment of each check."

"Well," Gene argued, "what if my brother or I wants to write a check that your auditor thinks is wrong?"

"Well, then, you go ahead and write the check because we believe you and Roger know what you are doing."

"Then why bother spending the money on the auditor?"

So they sent us to Yugoslavia with the money and no one to check us out.

Keeping books is really quite simple, and I have always been very cautious about whom we hire and what we pay and what we rent, etc., etc. The cost of a film is the sum of actual expenses, plus a small percentage for overhead. It was—and has remained—for us a matter of pride to get the full production value on the screen.

The six-week, thirty-six-day shoot that summer turned into a most complicated and difficult ordeal—the kind of shoot that proves films *never* go easily. I was trying to make a very big-looking film in thirty-six days on $500,000. It was just too tough.

For one thing, we never got all the military equipment and troops we were promised because there had been a huge earthquake and the men and materiel were needed for the relief effort. Or, so we were told. And we had a Yugoslav production assistant named Rolf, whose job it was to maintain order on the set. While shooting a beach sequence at an Adriatic seaside resort, I asked him to clear the background. There were scores of tourists and vacationers in frame and Rolf started walking toward them. Suddenly, he pulled a gun and waved it over his head as he got near the crowd. "No, Rolf," I shouted. "Please don't clear the beach with a gun. Just ask them to move."

Another slowdown in the middle of the shoot had to do with putting red stars on the uniforms of the Yugoslav Resistance partisans fighting the Nazis. Local officials wanted red stars on the uniforms and clothing of the guerrillas, many of whom I had understood to be simple peasants and farmers. So I said no, it didn't make any sense. The last thing people working in an underground resistance under Nazi occupation would do is sew red stars on their clothing. The Germans would just shoot them on sight as soon as they spotted the star.

They insisted, but I worked out a compromise. I agreed to put stars on certain extras. Then I moved them to the background, shot from angles that obscured the stars, and filmed montages of marching boots and guns rising up. That way, any time a red star did intrude I could cut away.

There was another ludicrous waste of time during a night sequence we were shooting out in the Adriatic. We had three boats: the camera boat; the boat with two of my male leads, Edd Byrnes and Stewart Granger; and a fog boat. Stewart announced at about three A.M., "I want Edd's line for this scene."

"It's Edd's line," I said. "It's in the script. How can you ask for another actor's line?"

"There's no way I'm giving you this line," Edd told Stewart. "It's a key line." The line was critical in establishing power within their group of men.

"I'm not playing the scene if I don't get that line," Stewart insisted.

"What do I care if you don't play the scene?" Edd said to him. Then he turned to me. "Can we shoot the scene without him?"

"Actually, no, we can't," I said. This impasse went on for over half an hour. The solution finally came to me. I invented another line, which Edd didn't like at all—and I gave it to Stewart. It was getting cold and late and tempers were fraying. We needed a way out.

"This new line is the *equivalent* of Edd's line," I assured Stewart. "Edd won't give you the line and if *I* give it to you, Edd will quit." He seemed placated, but now Edd spoke up.

"Look," he said, "here's the script. He read it before he accepted the project. How can he, in the middle of this scene, suddenly decide—"

"Okay, enough," I said. That was it. No more discussion. "Just let him say the line and let's get on with it."

In its final cut, *Secret Invasion* looked like a big movie and we did it for exactly $592,000. It grossed somewhere around $3 million. The reason I remember the exact negative cost was that we got a distribution report from UA that said we were still a couple hundred thousand dollars from breaking even. I called the head of UA and said, "Look, either straighten this report out or I'm sending in the auditors. There is no way $3 million in collected gross still leaves us $200,000 short of breaking even on $592,000."

"Tell you what," he said. "Don't audit. We'll buy out your participation for $400,000. You can have a check tomorrow. But," he added, "you sign away all your rights, your piece is paid off, and you attest that our books are true and accurate."

"That your books are true and accurate?"

"We don't want anybody claiming our books aren't true and accurate."

Gene and I signed the paper attesting to UA's true and accurate bookkeeping methods and collected the $400,000.

Chapter 10

A year or so later, after the settlement with United Artists, while I was in England doing my last Poe film, *The Tomb of Ligeia* (which Robert Towne wrote), I was approached by Columbia Pictures. "Sign with us," they said, "and you'll do bigger, better films." I thought this might be the time to graduate to more important pictures, but it soon became apparent that the studio didn't want more important pictures from me—they wanted slightly bigger versions of just what I'd been doing. I grew so restless from the way things worked at Columbia that I asked for a leave of absence from my contract so I could produce and direct a motorcycle gang picture called *The Wild Angels* for AIP in the early months of 1966. Five months later I had a rough cut of a movie shot in three weeks on a $360,000 budget.

Scene from *The St. Valentine's Day Massacre*

It wasn't that I had wasted any time in development at Columbia. While still wrapping *Tomb*, I contacted a very fine young Irish playwright named Hugh Leonard in London and asked him to adapt for film his own BBC teleplay of Joyce's *Portrait of the Artist as a Young Man*. He gave me a verbal commitment to go ahead as I worked something out with the Joyce estate enabling me to proceed.

I visited Oxford University and put up a notice that read: AMERICAN PRODUCER WANTS ASSISTANT. I also called one of the tutors at Oxford and told him I was looking for his very finest student. The tutor sent me a letter recommending a twenty-two-year-old woman named Frances Doel, an English literature scholar whom he described as St. Hilda's College's "most brilliant critical mind." I met Frances and soon learned from her that she did not type, drive, or do math. I asked her what her main interests were and she said, "theater and writing" and I assured her that she wouldn't be doing much of either if she came to work for me in L.A. I did not offer her the job right away; I returned to the States to get working on my Columbia deal. I was signed to a yearlong contract with an option to renew. I came home with great enthusiasm for the Joyce project; *Portrait* was a great story and I believed I could make a very good film of it in Ireland for not much money. Columbia, however, promptly told me they had no interest in *Portrait*.

Meanwhile, I kept looking for an assistant. I asked for recommendations from the USC and UCLA placement centers. One of the young women who showed up was Julie Halloran from UCLA. Julie was very bright, very pretty—beautiful, in fact. A charming woman in her early twenties. Another young woman who came in, Stephanie Rothman, was Phi Beta Kappa in English Lit from Berkeley, top of her class with a master's degree in film from USC. She had just won the Director's Guild Award as the outstanding student director at an American university. There was no way I could not hire Stephanie. So I offered her the job and I asked Julie for a date. Both said yes. Stephanie began a fine career that led to several directorial efforts for me; Julie and I began a dating relationship that was often broken up by location work but which led, six years later, to marriage.

My search for a project then shifted to a giant, wonderful $500,000 South Pacific World War Two era set for the movie version of James Clavell's novel *King Rat*. "Can you use this set?" they asked me, the way AIP might have done for a Poe project. To find out, they sent a limo to drive me to the set. I walked around all morning thinking, I've never had anything like this to shoot in my life. I could come up with a really big-looking film, because the money's already been spent on this set.

I decided to pursue a film adaptation of Kafka's *The Penal Colony*.

There was some issue as to international copyright and Czechoslovakia being a Communist-bloc country, yet the studio for some reason was never able to clear up the confusion over the copyright. "We
can't take the chance," I was told.

"Look," I said, frustrated and angry, "you're a major studio. You
have lawyers here, in Europe, everywhere. I cannot believe that
with all this legal talent you can't figure out whether *Penal Colony* is
copyrighted or not."

I did a little checking myself and learned they were, indeed, in
the clear. Kafka was dead. Czechoslovakia did not recognize international copyright agreements. There were no Kafka heirs. There
was nobody to get in the way, except, obviously, Columbia Pictures.
Orson Welles, I pointed out, had already filmed Kafka's *The Trial* in
Yugoslavia. Columbia seemed so busy looking for people to buy the
rights from that they failed to see that there were no rights to buy.

We drifted and the picture never got made. They let me develop
a strong script by the novelist Richard Yates about Iwo Jima; I was
still trying to do a large-scale war epic. But the studio didn't want to
go ahead because we couldn't agree on a budget. They budgeted it
at some extreme figure that would have made it the most costly film
at the studio then. "I am *not* going to restage the entire battle of Iwo
Jima," I kept telling them, and they kept saying, "But you *have to*
restage it."

This was the longest I had gone without directing. Finally, in 1965
Columbia gave me the go-ahead to make a Western called *The Long
Ride Home*, based on a novel the studio had acquired. I got Bob
Towne the assignment to work on the script.

★ FRANCES DOEL

I learned something about Roger on my first day in the office. As Roger
was going out for some appointments around lunchtime, he pointed at
a closed door. "Behind that door, Frances," he explained solemnly, "is
a writer. His name is Robert Towne. He's quite good but very slow. By
twelve-thirty he should have pushed under the door six pages. It probably won't be six. It'll probably be five because, as I said, he is slow. But
if he *has* done his pages, you may buzz him on the intercom, ask him
what sandwich he wants for lunch, go get it, and bring it back to him.
But do *not*, on any account, open the door."

So of course as soon as Roger left, Towne opened the door and looked
around, asking if Roger had gone.

Scriptwriting seemed then to be a big bone of contention between
Bob and Roger. Roger seemed to think that in the first ten minutes you
should have some big piece of riveting and explosive action. Towne

maintained that was ridiculous. Once you got people to pay their money and enter the movie house you had ten or fifteen minutes to establish a character, imbue the story with atmosphere. This was a rather frequent conflict between Roger and any writer. The main thing that happened was Roger usually ripped up the first ten pages of someone's script and said it was "just dialogue."

★ ★ ★

Because I was under contract, I could not direct for anyone else. But I backed several films during this time. Two were Westerns written by Jack Nicholson and directed by Monte Hellman, *The Shooting* and *Ride in the Whirlwind;* there was a pair of beach pictures and a science fiction picture called *Queen of Blood.*

After a series of disagreements on *The Long Ride Home,* I finally left Columbia and moved to Twentieth Century–Fox for one more try at working within the studio system.

Here things went better. I made *The St. Valentine's Day Massacre* on a budget of slightly over $1 million, the largest I've ever worked with. I believe *St. Valentine's Day* to be the most accurate, authentic gangster movie ever. I hired a writer, once a young Chicago police reporter in the twenties, for the screenplay. So every scene was researched, based on or deduced from fact. Frances Doel even remembers me asking her to write psychoanalytic profiles of each of the main characters so that their motivations and behavior would be more vivid for the actors.

My only qualm was in casting. I had wanted classical actors to play the gangsters—Orson Welles as Al Capone, Robards as Bugs Moran. I was waiting for Welles's response and Fox moved up the start date. "What about Welles?" I asked. Welles, they told me, made trouble and tried to take over any picture he acted in. "You're buying trouble if you buy Orson Welles. Robards can switch to Capone. We've already talked to his agent."

"He's not really right. Robards is thin and Irish and Moran was thin and Irish. Capone and Welles are both big guys."

"Look," they said, "we're giving you a chance after Columbia. Don't give us problems. We want the picture. We'd like you to make it."

I realized I couldn't walk off projects at two studios. So I discussed the casting with Jason, a brilliant actor. We both thought he was better suited for Moran, but he was willing to try Capone and I was enthusiastic about working with him. Ralph Meeker played Moran and George Segal played Moran's chief lieutenant. For one of the key roles I wanted Jack Nicholson, but I had to hire an actor under contract to the studio. Jack was in my office and I broke the news to him. We had the production board laid out on a desk. The board shows, in strips, the way each scene fits into the production schedule.

This was the longest shoot in my career at that time—thirty-five days. I told him about a good little role that required a week and a half of work. But Jack saw something better on the production board: a seven-week "carry." It was a tiny part—a getaway car driver— that had to be shot in two locations spread out over the whole shoot. But SAG rules required payment for the entire span of time, though the actor only had to show up those two days. The shots are nearly consecutive on film but shot seven weeks apart.

"Jack," I said, "you don't want a nothing one-line part."

"Roger," he said, "forget that it's one line. I want the seven weeks' work."

"But look, I've also got this good supporting role, almost a costar for two weeks—"

"I'm taking the seven weeks' pay, Roger."

I also hired Bruce Dern for a similar "carry"—as one of the gun-men—that got him in the film and the full seven weeks' pay.

St. Valentine's Day got solid reviews. Physically, it is one of the best films I ever directed, because I was able to walk around the lot and pick those fantastic sets. But I had plenty to learn about budget-ing at the majors, especially since this was the only studio production I ever directed on a studio lot. When I shot for UA I was on location and in charge of costs myself. Here Fox's own accounting depart-ment was in charge of the costs.

They sent me the first report on costs for construction. It took me five minutes to see what was going on. It wasn't that they were out to get me, but they had a multimillion-dollar overhead, which they had to spread around to whatever was shooting.

"Throw that report out," I told Frances, "and never look at another one they send us. This picture is going to cost whatever Fox says it's going to cost and there's nothing we can do about it. This is a totally different ball game."

This report had to do with moving some lumber across the set. There was a certain number of Teamsters assigned just to *move the wood* into position so the sets could be built. I thought: The number of Teamsters involved here will be the exact number of Teamsters not working on anything else at that particular time. If they've got one available, it'll require one. If three are hanging around, I'll be charged for three to move the wood. They were sitting there on a permanent salary. Same with the grips. Why charge for one when there are *five* hanging around doing nothing?

In any event, *St. Valentine's Day* looked much more substantial than the cost even suggests. When you figure in the studio overhead built into the $1 million, it's actually hard to believe. We used sets from major, costly pictures. Al Capone's house, for example, had been the manor in *The Sound of Music*. The bar in *The Sand Pebbles* was used as a bar in a Chicago brothel. The exteriors from *Hello, Dolly!* were transformed into downtown Chicago of the twenties. I remember a very positive review—and most were quite favorable—in the English film journal *Sight and Sound*—that went like this: "If there has been a question as to whether or not Roger Corman knows how to spend money, this picture answers the question and the answer is yes."

Chapter 11

No two films in my career reflect more vividly my natural attraction for stories about the outsider or the misfit than *The Wild Angels* and *The Trip*—films about outlaw bikers and acid dropouts. I was drifting further from the Hollywood mainstream. My filmmaking instincts, like my stance in politics, were growing more radical. In the process, these films put me together with a group of actors—Peter Fonda, Dennis Hopper, Jack Nicholson, Bruce Dern—who would become known for their portrayals of alienated antiheroes and who, in the 1960s, were part of a vibrant new counterculture within Hollywood. There was a creative kinship among us and their work helped turn those films into two of the most controversial and most commercial projects of my career.

It was a *Life* magazine photograph that gave me the idea for *The*

Peter Fonda, in *The Wild Angels,* gets a kiss from Nancy Sinatra

Wild Angels. The photo, in a January 1966 issue, showed a group of Hell's Angels on their choppers going to the funeral of one of their members. I brought the project to AIP and they went forward with a treatment titled "All the Fallen Angels." Back in 1954, *The Wild One*, with Marlon Brando and Lee Marvin, told a story from the standpoint of a town terrorized by a gang of Angels, the bad guys. AIP wanted their picture to go the same way.

I vehemently disagreed. "This is really wrong," I said. "I don't want the town's perspective. I want to tell the Angels' story. They are the leads. I'm not interested in the point of view of the Establishment, but the outlaws', the outsiders' point of view."

This was a pivotal time for me. I was just months away from my fortieth birthday. I had produced/directed forty-odd features in little more than a decade and financed and produced another fifteen or so for other directors. My recent attempts to work with the majors had led to disillusionment, some bitterness, and anger. It was apparent that I was not about to emerge as a "star" director in the Hollywood Establishment. Perhaps that is why the photograph of those outrageous and defiant bikers, living as outlaws on the fringe, openly flaunting society's conventions, so intrigued me. I wanted to make a realistic, possibly even sympathetic, film about them.

AIP went along, and Nicholson, who always had a terrific knack for titles and campaigns, improved the title to *The Wild Angels.* I asked Chuck Griffith to help me with the research and write the screenplay. We started at a biker hangout in East L.A. called the Blue Blaze Cafe, and soon found ourselves in the Gunk Shop on Western Avenue in South Central L.A., waiting for an Angels chapter leader. Chuck and I wore our oldest, roughest-looking clothes but we were no match for the leader and a half dozen of his members. They roared in on elaborately customized Harleys, decked out in their denim "colors" with the Angels' insignias and Nazi swastikas.

We started drinking. I assured them this would be *their* story and that I'd pay them all for being in the movie. "Pay us for the bikes, too," they said.

"I'll pay each man every day he brings his bike."

"We want a little extra if we bring our old ladies—a little less money for the girls than for the bikes."

"That's not a problem," I promised. I offered to buy them booze and marijuana, if necessary, so we could hang out and hear their stories. Pretty soon we were drifting into an Angels party in a rough section of Venice. I drank beer, smoked grass, mingled, and listened. I heard all about biker culture from a pretty woman who, Chuck discreetly warned me, was the leader's lady and definitely off limits for anything but pure research. She worked in a factory. She said the

Angels tended not to work but instead lived off their women's earnings. She said some of the girls supplemented their income as hookers. I wondered whether these stories were exaggerated or invented. One story was about the Angels "busting" a comrade from a hospital room before he could be brought to jail on some criminal charge. I liked that and decided to build our movie around that and the biker funeral.

This was a story about a group of society's unskilled, even illiterate, high school dropouts in a technologically advanced society. Some were psychologically maladjusted. They don't answer want ads for Draftsman, Tool and Die Maker, or Aircraft Fabricator. What is the life of a man with an 80 IQ? Janitor? Street sweeper? Gas station attendant? So why work in a demeaning job? They say: "Fuck it. I'll run a petty robbery here, scrounge around there. Get a menial job and quit after two months so I can collect unemployment. I'll get a girl who'll work and she'll collect unemployment and we'll scam together and we'll end up living together almost as well as if I were working. But at least I'm free. It beats holding down some crummy job all my life."

I saw the Hell's Angel riding free as a modern-day cowboy. The chopper was his horse. The locales would be the wide-open spaces— the beach, the desert, and the mountains. I also remembered Sonny Barger's remark that "we're not losers." The most famous Angel of them all, and the president of the powerful Oakland chapter, was proud. A "winner" in society's terms meant being Mr. Assistant Sales Manager Barger, not Sonny Barger on a gleaming, growling chopper. The Angels were an intriguing social phenomenon, and I wanted to tell it like it was.

Another "winner," Big Otto, who was the head of Sonny's rival chapter in San Bernardino, acted as our liaison, if not quite our technical consultant. He read Chuck's script and had no objections. We stayed with a straightforward, simple plot about a fictitious San Pedro chapter. The leader, Jack Black, and his buddy, the Loser, lead a "run" into the mountains to Mecca, where they brawl with the Mexican gang that stole Loser's bike. Two motorcycle cops break up the fight and Loser steals one cop's motorcycle. The other cop gives chase and shoots him, but the cop's bike veers off a cliff and crashes. Loser is injured and ends up in a hospital. The Angels, knowing he'll be sent to prison, bust Loser out and get him to an Angels pad, where he dies. Loser's memorial service degenerates into a violent, blasphemous orgy in a church. The procession through Loser's hometown triggers a free-for-all with the outraged locals. As the police sirens wail, the Angels roar off, all except Jack Black, the film's impassive antihero, who stays on to shovel dirt on Loser's grave.

Chuck's script had been substantially revised before shooting by a young critic and cinema buff named Peter Bogdanovich. Peter had come to L.A. a year or so earlier to write about films for *Esquire.* I met Peter and his wife, Polly Platt, at a screening, and called a few weeks later to ask if he wanted to write for the movies. This was exactly what he had hoped would happen out in L.A. and he said yes.

★ PETER BOGDANOVICH

"I want a big picture," Roger told me, "something like *The Bridge on the River Kwai* or *Lawrence of Arabia,* but set somewhere that I can shoot on a reasonable budget. Maybe Poland in World War Two." I said okay. Then Roger called a few weeks later. This time, he was starting a motorcycle picture and wanted me to location-scout in the desert. "You can take your wife. I'll send you the script right away and you should go to Palm Desert immediately."

I read the *Wild Angels* script and called Roger. "I don't like it that much," I said. "It reads like a Disney film. It starts with a highway and it says, 'Frog jumps onto the highway' and then you cut and it says, 'Frog's point of view' and then you have motorcycles and then you cut to the frog's reaction and who gives a shit? I hated all the characters, it has no plot."

After scouting in the desert I reported in. "I want you to do a rewrite of the script," Roger said, "but you're not in the Guild so it will be for no credit." With Polly's help, I rewrote 80 percent of the script and the plot got completely revised.

★   ★   ★

Jim Nicholson wanted George Chakiris for Jack Black because he had been so good in *West Side Story.* I let it be known in casting that everyone would ride his own bike. Chakiris told me up front that he didn't ride. He agreed to take a lesson, but came back and announced: "You gotta go for a double. I can't do it."

"George," I said, "you have to do it or pull out. I'm sorry. I won't shoot the whole picture using doubles, stuntmen, and cutaways like in the old Westerns." George pulled out and I promoted Peter Fonda, who I had in mind for Loser, to Jack Black and moved Bruce Dern up to Loser. I had seen Bruce in *The Shadow of a Gunman* in New York and he was brilliant, one of the best young actors in the country. Peter had been the young romantic lead in *Tammy and the Doctor* and a few other pictures. AIP wanted Nancy Sinatra, on the strength of her family name and big hit, "These Boots Are Made for Walkin'," for Mike, the female lead role of Jack's lady.

★ **BRUCE DERN**

I never met Roger until I went into wardrobe my first day for the Angels shoot. He had hired me by calling my agent, and then he told me how good I had been in this Broadway play in 1958. And I only had six lines and was onstage for maybe fifty seconds. But a guy named Bill Smithers had the lead and he was fantastic. I always thought Roger had somehow superimposed my name over Bill's in his mind for eight years—and I never told him the difference. So I always thought I had Bill Smithers's career, as far as Roger went.

★ **PETER FONDA**

I first went to see Roger wearing weird, mirrored granny glasses. I was not dressed normally. My hair was slightly long. I had a badge on, an Office of Naval Intelligence badge.

"What does that badge mean?" he asked.

"It means I get to piss on your tires, Roger" is what I said. I had a real fuck-you attitude. So Roger told me he had a problem because George couldn't ride. I told Roger, "Okay, I'll play the lead but only if you call him Heavenly Blues and not Jack Black." And he asked me what that meant.

"Well, a Heavenly Blue is a morning glory that grows wild all around the place, and if you take three or four hundred of their seeds, grind them up in a peppermill and drink them with water, you'll have yourself quite a hallucination."

He said, "You're kidding." I said, "No I'm not. Trust me. I want them on my motorcycle tank." We closed the deal. Roger got the better part of that one because now he had me as the lead for the same ten grand I was getting to play a stiff.

I did some hanging out at parties with the Angels. Their beer parties were just like anyone else's, except they listened to the Stones doing "Satisfaction" about a hundred and fifty times in a row.

★   ★   ★

I agreed to pay the Angels $35 a day, plus another $20 for the bikes per man and $15 for the old ladies. We planned on a three-week shoot, entirely in natural locations around Venice, San Pedro, and the mountains and desert around Palm Springs. The budget was set at around $360,000.

This turned out to be one of the most grueling films I ever directed. The Angels did not have great attention spans. I worked with about twenty of them but on some days the number dropped; they'd collect their cash and just drift off. No critic ever mentioned it, but the background Angels tend to keep changing from shot to shot.

I analyzed the situation and decided to keep the direction extremely matter-of-fact, almost emotionless. I wasn't going to order these bikers around because they weren't ordered around by *anybody*. But I couldn't appear weak or subservient.

Still, to control the Hell's Angels while shooting at the beach, in the desert, and up in the mountains for fifteen days was a back-breaking job. Just getting the Harleys to start was a major problem, since it was cold in the mountains and they were already old bikes and in bad repair.

The film's first ten minutes moved from Venice to the oil fields near San Pedro to the mountains, over the freeways, and down winding off-road hiking trails near Palm Canyon. Transportation was everything, getting the shot and moving on. Just for the opening shots of Peter and the Angels on the freeway in the desert, I had to get someone to stand over the horizon to stop cars, briefly and illegally. We had great cloud formations but we didn't have money for a camera car. I flipped down the tailgate of a station wagon and shot straight out. I let some air out of the tires for a smoother ride.

The first day we shot out in the desert at Mecca, the setup was taking way too long and I was really mad. Suddenly, a group of World War Two armored Nazi half-track tanks rolled down the street and started attacking the swastika-bearing Angels in the center of town. They were spraying blanks all over the place. I had no idea what was going on and neither did the Angels, but I yelled to my a.d., "Photograph it, photograph it, I'll use it somehow for *something*."

My brother, Gene, was producing *Tobruk* with Rock Hudson a little deeper south in the desert—actually, it was supposed to be North Africa—toward the Salton Sea. He thought this attack would be amusing. That set the tone.

We had our own armed forces on the sets—California state cops and the county sheriff's deputies. They ran a check on just about every Angel with us. One officer told my production manager, Jack Bohrer, "Nearly all of them are wanted. We should really arrest every one of them." Jack knew exactly how to handle the situation diplomatically.

"Look," he said, "these guys haven't had a legitimate job in God knows how long. They're working. We're paying them. Why break it up now? Let 'em make some money. Isn't that better for all concerned?" The police said okay, but they stayed just over the hill the whole time and kept an eye on us.

By then I was really becoming comfortable with fluid and more complex camera work. For example, as the gang fight breaks up,

Loser runs one way, the Angels the other. I pick him up running from a storefront, down a dirt street toward the camera. The camera dollies back, tracking and panning as he goes. Then he gets to the cops' choppers at an intersection and the camera stops moving for a set shot. In the background, the Angels run ahead of the cops; the cops fire shots at them as Loser revs up one of the choppers. The cops spot him and run toward him from his right as he roars off to his left. I pan off with Loser, going with him 180 degrees until he is in the distance and heading out of town. That action is all in one continuous shot, and while it's not a phenomenal shot, it is better than what you normally get on a three-week shoot. Perhaps that is why European critics, who really knew more about film than American critics, had begun to comment that I was technically more adept than other independent low-budget filmmakers.

One sequence shows how hard I was trying to give movement and depth, which is also unusual for low-budget direction. I had maybe eighteen actors and another fifty bikers swarming around up in the mountains. The Angels, in fact, did camp out in the groves and in motel parking lots because we didn't put them up with the actors. I used a hand-held camera, which produced a quasi-documentary look as I tried to capture the almost tribal frenzy of the Angels. It also kept the sequences from looking too slick. I wanted a rough energy to match the Angels' lifestyle. After Loser's chase, the story moves to the Angels' party in the mountains. In every shot there is motion and compositional depth—members riding choppers and running in the background, others partying with their women in the middle distance, and a few, including Gayle Hunnicutt (in one of her first features) dancing in the foreground. I was dating Gayle at the time. She looked so glamorous that makeup had to add a facial scar to "rough" her up. There are close-ups of Blues and Mike with wild bongo playing and dancing in the background as Blues smokes a reefer. As the camera pans its way around the group, you can see a couple making out on the ground, Gayle eating chicken, two Angels jousting on cycles with palm fronds, another Angel charging like a matador on his chopper through a red cape held by a woman. Blues jumps up, runs to an Angel snorting heroin against a tree, and starts beating him up.

The key to staying on schedule and getting all these mountain sequences in a day, plus the approaches and exits on the choppers, was turning the Angels on, keeping the beer and grass flowing, playing some music on the set to get them going.

Getting the Harleys going was a lot tougher. They were always breaking down and stalling out in the sand and dirt. That drove me crazy. We were always sitting and waiting for the damned bikes to be repaired and I once said to one of the Angels: "Look, I understand what you guys do. You come into town. You beat up the men, you rape the women, you steal from the stores, the police come charging after you, you run to your choppers, and you *know* the fucking things aren't going to start. What do you do then? What is this all about, anyway?"

"They start, they start," he mumbled. "Bad luck, that's all." Peter told me he never liked riding them. "You know why they call them Harleys, don't you?" he asked. "Because they Harley ever start."

★ **PAUL RAPP**

This film was filled with violence, real violence. Very early on, all the bikes were stolen and it was a very big blow to us because they then had to be matched. They were locked up in a truck or something at the corner of Overland and National and it was an inside job by a gang member. I was an assistant director and there was nothing but trouble. I knew I had to have at least two heavy-duty boys in my pocket to keep the other Angels in line. Money talked. For one scene in a restaurant an Angel was to pull Nancy's chair out for her as she sat down. Her father had shown up one night from Palm Springs with two bodyguards. He very politely told me he was holding me personally responsible for her safety. So we were virtually handcuffed together for her protection.

Then the guy slid the chair back as she sat down so she'd fall during the take. I threw the guy up against the wall, praying I'd get some help from other Angels. Sure enough, the main dude jumped in and grabbed this guy and they took him out back and beat him up. They all made a few more dollars after that.

It was very cold when we went to Idlewyld in the mountains for the funeral. The next morning one of the actors, Coby Denton, didn't show up. Roger was upset. Nancy was unraveling. Peter was getting paranoid. We got to Coby's motel room. I knocked and then kicked in the door. Coby was out cold on the floor, unconscious from gas leaking from a pilot light that had gone out. A cop who had given me a ride there called an ambulance from Hemet. They revived him and put him in the intensive care ward. I went back and told Roger in front of the cast and crew. Everyone got unglued and shaken. It wasn't because he was unfeeling or cruel, but Roger ordered everyone to set the cameras and lights and get right to work.

★ **PETER FONDA**

When we heard about Coby, we all told Roger we weren't going to work. That made the Angels happy—to tell the man running the show that we wouldn't work. But Roger told us to keep right on rolling. And he was right. You *do* keep rolling. You have no choice. This is the most expensive art form in the world. I thought it was rather crass at the time. Later, I learned that tragic things can happen, but you keep shooting. Roger was not wrong; we were wrong in our perception of his attitude. Two days later Coby came out of the hospital and rejoined us.

★ **BRUCE DERN**

I got punched out by a couple of Angels because I was wearing their "colors"—the jacket. This was right in front of the church on North Argyle in Hollywood, where we shot Loser's funeral service. They said, "Take it off, motherfucker." And I said, "Wait a second, I'm making a movie." They said, "Nobody's making a movie about the Hell's Angels, not unless we're in it. Take it off." Before I could get it off, I was out cold on the sidewalk. It was, like, Hey, I'm not even alive in the movie, I'm dead, and still they're beating on me.

★   ★   ★

There were always wild stories being told, even two decades later. Paul Rapp never mentioned this one until recently—a good a.d. has to shield the director from needless hassles while shooting. He said the Highway Patrol was working with some high-level state intelligence division to infiltrate our shoot and conduct surveillance.

They had shown Paul a car trunk full of sophisticated bugging equipment. They came to his room with an attaché case full of surveillance tapes and photographs of the cast, crew, and Angels. Paul said they even played a tape that recorded Paul and his girlfriend in their motel room. Paul claimed—and he had worked with the CIA— that they told him they had 150 agents assigned to watch us, including an old lady we thought we hired as an extra to sit in a car in town. Paul said they finally told him they were trying to bust a San Berdoo chapter member wanted for killing a cop. Their informants had tipped them off that he and his chapter were coming into the mountains, to our location, that night to take on the Venice Angels. But the snows that night forced the San Berdoo Angels to turn back.

The interior church scenes—when the Angels run amok and remove Loser's body from the casket—had been shot inside the Little Country Church in Hollywood. The church people tried to toss us out once they caught on to what we were doing inside. We were often laying waste to whatever locations we used and Jack Bohrer and Paul had become very good at double-talking their way out of anything on my shoots. We moved a bunch of their pews out and put in our own breakaways. Once we got rolling, I wasn't going to stop. This was the high point of the picture and I knew I was getting something nobody had ever seen in a film. If somebody yells, I figured, we'll pay for the broken pews, but this is good stuff. And indeed we smashed some of their pews, some of ours, and banged up the walls and windows.

The funeral service was as outrageous and irreverent as anything I had ever shot on film. Loser's coffin is draped by a bright red Nazi flag with a giant swastika on it. A preacher delivers his eulogy before the sneering Angels. Blues stands in the aisle and I pan slowly from the rear of the church to show the large red Nazi flag and large crucifix against the wall.

The Angels sneer during the preacher's sermon. Blues stands, extending his arms as a mock-Christ figure: "We want to be free to ride our machines without being hassled by the Man," he says. "We want to get loaded. We want to party."

And all hell breaks loose. The Angels riot, destroying everything in sight. Blues knocks the preacher out with a punch to the stomach and a karate chop to the neck.

Again, I shot with a hand-held camera right in the midst of everything to bring the audience right into the melee. Richard Moore, my director of photography, held the camera and I was right behind him. The adrenaline started pumping and I would say, "Do this, do this," and the cast would say, "Yeah, yeah, let's do it." I shot these scenes doubly fast to sustain momentum and spontaneity. We walked through this crowd as they went berserk and I kept saying, "Over here, now over there, let's go in here," knowing I'd cut it together later with whip cuts and flash cuts.

As the party got wilder, I started making up scenes to shoot, moving as fast as I could. Beer and bongo drums arrive and the party scene picks up. The Angels lift Loser from his coffin—dressed in his "colors" and a Nazi leather aviator cap—and prop him up against a wall. A joint is stuck between his lips, he's wearing shades, and his fingers are bent to flip the bird. The unconscious preacher is dumped inside the coffin and beer is poured on his head. Angels and their women dance on the splintered pews. Gaysh, Loser's grieving old lady—played quite effectively by Bruce's wife then, Diane Ladd— is stripped by two Angels who force her to snort heroin.

I directed one of the Angels to carve a swastika into the coffin so I could come back to him when he was finished. But when I did, he had gotten it all wrong. It looked more like a capital Z with a slash through the middle. I thought, That's probably the way Angels are. They don't even know how to carve a swastika. It's all right. It's part of the party. So I left it in.

By the end, the scene borders on the nihilistic. Blues snorts heroin, rejects his old lady, and lies down behind Loser's casket with his new woman. Gaysh is raped in the corner. The preacher is dumped out of the coffin and Loser is lowered back in.

For the procession, I paid locals $10 each to be roadside onlookers. We shot the "cemetery" in a park in Idyllwild. We built the arch, threw in a few headstones, crowded the background with the bikes, the foreground with onlookers, and called it a cemetery. The final brawl is triggered when a kid tosses a large rock as Loser's being buried. This is where I just let it go. I didn't even care that snow in late March had fallen and melted and that the two days wouldn't match. I didn't care. No one would. It's four in the afternoon, last day, losing light. My d.p. doesn't like the light. "Doesn't matter," I say, "there's nothing we can do. The picture's over and we've got to shoot."

★ **PETER BOGDANOVICH**

Roger was tired and frantic by the end. That's why the Angels didn't always like Roger: he was an authority figure and he was always, "Hurry, hurry, hurry, no time, no time, let's go, let's go." And so the Angels didn't always like *me* because they figured I was the silent one next to him who's really the shit.

Before the fight scene, Roger said to me, "Go ahead, run in there," because we hardly had any extras. So I go running in there as the fight breaks out, looking like a townie. I hit the ground and covered my head as all these Angels just beat the shit out of me until Roger yelled, "CUT!" *The Wild Angels* was three weeks of the greatest film school anybody could ever put me through. You were doing it, you were under pressure, you had to deliver.

★ ★ ★

Peter was, like Francis Coppola, an early "graduate" of the Corman school. Right after *Angels*, I financed his first feature, *Targets*. It came about when Boris Karloff's agent learned *The Terror* actually made a lot of money. I had offered Boris a fee plus 10 percent of the profits above a certain amount, which was considerably higher than the film's actual cost. When the agent found this out, he demanded that Boris's cut start at the lower figure. I agreed on the condition that Boris give me two days' work on a future film. So I went to Peter and said, "This is your chance. You can write and direct our new Boris Karloff film."

★ **PETER BOGDANOVICH**

What Roger said was, "I want you to take twenty minutes of Karloff footage from *The Terror,* then I want you to shoot twenty more minutes with Boris—I've shot *whole pictures* in two days—and then I want you to shoot another forty minutes with some other actors over ten days. I

can take the twenty and the twenty and the forty and I've got a whole new eighty-minute Karloff film. What do you say?"

"Sure." In the meantime Roger asked me to work on one of those Russian sci-fi films he acquired, *Planet of Storms.* "It's got spectacular effects," he said, "and we're dubbing it into English for AIP. But there are no women. So run down to Leo Carrillo beach. It'll match the Black Sea but it's really supposed to be Venus. Shoot women. We'll cut it all in. I'll pay you six thousand dollars for the two jobs."

I hired the Gill-Women of Venus—just a bunch of stoned kids walking around Carrillo Beach dressed like mermaids, with seashells covering their breasts. Tackiest fucking costumes I have ever seen. And now they were praying to a pterodactyl or something and communicating tele-pathically with Mamie Van Doren. This was hell. We retitled it *Voyage to the Planet of Prehistoric Women.*

Later, when I watched *The Terror,* I remember thinking, Gee, I hope Jack makes it as a director or writer because he's not much of an actor here. My idea was to have Karloff play a retiring horror film actor; the old footage was used as a film-within-a-film he's making at the end of his career. So to contrast the illusion of horror in Karloff's gothic castle with real horror, a deranged Vietnam vet starts sniping at people at a drive-in. This was a few years after the Texas Tower incident and Charles Whitman. Roger really liked this idea. I showed my original script to Sam Fuller and he liked it too. Then in three hours in his office he virtually re-created the script for me off the top of his head as I took notes. Roger said of the revise, "This is the best script I have ever had to produce. But you've got Boris all the way through the film. No way you'll get this in two days." I think we got Boris an extra day or two. Roger came to the set once. He said, "You know how Hitchcock shoots, don't you? Plans every shot, writes everything down, totally prepared. And you know how Hawks shoots, don't you? Writes nothing down. Doesn't plan anything. Rewrites on the set."

"Right."

"Well, on this picture, I want you to be Hitchcock."

We tried to get the majors to release it instead of AIP. Roger said we could call it *Targets* if it got released by a major and *Blood and Candy* if AIP got it. No one wanted it, so I called Arthur Knight, the critic, who taught a film course at USC. I said, "Do me a favor. Let me invite a critic from *Variety* and run the film for you. If you guys like it, would you review it and say we don't have a distributor? And if you don't like it, don't review it?" Arthur agreed. Both critics liked it. The story went that Bob Evans circled the review and sent it on to Charlie Bludhorn, then head of Paramount. Paramount bought it.

★   ★   ★

I got a $200,000 or $300,000 advance against profits from Paramount—a nice deal on a $100,000 budget. But there weren't any profits. This was a film about a sniper. The assassinations of Martin Luther King, Jr., and Robert F. Kennedy in the spring of 1968 didn't help. *Targets* finally came out in August 1968. Peter recalls Paramount releasing only eight prints. It's now on Paramount's Cult Classics series in video.

I had much more immediate success with *Angels*. The film was invited to be shown opening night at the Venice Film Festival, a prestigious honor. *Angels* was anything but an official U.S. entry. In fact, the State Department tried to get the film disinvited because of its violence and sensationalism. This was like *The Intruder* at Cannes all over again. It was AIP's most controversial film ever. There was a very elegant opening-night reception in the Doge's Palace. We all arrived from the Lido Hotel in motorboats, the men in dinner jackets and the ladies in long gowns. The film was received well, with several bursts of applause during the screening and a big round of applause at the end. The festival director, Luigi Chiarini, called the film "one of the most important American films of the past ten years."

It rained a bit that night and as we left the Palace for the motorboats, we stepped out across the Piazza San Marco. While walking to the canal, I turned back for one unforgettable sight. There was all of Venice at night, glittering in the canals with the big statue of the winged lion, the symbol of Venice, in view. The guests were coming out of the palace, and two ladies were moving toward me, one in a brilliant red gown, another next to her in a deep emerald green. The colors reflected up off the glistening wet stones of the Piazza. I was on such a high. That moment, as I turned back before stepping down into the motorboat, lingers even now as one of the most beautiful images I can remember.

Angels was released in the summer of 1966. It turned into AIP's biggest hit. Even I was surprised. Audiences went wild. It took in well over $5 million in rentals right off. We hit capacity almost everywhere Friday night. At drive-ins, people were turned away. By Monday after the first weekend, Jim Nicholson and the rest of us were laughing and screaming: The AIP guys had never seen numbers remotely approaching these for a single weekend. Jim told us one motorcycle gang had insisted on seeing the picture together on their choppers and promised there wouldn't be any trouble. So the owner cleared the front row opening night and these guys sat there all in a row, watching on their choppers.

Variety ranked *Angels* the thirteenth top film of the year. It has, over the years, taken in more than $10 million. I had a fee plus a percentage of the net. I made it for only $360,000. I sold out my piece of the film to AIP, and as a result AIP actually paid me less than they would have had I stayed in.

Reviews were mixed, but everyone had strong feelings, either way. It definitely hit a nerve. *Variety* called it a "realistic leather jacket delinquency yarn with plenty of shock value." Bosley Crowther of *The New York Times* called it a "brutal little picture" with a cinéma vérité feel to it. But he felt it was "an embarrassment all right—a vicious account of the boozing, fighting, 'pot' smoking, vandalizing, and raping done by a gang of 'sickle' riders."

Vincent Canby was more generous in a Sunday *Times* piece. He praised the film as "the best work to date of the newest cinema *auteur*—the work of a filmmaker with a vigorous, highly personal cinematic style. As an *auteur*," he went on—and I can sometimes remember quotes verbatim—"Mr. Corman would thus be promoted to the pantheon that includes John Ford, Howard Hawks, Hitchcock, D. W. Griffith, Nicholas Ray, Charlie Chaplin, and Samuel Fuller, among others dead and undead."

That sure placed me in good company—though the Angels threatened to include me among the dead. First, the San Bernardino chapter sued me for defamation of character or something to that effect and made threats against my life. They were asking for $4 million and claiming I had portrayed them as an outlaw, antisocial motorcycle gang, whereas in reality they thought of themselves as "a social organization dedicated to the spreading of technical information on motorcycles."

If anything, the picture *upgraded* them by 2 percent and there was *no way* they were portrayed *worse* than they were. Big Otto called and threatened me. My money *and* my life. "You know," he said, "we're going to get your four million dollars and then we're going to snuff you out."

I reasoned with him that if they rubbed me out they couldn't possibly collect the $4 million. Worse, if I vanish, they're the prime suspects. "It is," I explained calmly, "definitely in your interest not only to *not* snuff me out, but you and the Angels should be protecting my life to make certain nobody *else* snuffs me out, because you'll get the blame. Plus, I'm insured and I don't really care whether or not I lose the four million. My advice is forget about snuffing me out. Go for the four mill."

Otto concurred with my analysis of the situation. No one ever collected a cent from anyone.

After *The Wild Angels'* huge success, AIP wanted a sequel, and indeed, dozens of biker films eventually got made. I agreed to produce *Devil's Angels* for AIP. Chuck Griffith wrote it and my art director Danny Haller directed. That one did close to $4 million in rentals; Richard Rush directed *Hell's Angels on Wheels* and that one did close to $3 million. We had clearly broken new ground and created a market.

For my next AIP project, I wanted a variation on the contemporary outlaw/antihero theme that Peter Fonda had handled so effectively—and which was clearly commercial. Jim Nicholson and I eventually agreed on another topical theme—a trip on LSD. It was 1967 and we decided to go with Peter, a highly intelligent and sensitive actor. Like the Angels and their bikes, the drug subculture was in the headlines. LSD, grass, hash, speed, the drug and hippie movement, dropping out, tuning in, free love—it was all part of a pervasive "outlaw" anti-Establishment consciousness in the country during the Vietnam era. More and more "straight" people were dropping out and "doing their own thing." I wanted to tell that story as an odyssey on acid.

Chuck spent three months on a script that simply did not work. I knew exactly what I wanted with *The Trip,* which was our title from the start. More than plot, I wanted an impressionistic, free-form trip in every sense: a straight guy spends eight, ten hours tripping his brains out, comes down. The trip ends, the film ends. What's happened to him? Where has he gone? He is reborn, his life continues, transformed.

I went to Jack Nicholson, who had written the two Westerns I had backed. He was good. I told him the character should be a burned-out TV commercial director in L.A., sort of a stand-in or alter ego for me. A film director would be too corny and transparent. Jack wrote a good script. If there were any problems it was that he wrote in millions of dollars in special effects.

I created some special effects of my own even before we had Chuck's original script. I had hung out with the Angels; this time I decided that as a conscientious director I should trip on LSD myself. Chuck, Jack, and Peter had all tripped. People—hippies, the flower children of the 1960s—back then were just walking into basements and parks and dropping acid.

I approached acid much the way I approached Freud and analysis. I did research. I read Timothy Leary, who believed you should trip with somebody you knew and be in a beautiful place. I got together a group of friends and decided to take my trip up north around Big Sur. I called Sharon Compton, a young art director I had dated on and off. I called Chuck Griffith. I asked my story editor and assistant, Frances Doel, to come and take notes. I also asked Frances to read the Tibetan Book of the Dead and prepare some research for me. A few other friends came along. I moved with hip people but I was always the squarest guy in a hip group. So when people heard I was taking LSD, they figured: If he can take it, anybody can. It must be really safe and all right. We got this caravan together and went up to a grove of redwoods near a waterfall in Pfeiffer Big Sur State Park. Some stayed at the Big Sur Inn; others camped out in the park.

I took my acid in a sugar cube and for a while nothing happened. I thought: Boy, what a waste. Four hundred miles up here for nothing. I'll wait a while longer, go out and get some wine, have some dinner, and go home to L.A. tomorrow.

I decided to lie down. And then the acid kicked in. I spent the next seven hours face down in the ground, beneath a tree, not moving, absorbed in the most wonderful trip imaginable. Among other things, I was sure I had invented an utterly new art form. This new art form was the very act of thinking and creating, and you didn't need books or film or music to communicate it; anyone who wanted to experience it would simply lie face down on the ground anywhere in the world at that moment and the work of art would be transmitted through the earth from the mind of its creator directly into the mind of the audience. To this day, I'd like to think this could work and it would be wonderful. I think of all the costs you could cut in production and distribution alone.

I recall one dominant image that was outrageously erotic and beautiful. I was floating through the sky during a golden-reddish sunset and emerging from this glorious sunset was a sailing ship, a clipper ship, sailing straight toward me. This ship was laden with brilliant gleaming jewels. The whole ship was crusted in spectacular jewels. Then I realized as it approached me that the sails were actually the movements and curves of a woman's body. This vision was a ship, jewels, and a woman.

My trip was so good, in fact, I decided that when I shot the movie it would have to show some bummer scenes or else the film would seem totally pro-LSD. So I consciously went back to some of the imagery of horror from my Poe films to represent the bad end of acid tripping. When I came down, I thought: There is no reason to exist in the real world. This is better. It was such a wonderful, heightened experience that I thought about just taking acid again and going right back *in there* and not worrying about the rest of the stuff *out here.*

LSD had gotten some bad press linking it to terrifying psychoses, suicides, and grotesque birth defects. But I always believed that the government stirred up a lot of that paranoia and that there was no evidence for genetic damage whatsoever. I frankly assumed that acid was going to become a major part of my life. But I never took it again. I wasn't foolish enough to believe I could actually *direct* on acid, but I thought it could unlock my mind, make me freer to create images and ideas that could be translated into the reality of films. It wasn't reality, though; it was a chemically induced nirvana.

As it was I became associated with drugs later in the 1960s. My own LSD trip and the film both got considerable press. *The Trip* became quite controversial, as it was probably the first commercial film to examine the effects of LSD. A few years ago President Reagan made a speech vehemently denouncing drugs. A *New York Times* reporter called me for my reaction. "Why do you want *my* reaction?" I asked. "Because," he said, "you're one of the spokesmen for the drug movement."

"I take one acid trip and I become a 'spokesman for the drug movement'?"

★ **CHUCK GRIFFITH**

Once Roger finally stopped complaining about wasting his time and getting ripped off on acid that didn't work, he got down on his stomach, grew very introspective, and went into one of the best trips I've ever seen anyone have—a classic, useful, contained acid trip. If there were manuals on acid trips this is the kind they'd tell you to have. I was his guru the first day—he tripped, I observed. The next day was my turn. I spent twelve hours staring at a piece of bark, feeling the energy of the woods flowing, hallucinating in the forest. Those were the days.

Roger kept saying, "The earth is a woman, the earth is a woman and I am *humping* her." Then it was, "I have invented a new art form with wires leading the artist's brain down into the earth and back out to everybody else." Then there was that golden galleon in the sky with the jewels. It was wonderful. *That* was the movie.

He wanted to make sure his friend Sharon Compton was there, a link to safety and reality. And Sharon was out there finger-climbing a cliff. What an amazing character!

"Okay, Roger," I said, "getting dark. Time to go. They're closing the park." Roger got up to pee.

"You're just a jealous guru," he mumbled. "You just want me to get out of this state. Finally after all these years of experience I reach this point and you want to take me out of it?"

★ **JACK NICHOLSON**

Roger knew I had taken acid and we were both serious on the subject. Both of us had tripped in kind of clinical situations. I told him I didn't want to write a flat-out exploitation film. He had higher aspirations this time. Roger was my whole bottom-line support then. I had done the Westerns but I had pretty much given up as an actor. I really didn't have much else going then, kind of a journeyman troubleshooter. He knew he couldn't get a writer as good as me through regular ways. I was happy to write it and make a more demanding picture out of it.

The first guy who read it—an actor friend of mine—finished it, walked outside, and fell off my front porch. I wrote the lead for Fonda and I knew he and Dern, who did *Rebel Rousers* with me, had done the biker film. I hoped to get the part Bruce Dern played—the guru. But I knew—from *Wild Angels* and *The St. Valentine's Day Massacre*—that Roger always preferred Bruce. The picture was very McLuhanesque. It was about the juxtapositions of reality. I had no illusions about it. The theory was to show how quickly things move. It was so dense with material you could see a one-frame cut.

★ BRUCE DERN

I was bugged in *The Trip* because my character gives Peter the acid, I guide him through the first part of his trip, he panics, runs away, and then you never see me again. And they said, "Well, that's what happens on acid." And I said, "Well, I don't fucking know that because I don't *take* acid." I'm just looking at my part as an actor and suddenly I'm out of a fucking movie. I though I'd be in the whole movie, I've worked three days and I'm gone and yet I'm one of the stars.

Roger was moving up in class with the movie. Jack's script showed a lot of imagination. I helped get *Rebel Rousers* made and I made sure Jack was in it. A couple years later he returned the favor by asking me if I wanted to be in *Drive, He Said.*

★ ★ ★

Bruce was straight, a distance runner, an Olympic team alternate. Everyone else was fairly counterculture. I wanted Bruce to give some validity to the picture. The story was simple but typical of many "straight" people's experiences back then when there was tremendous social pressure to "turn on" and "drop out." When we shot the film it was the spring of 1967 and the Beatles' *Sgt. Pepper's Lonely Hearts Club Band* LP was just coming out. The Summer of Love was around the corner.

In the film, Paul Groves, the ad director, is getting divorced and he feels he's sold out creatively. His friend, John, the drug guru, recommends a psychedelic journey of self-exploration on acid. He introduces Groves to the psychedelic hangouts on the Strip; Groves meets Max, a hippie high priest, played by Dennis Hopper, and Glenn, a tall, blond flower child. Groves drops acid at John's and everything is blissful, flowing energy and colors more intense than any he's seen before. Then the trip suddenly turns into a hallucinatory past-life bummer set in the Middle Ages; he is chased through a forest; Max and Glenn reappear; he has visions of his own funeral. He runs from John's pad and ends up on the lurid, teeming Strip at night. It's no better out there. He finds Max and Max brings him to Glenn. By daybreak, he's come down and begun his life anew.

This was one of the finest casts I ever used. Dern was excellent. Peter's role—my surrogate, in a sense—fit even more correctly in *The Trip* than in *Angels*. Dennis, who was recommended by Peter, since they had been trying to do films together, gave an exceptional performance as Max. The scenes in his hippie drug den worked wonderfully. He got Max's stoned apocalyptic ramblings down just right. I let them all improvise a little and have some fun and make the dialogue their own. As a joint passes around a circle of hippies seated on the floor Dennis has lines like "Anyway, I'm flashing and I'm strung out in the stream and then the fuzz drive by. I say, 'Hey, baby, get a hold of yourself and pull yourself in, man, 'cause this is it.'"

The shot was a complicated circular dolly movement in the middle of the group as each friend took a hit. Peter Fonda insists to this day it was not real grass. I wasn't listening too closely to Dennis because of the intricacy of the shot. When it was over, I said, Print. The soundman came to me and said, "Dennis just broke the all-time record. He used 'man' thirty-six times in one speech." "Great," I said. "Print it, man."

My three-week shoot was in town. The medieval flashbacks were done up north around Big Sur. Peter's sequence on the Strip was incredible to shoot. The Strip then was a melting pot of flower children, derelicts, burnouts, acid casualties, sleazy hipsters, and tour buses. I went out with Dennis Jakob and used a hand-held camera. Dennis was in a wheelchair to keep the ride smooth. There were sun guns strapped to the chair to kick light into Peter's face as he moved through the night crowd.

★ **PETER FONDA**

When we were at Big Sur, someone said, "Let's do a little somethin' before dinner." "You guys crazy?" I asked. There were twenty or so of us up there and for some reason, everyone showed up at my cabin before dinner the last night. So we did "a little somethin'" on a pin. You just open the safety pin, stick it into a small block of a certain substance I will not name, put a lighter underneath it so it flames, blow it out, and make that smoke go through a tiny little hole you make with your lips just like you were sucking in hot soup. And everyone got ripped. It was hilarious at Nepenthe. Roger was there—one director who was hip—the cast and crew. We're trying to read the menu, ordering wrong things, tears rolling down our cheeks.

★   ★   ★

After the fifteen days, I still needed some nonunion shots in the desert. I asked Dennis Hopper to go with Peter. I gave him a wild camera—a nonsync camera, no sound. They got some long shots of

Peter walking in the desert, which I cut into the other medieval scenes.

★ PETER FONDA

Dennis needed a job and he was very pleased to get this one. We had already written two scripts together, figuring if we keep going like this, we're never gonna make any more movies. People didn't want to hire Dennis because he was a tough cookie to work with. So we shot for a couple days in Yuma, to Big Dune and back toward L.A. Dennis got some beautiful, beautiful stuff of me in the dunes, with water behind me, water going into my profile and bursting behind me, water lit by the sun. We pulled off what I felt were some of the best shots of the film. Roger used it all.

★ ★ ★

We were shooting outside a club we called the Bead Game. I was filming a nude dancer from the Playboy Club, another first for me. We were running late. The club owner wanted us out; patrons were lined up waiting to get in. My art director, Leon Erikson, was still painting the club's front door while we were shooting the last interior shots of the dancer. There was time for only one exterior shot.

"The door's going to be wet, Peter," I said, explaining how he should enter the club. "Be very careful. We can't wait for it to dry. Just put your hand on the doorknob and go through. Don't brush up against it."

"You gotta split now," the owner complained.

"I'll get it in one take. Relax."

Peter has to come along the sidewalk, the camera pans with him to the door, he opens it and goes in. It's a simple shot with a dry door. I made no attempt at dialogue. When in trouble, get the shot, loop it later. There was no time to rehearse. Leon was still crouched over with his brush, madly slapping paint. These were the directions to Peter and Leon as we started to roll:

"All right, Peter, you're coming down here, you come down the ramp, you move along toward the door. Okay, fine, fine, keep it going. We're panning, Peter, you get closer to the door, now, LEON! GET OUT OF THE SHOT WITH THE PAINTBRUSH NOW PLEASE and, thank you, Leon and, okay, Peter, open and go right through the door, yes! CUT. PRINT." Leon just ducked out of frame as we panned the door. It was all in one swift movement, the only time I had to direct a painter to hit his mark. It was the kind of shot you'd try to get if you want to make a picture look more intricate than it was.

Dressing the sets wasn't nearly as intriguing as undressing the

dancers. When the Playboy dancer's scene was shot, men were vol-
unteering to paint her body in psychedelic patterns. Young actors
were all over the place, asking to be unpaid extras in the dance
scene.

For some of the light effects I asked my ace cameraman Arch Dal-
zell if he could find some trick lenses. He tracked down some old
special effects lenses at a camera warehouse that had not been used
in years. They had multiple prism effects. You rotated the prisms so
one nude dancer became eight nude dancers and then the eight girls
would start swirling in a circle. We also brought in a guy who did
effects with moving colors. We were trying anything we could think
of to get optical effects that mimicked acid-tripping.

Some actors smoked grass on the set. Some of the dancers and the
patrons in the club were stoned. It gave them more energy for the
scene. These dancers were in great shape and they moved well. I was
behind "the movement" as it was called then but maybe 75 percent
behind it. Peter, Dennis, they were a hundred percent committed.
This was, as far as they were concerned, the dawning of the Age of
Aquarius. They had no skepticism, whereas I said, sure, possibly it *is*
a New Age.

★ **PAUL RAPP**

In the topless dance nightclub scene Arkoff was at a back table. I bought
hundreds of boxes of amyl nitrate, which was then sold over the
counter. I was working with dozens of extras in the scene and I needed
to get their energy up to a pitch. They thought I was filming when I was
only rehearsing. I wouldn't run any film through the camera and waste
it on rehearsals. When I was ready to shoot, I got everybody higher and
higher and brought out the poppers. My own girlfriend was dancing topless and I put a police helmet on her. The girl Frankie.

★　　★　　★

I had no trouble getting Peter's energy up for a very different kind
of scene that also involved nudity. It was the bedroom scene with
Groves and Glenn, played by Salli Sachse, at the end of Groves's all-
night trip.

★ **PETER FONDA**

I freaked Salli out when I said, "I hope you don't mind but I don't like to
wear clothes for these scenes." We were in a house in Malibu on the
water. She was very nervous. I tried to teach her biofeedback about
being calm. "You have to realize I have intimate knowledge of your char-

acter, Glenn. You're going to be naked on top. And underneath me. Don't worry about it."

They pushed two twin beds together and they kept sliding apart so a couple guys off-camera had to lean against the frames to keep us from slipping through. Roger is shooting this scene from an angle straight over us. He moves the camera around the bed thirty times during the scene. We keep on working. At one point while she is on top of me Roger says, "I want to follow your hand moving over her body."

I put my hand on her back, her rib cage, and was moving to the breast. That's about when my Little Mister decided to pop up and say, "Hey, guys, I'm in this film too!" And was he ever. Right there on camera. It was hilarious. Salli just clamped her legs together to keep it out of sight. I looked up and there was Roger, still photographing.

★   ★   ★

AIP gave me a lot of freedom to make the movie. Then they were concerned that it might be construed as a pro-LSD film when passions were high about drugs. They made changes after it was finished. Before *Angels,* that had never happened. I handed in an answer print and went off to Europe because I was shooting a film there. When I came back they had cut material they found objectionable. They tacked on a warning at the opening that the film was a "shocking commentary," that "mind-bending chemicals" can be fatal, and that the producers deplore drugs.

What really *was* mind-bending was AIP's altering the final sequence without my knowledge. After his night with Glenn, Groves awakes and walks out to the beach and gazes over Santa Monica Bay. His trip is over. He is reborn. I wanted to leave the ending open-ended as to whether the drugs were good or bad. It was an intricate series of dolly movements to get him from inside the house to the deck in one shot. It looked great.

AIP cut up the dolly shot and then froze the frame and put a jagged crack over the image, ripping it in half, as if to say that his life had been shattered by drugs. Everyone—Jack, Bruce, Peter, Dennis—objected along with me. It was the wrong message. Plus, from a purely cinematic standpoint it messed up and garbled what was really a rather well-executed and graceful shot. Privately, I wondered *who* exactly would understand what that shattered frame meant.

I had come back to AIP after the frustrations and constraints at the studios. But now, it seemed, I was on a collision course with AIP. I had to assume it was Jim Nicholson and not the more liberal Arkoff who was messing with the films. Jim was turning increasingly conservative and I was getting wilder in my films, more radical in my politics. After *Angels* I saw a pattern taking shape.

AIP had made a bizarre cut in *Angels* that made no sense what-soever. They changed the pan shot outside the church, before the orgy sequence, to a shot of a sign that said it was a funeral home. It wrecked the shot. Just as I had no special empathy for the Hell's Angels and did not glorify them, I was not out to defend or promote acid. I wanted to be dispassionate and make the film with a semidoc-umentary tone. But Jim was objecting strenuously to the statements he believed I was making in my AIP films.

My statements were implied. Even if acid seemed bad, Groves had possibly learned something about himself by taking acid. And in fact, so had I. At least opening oneself up to new experiences was posi-tive. That's what these two films were all about—alternative life-styles that challenged the Establishment norms and values.

Clearly, I was behind that message all the way. So, apparently, was the public: *The Trip* took in well over $6 million in rentals. We were clearly on to something here: two films, about outlaw bikers and psychedelic drugs, with combined budgets of roughly $700,000 and rentals totaling over $16 million. And just as *The Wild Angels* had been at Venice, *The Trip* was well received at the Cannes Film Festival, where it played to overflowing crowds.

When Peter Fonda and Dennis Hopper asked me to back them for a movie that combined bikers *and* drugs in a journey across America, I was listening.

Chapter 12

Having enjoyed success with films about outlaws and drop-outs, I did two more pictures in the late 1960s that were about different kinds of outlaws and dropouts—a Depression-era woman gangster and a band of roaming hippies looking for Utopia. But they appealed to the same counter-culture spirit of rebellion and alienation that helped make *Angels* and *The Trip* so successful.

When I finished these pictures—*Bloody Mama* and *Gas-s-s-s!*—I was just about ready to drop out of directing. I was tired, but more important, I was frustrated with the way things were happening at AIP, which released them. I had come back to AIP after a discour-

Top: Shelley Winters is *Bloody Mama* (note Robert De Niro at right)
Bottom: Robert Corff and Elaine Giftos are the parent figures in *Gas-s-s-s!*

aging attempt to work with the majors but now they, too, were becoming part of the problem. I realized I needed to take a break.

I was traveling almost constantly, either to make pictures or produce them. I was basically living out of suitcases and still a bachelor. And though I may have become identified through my films with political radicals and other elements on the fringe of society, I was, at forty-plus years of age, hardly a member of the youth culture. It was time to make some substantial changes in the way I was living and working.

Things had gotten to where I had regrets not only over pictures I did, but also, in the case of *Easy Rider,* a picture I walked away from. Peter and Dennis Hopper had been developing an idea that basically was a fusion of the dominant images of *The Wild Angels* and *The Trip:* two hippie dropouts set out to discover America on choppers, fueled by mind-altering drugs. This was like the definitive Corman project. I was sure they had a hit on their hands.

"Will you produce it if Dennis and I write it and act in it?" Peter asked me. "Sure," I said without hesitation. I made the deal and talked to Sam at AIP. They went to work on the treatment. The cast I had in mind would be Hopper, Fonda, and Bruce Dern—all from *The Trip.* Bruce was going to play the straight lawyer.

I found out that Jack Nicholson had an arrangement with Peter that if Jack arranged financing at Columbia, he'd get Bruce's part. Jack had been developing projects with Bob Rafelson and Bert Schneider. Rafelson, who directed Jack in *Five Easy Pieces* a couple years later, was a friend of Hopper's and Fonda's. Schneider's father was a top executive at the studio. They had been successful with the Monkees' TV series and they had an in at Columbia. So Jack's "fee" for brokering the deal would be the role of the straight lawyer.

Dennis and Peter came to my house to discuss the film. Peter asked to see the top sheet on *Angels* and I gave it to him. It showed how I budgeted it out to $360,000. We decided to go ahead but the whole thing blew up at AIP when the three of us went to Sam's office. Sam didn't want Dennis to direct. I didn't want to direct it. I had other things going. I decided to stick with Dennis, who had done some fine second unit work on *The Trip.*

Sam reluctantly said yes but later insisted on a clause in the contract stipulating that if Dennis fell three days behind, AIP could fire him and take over the film. I broke the news to them at my house. That infuriated Dennis and Peter. "I can't let that happen, man," Peter said. "He's the writer and the costar. I hired him because he has a certain eye and ability to see form and substance, to understand art and framing. This picture's going to be nothing but a travelogue unless we get some really fine shots. I can't go along with this."

They backed out and there was Jack with his chance to take the project to Columbia and replace Bruce as the lawyer. When Jack directed his first feature, *Drive, He Said*, the first actor he called to be in it with him was Bruce. That's the kind of guy Jack is.

★ PETER FONDA

While we were trying to figure out where to go with *Easy Rider* Dennis and I had this other story going called "The Queen." It was McGeorge Bundy, LBJ, Dean Rusk, and Robert McNamara all sitting around a table wearing off-the-shoulder white beaded evening gowns, eating lobster with their hands while plotting the assassination of Jack Kennedy. This was right before Bobby. We were going to shoot this in four days for $60,000. We were pitching this to Rafelson. He had the sixty grand. Nicholson was sitting there. We were all friends. Then this tall guy comes in and it's Schneider. He listens, then pulls a chair beside me and says, "How much you need for that movie?"

"Sixty. Real cheap. Can't lose."

Then, either to defuse the situation or change the topic, Rafelson asks, "Peter, how's that motorcycle movie coming?"

I start telling him the troubles we're having with AIP. Bert looks curious and Bob fills him in. "This is the most incredible story you'll ever hear in your life," Bob tells Bert. "And the most commercial."

"Well," Bert says, "how much do you want for *that* one?"

"Don't have a top sheet yet because there isn't a script yet," I say. "But let's just say $360,000—no Teamsters, no carpenters, no Nancy Sinatra salary." Pulled it right out of the air.

"Be at my office at two o'clock today," Bert says, and Dennis and I are off to the movies.

The lineage from Roger to *Rider* was obvious. I'm thinking, okay, I see how Roger's doing this. He was a teacher without being a teacher. He taught by example and by sheer disbelief—showing what he could do if given the chance. He always kept a calm countenance. Dennis doing *Rider* was never a calm countenance. The moment when the fuse has been struck and before the bullet bursts from the shell is called the hangfire. *Easy Rider* was the hangfire moment for both Dennis and me, for sure, in an artistic and wonderful way. And I would not have been able to keep my countenance had I not watched Roger keep his countenance against incredible odds.

★　★　★

I thought *Easy Rider* was a good project and would do well. I didn't think it would do *that* well. It was going to cost between three and four hundred thousand dollars. I was eager to produce it when AIP was backing it, but when they pulled out I was reluctant to put that much money up myself. I had only backed films costing $100,000 or less. Sure, I regret pulling away, but those are the breaks of the game in Hollywood.

★   JACK NICHOLSON

I did not feel disloyal taking this project and telling Bert and Bob that I was absolutely sure it would make endless amounts of money. When it did make all that money, I felt I had won that ongoing discussion with Roger. If he had owned that film, he would have made $26 million. You gotta pay a lot of people scale to make up $26 million. Get it? In that case, his theory of making movies the cheapest way possible proved absolutely wrong.

★   ★   ★

In the spring of 1969, I agreed to do another AIP picture, but I had nothing in mind. I was simply beginning to burn out. They sent me a half-dozen scripts in development. Most were really bad and didn't deserve to be shot. *Bloody Mama*, written by Robert Thom, was quite good. I hired another writer to polish the story. It was a Depression-era film set in the rural South. It traced the story of the notorious Kate "Ma" Barker and her four criminal sons on a spree of violence and depravity involving rape, incest, kidnapping, drug addiction, and murder. She and her four crazy sons all die in a shoot-out at the end in Florida. Ma Barker made *The Wild Angels* and *The Trip* look about as menacing as fairy tales.

Both Jim Nicholson and I agreed that the perfect—the only—actress to handle Ma Barker was Shelley Winters. This was a tough, unrelenting gangster film with its own peculiar ironic humor and vision of rural America in the 1930s. Once Shelley accepted the role, she and I worked together on casting, the only time I worked that way. Later, she and I celebrated ourselves for putting together a truly extraordinary cast. For her sons we got Bobby De Niro, Don Stroud, Bobby Walden, and Clint Kimbrough. Bruce Dern played a young ex-con who joined the gang. Pat Hingle played the kidnap victim. Diane Varsi did fine work as Stroud's prostitute girlfriend. Shelley knew some of these actors from the New York theater scene and Actors Studio. She showed me a tape of De Niro in a low-budget underground film for Brian De Palma made around 1968. He had never done a major feature. That was all I needed to see. It was also the first feature film by the gifted cinematographer John Alonzo.

I took a scouting trip and settled on the Ozarks in Arkansas and the Little Rock area. The four-week shoot turned out to be one of

my smoothest and most successful. There was a strong sense of cama-
raderie that helped me get terrific performances all the way around.
And Shelley was simply exceptional. Not that she wasn't a bit tem-
peramental. As I told Bobby Walden, "I'm not getting along that well
with Shelley." And Bobby said, "I know Shelley real well and I have
never seen her get along with a director so well. You two are working great together." She could have fooled me.

Shelley was certainly unlike any actor I had worked with before.
Right before her important scenes, Shelley liked to play, at top vol-
ume, arias from favorite operas, usually sung by women, right up to
the moment the camera rolled. Shelley was a great believer in
Method acting and arias intensified her concentration. When the a.d.
yelled "Rolling!" she would turn off the record and come on, ready
to play.

There was a scene where Lloyd, the glue-sniffing junkie played by
De Niro, dies and is buried in a shallow grave by a lake. I had an
early morning sequence with Don Stroud and Bobby Walden first
and Shelley was due a little later. So I finished the scenes with the
two brothers and set up the grave shot. We couldn't find Shelley all
morning. Suddenly she ran down a hill toward the lake, screaming,
"No, no, no, what have you done, it's no grave, my boy is not dead,
why are you digging a grave?"

"Shelley, this is the scene, what are you talking about?" She was
totally lost in another world. Walden, also trained at the Actors Studio, took me aside. "Shelley's been up almost all night preparing for
this scene," he explained. "She called the funeral parlor in town and
asked them to open it up for her. She went over there and she's been
sitting up in there all night and morning, staring at a coffin. She is
definitely *into* this scene. Go with it."

★ SHELLEY WINTERS

That funeral scene was a real chancy thing to do. I sat in that funeral
parlor a long time, but since I didn't know the person in the coffin, I had
to do something called personalizing or substitution. This was what,
'69? Was Vietnam on then? I didn't have that big a TV. When I saw the
war I thought it was a movie but it was live from Vietnam. I saw the
bodies falling, faces being blown away. I was stunned. So I used that.

De Niro was probably the most intense actor I have ever worked with.
He prepared in great detail and came in with powerful emotions for his
scenes. Bobby came early to the Ozarks to master his accent by roaming
and absorbing. We hired a local guy to give us the correct accents and
pretty soon Bobby, born and bred in New York, was helping *him.*

For Lloyd's part, he reversed what he did later as Jake LaMotta in

Raging Bull and Al Capone in *The Untouchables:* he stopped eating and lost weight as his addiction progressed. We shot roughly in sequence. He consumed vitamins, water, fruit juices, and a little bit of nourishment. He lost close to thirty pounds and took on the haggard, sickly look of a junkie. The man is as dedicated as any actor in America.

★   ★   ★

De Niro would try anything. One scene had Lloyd driving a period car down a steep dirt road while Ma rode shotgun and shot out the window at someone chasing them. I was strapped to one fender of the car and Johnny Alonzo was strapped to the other fender by fireman belts. Johnny's camera was lashed to the car as well. We were both a little nervier than we should have been. And De Niro was behind the wheel as the car—and camera—started rolling.

De Niro took this road as fast as he could get this car—a Model A or something like it—to go. He gets this thing screaming downhill, driving like crazy. We did it a few times and it was a really tremendous shot. We were all into it.

Between the second and last take Shelley went to Bobby and said, "You're driving great, you're really looking like a guy driving out of control."

"I *am* driving out of control," he said with a grin. "I have no idea how to drive. I'm from the city. I don't even have a license." He would never have mentioned that because we'd have gotten a stunt driver. If anything had happened—if the car had rolled while careening and skidding down this hillside—Johnny and I would have been finished. Somehow, when you're making a picture, you get caught up and never imagine anything can happen to you. Directors must sometimes believe in their omnipotence, or at least their invincibility on the set.

★   JOHN ALONZO

I had been shooting *National Geographic* and Jacques Cousteau documentaries when a friend of mine, Bill Asher, made a deal to direct a movie that Roger would produce. Bill had asked me to be d.p. on that film but then it fell through. Unknown to me Roger agreed to honor the obligation or understanding that I was to shoot the film, and he offered me *Bloody Mama*. He just trusted his instincts. I was quite flattered.

Roger was never demonstrative, never one to insincerely gush, "You're wonderful, everything is terrific." I was spoiled by Roger and I've made almost fifty movies since then. I thought being a d.p. was a piece of cake. He was never intimidating. He'd just look through the lens and say, "That's fine."

Roger had his hands full with all the strong personalities in the movie. Shelley was supposed to hit Stroud, her biggest son, because she was pissed at him. So she hit him for real and his natural reaction was to hit her right back. It knocked her down. I looked at Roger. He was laughing, shaking his head.

In the big funeral scene, Shelley's got to wail and shoot a gun in the air at God in her rage. So there's Shelley over there to the side with a gun in her hand, playing some opera in her head, crying, working herself up emotionally. I'm looking over at Roger and he's smiling. And he says gently, "As soon as you're ready, let's shoot this thing."

He tells me, "Hand-hold the shot, very simple. Take Shelley all around the grave and be sure that you end up on the gun when she fires into the sky." I started to think: How can I get her to hit all these marks to make sure I focus on her? So I go over to Shelley and start, "Would you mind if we—"

"Don't *talk* to me," she says. "I'm preparing. I can't discuss anything right now."

"Well," I insist, "I have to follow you around and make sure you hit certain spots and that I get your face and the gun."

"I can't hit any marks. I'm preparing."

Meanwhile, Bobby is lying off-camera in the ground. And we start rolling. Shelley, somehow, hits *every single mark* perfectly. She knew *exactly* what she was doing—a truly professional lady.

★ SHELLEY WINTERS

Roger understood the delicate mechanisms of the actor, of working in Method. Actors liked working with him. He would take chances on all kinds of actors, writers, producers, and directors but never had the confidence to do the big movies himself. But he was in control. He storyboarded in his head. I've done pictures with directors who turn the set into a democracy because they don't know what to do and can't decide.

Roger did what the great directors all do. He rehearsed quite a bit, then he'd get a take right away. That way, you can't plan anything and you get a spontaneous quality to it. If an actor sees a director look at his watch, he's dead. A director must never look at his watch. You think, "I'm not going fast enough, he's bored." Roger never did that. We were never aware of Roger. I knew he did his movies fast but I was never pressured. We rushed *in between* scenes. But he knew instinctively that what went on behind the camera was as important as in front. The atmosphere you create shows up on-screen or onstage. Roger created a relaxed comradely situation.

Then there was the scene I throw a bottle at Bobby, after he sniffs glue and starts to weep. It was supposed to be a fake bottle. He got so involved playing a junkie that he forgot the story. He developed scabs on his body from eating nothing but water and fruit juices. I told Roger I was worried about the kid and Roger said, "Don't worry, he's an actor. Leave him alone."

But I felt he didn't act until the middle of the shoot. He wasn't doing the real feelings. So he sniffs glue and has to cry and he couldn't—or wouldn't. Roger's been known to tear out a page of script when he's falling behind so he can catch up. Roger's also been known to shoot an ending first so the in-between pages can be ripped out.

So before like the seventh take, I grabbed a real wine bottle and looked over at Roger. He knew what was going on. The camera rolls and Bobby's cowering in the corner for the shot and I toss this wine bottle at him. He had to cover his head and duck. He was so startled that he cried. He was so upset that *Shelley Winters*—rather than Ma Barker— would do that to him that he was stricken.

Roger shot every scene of *Bloody Mama* but we begged him for another three days. With another hundred thousand this could have been *Bonnie and Clyde*.

★ ★ ★

Bloody Mama is still one of my favorite films, even though it was viewed as a little picture here and got somewhat passed over by critics. But it got rave reviews and serious attention in Europe. It did less well than *Angels* and *The Trip* because they were slanted to the 1960s youth culture and had young leads; Shelley was a middle-aged lead and this was a historical film.

It was about the power of family, blood ties, clans—which is, historically, where countries can trace their beginnings. It was about the breakdown of rationality. Clans grew into extended families and tribes and then nations. So the film played back to a state of pre-civilization when the most important, the only important, bond of loyalty is family.

The film still does well overseas and in video and it led to fictional sequels and spin-offs for my own company a few years later with a younger, more glamorous lead, Angie Dickinson: *Big Bad Mama* and *Big Bad Mama II*. Angie led her two daughters in crime. These films have become huge favorites in video rental.

Bloody Mama was also quite a violent film. We are a violent people, a violent species. If we weren't violent, the saber-toothed tiger would be roaming the earth as the dominant species. But the humans killed them. I touched on this in *Death Race 2000*, which was a New World film in the mid-1970s. For the human race to endure and not be wiped out, we had to be violent in the jungles and forests of predators who were bigger and tougher and swifter. Violence was absolutely necessary. The ironic, or perhaps tragic, twist is that violence is no longer necessary. But the violence that enabled us to survive is now the violence that may defeat and destroy us. The A-bomb is the easiest example. There's bacteriological warfare. There is gang violence, random street violence. We are, indeed, capable of wiping ourselves out one way or another.

Certainly that theme—and possibility—was at the core of the protest movement as the war in Vietnam escalated. After *Bloody Mama* I returned to an irreverent youth-oriented film that I hoped would be an apocalyptic, Strangelovian political satire: *Gas-s-s-s! . . . or It May Become Necessary to Destroy the World in Order to Save It.* The idea came mostly from Jim Nicholson at AIP and was inspired, simply, by the 1960s slogan about not trusting anyone over thirty. The idea was to present a world where there were no people over the age of thirty. Here's how we set it up: an experimental gas developed by the Army in Alaska escapes into the environment and, because of its effects on aging, only kills people over thirty. I wanted to do a dark comedy. I worked with a young writer named George Armitage and we tried to use the film to examine certain trends in society through humor. The problem was we were already into the fall of 1969 and I was committed to doing another picture—*Von Richthofen and Brown*—for United Artists next spring and summer in Ireland. I had to go into production without a finished script.

Gas-s-s-s! was another picture shot from location to location, as were *Angels* and *Bloody Mama*. A couple from Texas sets out to escape the toxic gas and find Utopian life at a commune in New Mexico. Along the way, they run into a man calling himself Billy the Kid, join up with a hippie "family" seeking the same communal salvation, go to a rock festival, encounter a fascistic football team known as Jason and the Nomads. The family realizes the commune is no Utopia. There's a surreal procession of heroes back from the dead—JFK, Martin Luther King, Che Guevara, even Edgar Allan Poe. There were some truly imaginative, off-the-wall ideas being thrown around.

The cast was solid and talented—Bob Corff, Elaine Giftos, Talia Coppola, Cindy Williams (who would star in TV's *Laverne & Shirley*), Bud Cort, and Ben Vereen. But it was extremely difficult to shoot.

The big lesson learned was never start a shoot with just a first draft. I got away with it on *Last Woman on Earth*. But that was a very simple little film. This time I brought George along and he played Billy the Kid as he rewrote. We started shooting in Dallas and then moved to New Mexico, ending production on top of the Acoma Indian Pueblo, which is at the peak of a spectacular mesa in western

New Mexico. So we were traversing a significant portion of the Southwestern United States. Winter was closing in. I had to finish by Christmas. We got perfect weather in Texas during preproduction and then we had icy sleet the two days we shot in Dallas and it was a complete mess. We all left Dallas totally discouraged. The days were getting shorter and colder; we couldn't hold the company through Christmas.

George and I worked hard at nights and on Sundays to pull the script together as we made our way west to New Mexico and then north toward Acoma territory. I had Stephanie Rothman and her husband, Charles Swartz, doing second unit work.

We ended up with some pretty wild and surreal images. We had a group of Hell's Angels riding in their colors in golf carts instead of their choppers. The Texas A & M football team became a band of marauders on dune buggies, terrorizing the Southwest. We had Edgar Allan Poe speeding through the frame on a Hell's Angel chopper with a raven on his shoulder, making comments from time to time.

We wanted a scene showing an Edsel convertible and a National Guard truck driving through and around wrecked cars littering LBJ Freeway in Dallas, which was completed but not yet open to the public. We got permission to shoot there. Paul Rapp managed to get fifty junk heaps towed out there for about ten bucks apiece. I got a sensational dolly shot around and through the wreckages. A highway cop came to us and said they had had five hundred calls referring to a major accident on the LBJ.

We re-created the Kennedy assassination while it was sleeting. Then we finally got to the Acoma mesa, which is virtually cut off from civilization, accessible only by a steep and winding dirt road. We had to set up scores of extras on top of the mesa. Dealing with the Indians was rather difficult and they tried to get a bigger location fee. Their reasoning was that this had been their hallowed ground for centuries.

We had money troubles with not only the ungrateful dead but the Grateful Dead as well. In Albuquerque they were supposed to play a concert in a drive-in for the film. At the last minute they demanded a huge increase in money. We got Country Joe and the Fish instead.

★ PAUL RAPP

The *Gas-s-s-s!* shoot was the toughest one I ever saw Roger go through. I had never seen Roger in a nasty, bad mood like that. He seemed very down, snarling and weary. The Dallas sequences were around Thanksgiving and they had all-time record cold and blizzard conditions. It was miserable. Roger was shivering the whole time, wearing the same parka he had for *Ski Troop Attack*. But he did take us all to Thanksgiving dinner at Brennan's, where they gave us a private dining room.

The day we set up the last sequence at the mesa Roger seemed really adrift. The Indians were terrible to work with. He seemed isolated, almost directing like a robot. The last scene was a big action shot with the entire cast, dune buggies, motorcycles, and the whole Indian tribe coming together. The first take was a complete mess. Roger just sat there. I got everybody back in their positions for a second take and looked over to Roger. He just nodded. I called action for him, and surprisingly, this time it went perfectly. Roger got up from his chair slowly, thanked everybody, and said very quietly, "Let's go home."

★ ★ ★

My films and politics were getting more radical, more "liberated," as the 1960s were coming to a close. I was truly beginning to believe I could do anything, which is why the picture ran a little out of control. Any idea that came to either of us we would put in. Writing at night and shooting the very next day didn't give us the right perspective. Once we awoke in the middle of a snowstorm and so we tossed out that day's pages, rewrote a scene, and raced out and shot it in the powder. We were a pack of nomads, moving every second or third day. But by the end the morale had come back up and we were doing really wild stuff.

I was spending a lot of petty cash. It was just easier to pay cash for materials and other expenses. Dave Melamed, AIP's treasurer, told me, "We know you're honest. But you're spending a larger percentage in cash than anyone else. Nobody in the company questions the actual cost of your films and no one makes such big-looking films for so little money. But we get audited from time to time by the government. And it really looks bad for you to spend seventy-five of three hundred thousand on petty cash."

I explained why I did it that way. "Okay," he said, "at least bring me the receipts. Bring 'em back in a bag if you have to. I don't care. I need something to show the IRS."

I instructed Paul to get everyone to save receipts for everything but to go on with business as usual. Weeks after the shoot I was in Jim Nicholson's office when Paul came in and dumped an enormous bag of thousands of receipts out on the floor. Dave came into Jim's office. "Greatest petty cash receipts I've ever seen, Roger. Sixty thousand dollars in petty cash spent. Ninety thousand in receipts."

That was about the only amusing moment in postproduction. I went off to Europe to plan for *Von Richthofen and Brown* in Ireland.

I should have known something was up. It had happened on *Mama* and *The Trip*. I turned in the final cut, left for Europe, and changes were made without my knowledge. When I saw what AIP did to my film I realized we had come to the end of the line as a team.

The unkindest cut of all was the last scene. I ended the film with a spectacular shot from on top of the mesa, with a view sixty, seventy miles to the horizon. We had the entire tribe there and everyone else who had been in the film. It was a celebration. The leading man kisses the woman and I zoom back. It was a cliché I had never used to end a film. I did it precisely because it was a cliché. I had the entire marching band of the local high school. I had a whole group of Hell's Angels. I had a bunch of guys on dune buggies. I had a football team. I had our whole cast in this wild celebration as the camera zoomed back and over the shot. God, who was a running character throughout the film, made his final comments on what went on.

There must have been three hundred people on top of that mesa. It was one of the greatest shots I ever achieved *in my life*. And AIP cut out the entire shot. They ended the picture on the couple's clichéd kiss—because they didn't like what God was saying. The picture ended and made no sense.

While I was in Ireland to shoot *Von Richthofen* I attended the Edinburgh film festival and *Gas-s-s-s!* was invited. Weirdly enough, it played very well, got a huge round of applause and strong reviews. But I was shocked. They had again waited until I was out of the country to cut the film.

Final cut approval had never been put in writing at AIP. It was more a tacit agreement. But only my last four films were anti-Establishment; AIP had grown into the biggest independent in the U.S. It was now a publicly held company. The more irreverent the film, the greater the financial risk. The political stance or "image" of the company, as seen through its releases, had an impact on its stock. And I was going against Establishment taste and sensibility in my films of the late 1960s. AIP was losing its nerve, maybe shaken by the controversy around the biker and acid movies. I felt, morally, politically, that our films should be on the counterculture side.

Hollywood was deeply split during Vietnam between two camps. The power structure, the financial people and some conservative big-time actors—John Waynes, Charlton Hestons—generally supported the war and Nixon. It was my feeling that 80 percent of the creative community in town was counterculture and 20 percent, the older segment, was Establishment. But Jim Nicholson, AIP's president, had become a true—and increasingly conservative—pillar of Hollywood's professional and civic community. Arkoff remained liberal. Always a good and decent man, Jim had grown conservative and it was his objections to my work that led to the cuts.

Jim had done this on four films in a row. *Gas-s-s-s!* was the worst case, the one that really did it for me. And it turned out to be the last of thirty-three films I directed for AIP and my forty-eighth feature film in fifteen years. I was pretty tired. I would turn forty-four the following spring in 1970.

It was the end of an era at AIP, but it was also the beginning of a whole new way of living and working for me.

Chapter 13

T hough *Von Richthofen and Brown* is not among my best-known films, the shooting of the World War One drama—with stunning aerial dogfights in period biplanes—became a critical turning point in my life. It was while doing that film in Ireland that two major decisions were made that would profoundly change the course of my life: I decided to stop directing films for other people and set up my own production-distribution company; and Julie Halloran and I decided to get married.

At the time, I intended only to take a yearlong sabbatical and get back to directing. But *Von Richthofen*, which I shot in Ireland in six weeks for under $1 million dollars, was the last film I would direct. There was never a conscious, deliberate plan to quit directing,

Top: On location filming *Von Richthofen and Brown*
Bottom: Julie Halloran marries Roger Corman, December 26, 1970

marry, get behind a desk instead of a camera, and settle down with a family. Yet there may have been an *unconscious* intention to change the direction of my life. In any event, that's essentially what happened.

I had been interested in the theme of aristocrats at war since the early 1960s, when I developed an idea and first draft for a film about General Robert E. Lee. I offered it to UA and they refused to believe I could do it for $500,000. "That's a *giant* film for me," I explained.

I had arranged to restage the significant battles of the Civil War by using the cadets of a military academy in Virginia as part of their senior class exercises. The academy was willing to put some five hundred extras on the field. Weirdly enough, their uniforms almost perfectly matched those of the Confederates. I was going to give a donation to their building fund and this would be a yearlong school project.

"It won't happen," UA insisted. "This is a multimillion-dollar film." And I said, "You know, I've been doing this for fifteen years now and I know what I'm talking about."

"You cannot make 'Robert E. Lee' for five hundred thousand," they insisted, and that was it.

So several years later, my curiosity about aristocrats in war turned to the legend of the Baron von Richthofen, Germany's ace World War One fighter pilot and the last knight at war. The Red Baron was aristocratic, Prussian, a product of a military academy, a member of an elite branch of the German army before the war. He had requested a transfer into the flying corps because he was a great hunter and sportsman.

And the man who eventually shot down the Red Baron was Roy Brown, a garage mechanic from Ontario who flew for the Royal Air Force. Brown got so nervous before missions he lined his ulcerous stomach with a quart of milk. But he was a natural pilot, a man who possessed astonishing instant reflexes.

I had read some books about the Baron and Brown and concluded their story would make a fascinating film. The theme was the end of the chivalric tradition in warfare, the end of knights, the beginning of the era of tanks. War changes from an honorable, almost gentlemanly, sporting combat to mass slaughter in the trenches. The symbol of this transformation was von Richthofen—the greatest ace pilot with the greatest number of kills, a true aristocrat, and a fearless hero to his country.

Before he was the Red Baron, he refused orders to camouflage his plane. The actual wording of the order was just to repaint all planes. So he chose his own color—and simply repainted it red. Hence his nickname. And he insisted on flying the slower Fokker D-6 triplane, even though the Germans already had the D-7 biplane and the single-wing D-8. He said he preferred giving up a little speed for maneuverability; he wanted to be able to flip over instantly, dive down, and make a kill.

I had great admiration for a guy like that—sees a loophole in the regulations and defies authority. His reasoning was brazen: Anyone who's got the nerve to go up there against me, I'm the one in the bright red Fokker D-6 triplane. I'm ready. I'm waiting for you.

The other symbol of the transformation of warfare in the modern age was the humble garage mechanic who was terrified to sit in the cockpit—and who shot down the Red Baron.

This time, UA gave me a green light and my brother and I were off to Ireland, where two other flying films—*Darling Lili* and *The Blue Max*—had been shot in the 1960s. I'd made a deal to rent the planes built for those films. Before I left, though, I took care of one production detail that would make the shoot much less of an ordeal than my most recent films.

I got in touch with Julie. She had worked in films before and had worked in market research at the *L.A. Times.* She had just completed a six-month study in Mexico City and was heading to Europe for a vacation. So I suggested, as we went into preproduction, that she should stop off in Ireland and visit before going on to France. I thought she could stay on as a production assistant, as things were likely to get overloaded and pressured.

I planned to do all the dogfight sequences in two weeks. The *Blue Max* aerial sequences took five months to shoot. *Darling Lili* took two summers.

I would match the aerial shots I got in two weeks with anything in either of those two films. I was able to accomplish that by having three units shooting aerial sequences simultaneously. I had the Irish Air Force—again, a modest contribution paved the way—flying for me, as well as several stunt pilots.

I started by building a thirty-foot wooden tower on top of the highest hill I could find in this section of the Irish countryside outside Dublin. I put my stationary camera in the tower, so that I could shoot low-flying planes horizontally to create the impression that the camera was in the air. And I hired an Air Force helicopter for my art director and second unit supervisor, Jimmy Murakami. This way we could shoot two battles simultaneously—one from the tower and one from Jimmy's helicopter. Jimmy had been a cartoonist and animator and wanted to break into features so I gave him many of the aerial sequences. His storyboards were extraordinarily detailed.

But as we mapped all this out it occurred to me that, due to the schedule and the budget, I'd need a *third* camera for a third battle going on at the same time. I couldn't build another tower, and a second helicopter was too expensive. So I asked around and learned of a plane specially developed by oil companies for aerial surveys and oil exploration. This plane was designed to fly at any altitude at a very low speed—somewhere between fifty and sixty miles an hour. This was ideal; a plane zooming in at 150 miles an hour would be moving too fast to control the images. I chartered this plane and a pilot out of England for my third battle sequence.

So the plan then was for Jimmy to shoot from the helicopter, another camera operator to shoot from the oil plane, and I would be on the tower with the fixed camera and radio controls to the pilots, the chopper, and the oil plane. I was working partly as a director, partly as an air traffic controller guiding ten aircraft into and out of three dogfights. It seemed feasible enough.

The early morning routine that got us going was the most fun of the shoot. We would all meet at a small private airfield outside Dublin with the pilots and crew. The actors came a little later for the close-ups in the cockpits. We'd have coffee and bangers as the sun came up and look over the storyboards. I even had small wooden model planes built and, like kids, they would hold up the planes in their hands and move around me—I was the control tower—to coordinate the flight patterns. Having been a builder of model planes with radio controls as a kid, I was reminded of what Groucho Marx once said, getting out of his car at Fox, "This is the greatest electric train a boy ever had."

The pilots were a mixed crew—the Irish Air Force, a couple of U.S. ex-fighter pilots who had signed on, an Englishman, and a Canadian. Two of the planes had two seats, one behind the other. I put the pilots in the front seats with an Arriflex bolted between the two seats, trained on the actor in the rear seat. One of the American pilots we used was Richard Bach. He told me he was writing something about flying too. I asked him to show it to me. It was a book called *Jonathan Livingston Seagull*.

As I did in *Young Racers*, I had the actor control a switch that turned the camera on when it seemed the time was right. The pilots did the stunts. As the planes spun, rolled, and dived through the simulated aerial combat stunts, the actors could sense when it was just right and flicked the switch. They loved this because it let them be something of a director and a dogfight pilot at the same time.

It worked wonderfully. There was no faint blue halo of the matte process and it was better and cheaper than matte. You could really see their faces on a tight spin, see the flesh on their faces move just a bit from G-force.

One reason my predecessors took so long for the aerial shots was that they waited for perfect weather. We worked from three books: Blue Day, Gray Day, and Doesn't Matter Day, depending on the early weather report. There were seven battles to shoot and these books were like bibles. Who ever said they only scheduled dogfights in World War One on blue sky days? They were not waiting for light. But we did have to remain consistent within a battle scene so we kept the books for matching shots. The Doesn't Matter Day book was for battles that start under blue skies, say, and the planes fly *into* clouds and gray. That was my hedge that allowed me to never lose a day's shoot except for rain.

The aerial photography was the most fun, I believe, I ever had shooting a film. Julie came to the location from her travels around Europe. The BBC was due to interview me and do a piece on the shoot, so I told her to function as a public relations liaison and talk to them because I didn't have much time for it. She showed them around, told them what was going on. The director asked her how long she had been in public relations and she answered, "Oh, about a half-hour." Julie was really quite impressive over there.

I had one great flying day when the RAF raids the German base. I was on the tower, thirty feet off the ground. It is amazing what you can get with an ace stunt flyer if you are off the ground because he can perform stunts below you. One guy came in so low he grazed the ground and the wing picked up grass on its edge. "Look here," he said, "you can't get any lower than that." We were all truly exhilarated.

Then for the raid I had cameras positioned all over the place— the big set piece. Smoke bombs wired to go off everywhere. We were all set but for some reason one plane was one gunner short. No one to swing the rear gun. We didn't know what to do. Six weeks, giant film, the big payoff shot coming up. No time to lose. Julie was standing next to me. "Give me a helmet," she said, out of the blue. "I'll get in there and do it."

I was stunned. "You want to do that?"

"I'll just tuck my hair up, pull the helmet way down, and put on the goggles. Nobody'll ever know."

Sure enough, she got in the cockpit and took off. Then her plane was coming in right at my tower, with all the others swarming around it, hitting 120, 130 miles an hour, zapping along, spitting out blanks, and my eyes were glued on Julie in the rear seat, swiveling that machine gun like a pro, coming through the smoke bombs flying up all around her. And there I was, yelling directions into the radio, with tremendous static and engine noises making communication all but impossible. It was clear Julie liked the way we functioned and I sure liked the way she responded to it. Some people come to a location, look around, and say, "This is great. I want to be part of all this." They catch on right away. Others say, "This is awful, I want to go back to my desk at the office." Julie was definitely into it.

★ JULIE CORMAN

What I noticed most about Roger on location then was the *physical* aspect of his directing: get the shot, move *immediately* to the next shot. There is always a tendency on location for inertia to set in, for a director to stop after a shot and say to the cameraman, "How's that for you, camera?" "Sound, was that okay?" A little discussion with everybody. Four or five minutes go by that way every time out. If you get twenty setups in a day, that's about 100 minutes a day to discuss "How was it for you, sound?"

Roger never took time for such discussions and never understands why other people do. As a director he is always looking, listening, and unless he hears something from sound or camera, he knows he got the shot.

One time early in the shoot he called: "Cut, print, next shot is over here." He walked the twenty feet across the field for the next setup and waited about ten seconds. This was an English crew and the a.d., the soundman, the d.p., and the gaffer were chatting. Roger walked back to them and said, "Gentlemen, I *said* the next shot is over here." And they followed him immediately from that point on. It's keeping the momentum going that's allowed him to make films efficiently. Watching Roger direct is like watching a dance. He has flow and rhythm and concentration. Roger, even when there were two hundred people on a location, was never distracted from what was in front of the camera.

★   ★   ★

Until Julie, most of the women I had dated and known socially had been actresses. There are many very bright and pleasant actresses. But Julie's background and experience were much closer to mine— a more literary, educated orientation, and a different set of values. Very few actresses, for instance, were college educated then. Not that they couldn't be, but they decided on acting as teenagers and never went to college.

Julie had been an English major at UCLA when I first interviewed her for a job as my assistant. She had done location scouting work and some film production research. She eventually took a market research job at the *L.A. Times*, where she got the paper's book review section started. But she was interested in film, and she brought with her a real passion for research and digging things up. And there was the fact that Julie was, and is, a beautiful woman.

We had dated on and off for a few years. There were always trips and shoots and other involvements keeping us from getting closer. But I was tired of directing, living on the road, dealing with longer and tougher shoots. Also, it was clear I was in love. Our dating had been fairly traditional—dinners, parties, movies. We became closer and closer and finally got engaged, almost without being conscious of it. But once we finished *Von Richthofen*, we decided to marry.

After the flying sequences, the rest of the shoot was standard for dramatic scenes. It was becoming a routine I dreaded. What did ease the grind for us was shooting at the magnificent Powerscourt Castle outside Dublin. It was beautifully furnished with nineteenth-century decor, art objects, a handsome library, and a spectacular view over the Irish downs in late summer. I'd sit there before the first shot, sip coffee, read my script and notes as the morning light poured in. That was the nicest time of the day for me, even though I knew eventually I'd have to go out there and go to work.

One morning the man who owned the period planes we leased, Birch Williams, came to Powerscourt Castle in a rather grand manner—landing a helicopter on the lawn. Birch was an American living in Ireland. He had hosted us generously at parties, serving Irish whiskey; now he was acting in a grand manner himself. He announced that he had signed a deal to lease his fighter planes—we were finished, essentially—for another film about zeppelin raids over England during World War One. "I've seen what you and Jimmy have been doing and I decided I wanted to direct the aerial stuff myself from the helicopter."

"Two problems," I said. "One, you leased the planes to us for the summer. You can't charter them to someone else now. What happens if there's an accident? I've still got a few close-ups with the actors to shoot in the air."

"No problem. There won't be any accidents." I didn't want to be a bad guy. So what if he could pick up a little extra money?

"But there's another issue," I said. "Directing's not as easy as you think once you're up in the air. You've never directed anything *on the ground.* It's really pretty tough in a helicopter. I know because I tried it and I've done fifty films."

"It'll be all right. I've got one of the greatest cameramen in the world with me." He was a Frenchman and he was, indeed, considered the top aerial cameraman in the world. I wanted him too but he charged much too much money. The camerman I used, an Irishman named Seamus Corcoran, *became* one of the great aerial specialists because of this film.

"Okay, Birch," I said. "Go ahead. Good luck."

He finished his coffee, got in his helicopter, and took off. We were all feeling very grand about now. We owned an air force. We sipped coffee in a castle. And as the rotors of the chopper whirred and roared, Birch waved silently from his seat. He was with a pilot, the cameraman, and the film's director. The helicopter rose above the trees, spun around, and veered off.

And that was the last any of us saw of Birch Williams alive.

The way I heard it, Birch was directing the aerial sequences for *Zeppelin* later that same day in his chopper out over the Irish Sea. He was calling two planes in on him for a dive as they fought in the air. And he called them in wrong and the planes collided with the helicopter. Birch and everyone in the chopper were killed, as were two pilots from the Irish Air Force.

When I got back that day to the apartment I had rented during the shoot, all hell had broken loose. There were calls from all over. The word had gone out on the radio that a crash had killed four or five people—including the director—connected to a World War One flying picture.

"Is Roger dead?" people were asking. Everyone assumed I was.

The crash had a devastating impact on all of us. The Irish government halted all flying as too dangerous. Even though the accident had not occurred on our film, the insurance company canceled our aerial insurance. Julie negotiated with government officials. Gene managed to get the insurance reinstated and returned to Dublin with cash to pay cast and crew since a bank strike precluded our banking in Dublin.

The Irish government wasn't satisfied with the insurance coverage and demanded that the production post a bond before we could resume aerial shooting. Gene agreed to put up the cash he had brought back as the bond. He signed the papers and we were set to fly again.

"One small problem," Gene then told the government men. "We've given you all our money and we're shooting with Irish crew members and actors. We can't pay hotel, equipment bills, or anybody. What we'd like to do is borrow against the bond. Lend us a hundred thousand pounds, using the bond as collateral."

Incredibly, they agreed and Gene borrowed the money *back* from the government.

I had dinner with Julie that night. She was impressed with what my brother had done. "I have never seen anyone work so smoothly and convincingly in my life," she said.

It was my relationship to directing, however, that was coming apart by then. I had begun thinking while in Ireland that I should start my own production and distribution company. Gene would run the production end. I could get Larry Woolner, the distributor from

New Orleans who had worked with me early on, to run distribution. I would oversee the whole thing.

Each morning I had to drive from my Dublin apartment to the airfield. There was a fork in the road along the way. One road led to the location; the other led up to beautiful Galway Bay on the Western coast of Ireland. And every time I passed the sign for Galway along the road, I felt a temptation to just keep on going up to Galway with Julie and say, "Forget the picture."

We managed to wrap and get back to Los Angeles. I still needed some crash shots. I went out to a field and found some kids who were building and flying radio-controlled gas-powered model airplanes, the kind with long wingspans that I used to build as a kid. I asked them if they were into building World War One models for me and I offered each one a couple of hundred bucks.

They loved it. One kid, the oldest, built a Fokker triplane just like the one we flew in Ireland. I made a deal with Andrews Air Force Base because I needed to match closely the clear skies of Ireland. We went up there on a Sunday and flew the planes, stunted them, did all kinds of things. They placed little balsa wood dummies in the cockpits and I could get them in close-ups with the zoom lens. We built a few smaller ones with little engines and hung them on wires so we could make them collide head-on.

We had a terrific time. I was shooting it all. At the end of the day every kid slammed his plane into the ground for the crash shots. Two of them were radio-guided into each other for a great collision. Then I could cut away and we set fireballs up underneath the planes so I could cut back and get the explosions. It was a wonderful day for me and these kids. We just wiped out all these planes. It was very much the way it had been as a child with those giant lifelike planes.

If I was finally ready to take a break from directing, I was also about to begin a new role in my personal life. On December 26, 1970, several months after finishing *Von Richthofen*, Julie and I were married. We had a small family wedding at St. Paul's Chapel in Westwood. Afterward, we had a party for a hundred or so friends at the home of Danny Haller, my art director who had moved on to directing, and his wife, Kinta, my one-time assistant. The name I had chosen for my own production-distribution company, New World Pictures, seemed fitting.

Chapter 14

had no idea then that this new venture would become the major turning point in my career—that I was about to retire as a director and become a one-man studio. Nor could I have known that within a couple years our company would become the most successful independent operation in the business and enjoy an utterly unique image in Hollywood.

We not only began to attract a new generation of creative, energetic filmmakers who saw exploitation genres as a path to big-budget studio features; we also became pioneers in the distribution of art films by the world's greatest directors.

I chose the name New World. I had read a book by an advertising man who said the two most significant words in the ad business are new and free. "Free" obviously had nothing to do with the way I

Top: Roger Corman with Japanese director Akira Kurosawa
Below: Scenes from *The Young Nurses* and *Candy Stripe Nurses*

wanted to make films. I was going to go with New World Films, but I had the feeling that film might someday be a transitory phenomenon, replaced by lasers or tape or something else. So I went with New World Pictures, figuring whatever they use to make movies, the result will always be pictures.

This new venture got underway while I was still in Ireland. The idea was to give me something interesting to do and find a source for investment. I had invested almost entirely in the stock market. My father, who had retired from engineering at forty-three, had become an investor. He had coached me on my own investments. I had done quite well and actually could have quit working and lived off dividends the rest of my life. But I still wanted to play the filmmaking game, calling all my own shots.

I also wanted to diversify. Rather than invest in real estate or stocks, I thought I'd invest in a field I knew well. There were business reasons to go into distribution. One was that the film rentals go to the distributor first to cover his fee and expenses—prints, advertising, mailing, etc. There was money to be made there.

Another major justification was that you can determine with much greater control when and in which theaters you book your films. You decide how much money to spend on advertising your films. You control the negotiations for terms with the theater circuits. As a producer, or producer/director, you basically reclaim all the control you give up when someone else releases your films. Otherwise, the risk is that the distributor, who, like AIP, is likely to be in the production business, may give a good play date to a picture he owns 100 percent rather than yours. With AIP, I was always competing with the films they had backed. Still, they treated me fairly and we kept the bickering to a minimum.

It was simply that I stood to earn a profit and maintain greater control. Very few independents control their own distribution and turn out consistently commercial products. I wanted to be one of those who did.

I was offered another deal, however, with UA—an adaptation of John Updike's popular novel *Couples*. The studio had spent a huge amount of money on the rights and a first draft. But it wanted that film to be the second of a two-film deal and they wanted to cross-collateralize the projects—a possible trap.

I didn't like the screenplay and wanted to start over. The first film had some profit potential. But the profits from *Von Richthofen* would be used as collateral against the second picture and they already had close to $1 million invested. If the second film didn't work, out went all the profit from the first to pay for the losses on the second. So there would be no profits at all until the negative costs of *both* films were recouped.

Perhaps had I been a more committed artist I might well have said: "I don't care. This is an opportunity to do a more significant piece of work. The possibility of losing my profit is immaterial compared to my chances of moving ahead as a serious filmmaker." But I didn't. I turned down the offer. Perhaps I was afraid of failing on a literary project that would attract much attention. This wasn't a clear-cut conscious stance, but a plausible motive in the unconscious. Certainly, my bitter experience with *The Intruder* could have contributed to my decision.

So it was on to New World. I had wanted my brother, Gene, to run the production side but Gene had many of his own projects working and that never really came off. I contacted Larry Woolner, who with his brother, Bernard, had released *Teenage Doll* and *Swamp Women* years earlier. They owned a chain of drive-ins throughout Louisiana.

Larry had an idea for our first film—a student nurse. As soon as he told me this, I said yes. But I said we should turn it into the stories of four nurses, blend them, and call it *The Student Nurses*. He said fine.

Stephanie Rothman directed *The Student Nurses* in three weeks for $150,000. She had been my assistant for about a year. The nurse picture, which her husband, Charles Swartz, produced and wrote with her, took shape out of a formula I had been working on for some time: contemporary dramas with a liberal to left-wing viewpoint and some R-rated sex and humor. But they were not to be comedies.

I frankly doubt the left-wing bent, or message, was crucial to the success of the films we would do. But it was important to the filmmakers and to me that we have something to say within the films. One nurse was black, another was involved with street protests. This was 1971. The "sixties" was still an active cultural movement. We had four very attractive nurses; I insisted each had to work out her problems without relying on a boyfriend.

We had an amazing start with an instant winner. It took in over $1 million in rentals, which not only meant a solid profit to New World, but also established us in the minds of the theater owners.

Everybody was thrilled. Well, *almost* everybody. Larry came into the office one day and read a letter from the Private Duty Nurses' Association, stating that they felt we had portrayed nurses in a sexual manner that was not an accurate reflection of the nursing world. "What do we do with this?" Larry asked.

"What do you mean, 'What do we do with this'?" I asked.

"They've just given us the title of our first sequel—*Private Duty Nurses*."

New World was soon in production with biker films like *Angels Die Hard* and *Angels Hard as They Come*, which was the first of several projects cowritten by the team of Jonathan Demme, who produced, and Joe Viola, who directed. Then we had our women-in-prison films like *The Big Doll House* and *Women in Cages*. We had three or four straight winners out of the box, with our distributor's fee set at around 35 percent. This was the amount of money charged by the distributor to cover his major costs—prints, shipping, promotion, lab costs, etc.

Larry had never seen money like this. But after a year he felt he wanted his own company. It was a most amicable split. When I bought him out we went for a drink and Larry said it was the greatest year of his life. He walked away with a lot of money for a year's work and we stayed good friends.

Many of our early pictures that first year or two were in part backed by the franchise holders. Many of them had been in production but had never enjoyed returns on their investments like these. There were about twenty involved around the country. They would get, say, a piece of the 35 percent distribution fee and then a piece of the profits.

Their investments were gauged by a formula that reflected the size of their territories. For instance, there was the New York territory, Dallas, Denver, New Orleans, etc. The size of their investments wasn't negotiable, but fixed. A franchise holder with, say, a 5 percent territory put up $10,000 on a $200,000 film, if all the money came from franchise holders; and $5,000 if we were putting up half the money. The territorial cuts were generally known within 1 percent. And their return on their investments was based accordingly.

I will always remember when the franchise holder in New Orleans, a heavily Catholic city, told me that after he saw the numbers on *Big Doll House* Friday night, he lit a candle in church on Sunday to the film. He said he had never made a profit like that in his life—and he had been in the business forty years.

These men had instructions to call us Friday nights and tell us how we were doing on the first show. For the 7:00 P.M. opening we would hear by 7:15 and then get the full night's figures. Then the weekend grosses were phoned in to the distribution office on Monday morning. At that point, you see the pattern.

It wasn't as if we were popping champagne bottles in the office all the time, but there was a frequent sense of elation when we knew we had a hit on our hands. You almost always knew after the first date how you were going to do—approximately nine times out of ten.

We started early with saturation bookings. That became our stock-in-trade. We would move one hundred prints into a town and then move those prints from market to market. Then we'd send out another one hundred someplace else. It was not unusual, once we got rolling, to have three hundred to four hundred prints working. And we would usually cover the country in four to six months with a release.

But I have never believed in the cost efficiency of massive national or "wide" openings of, say, one thousand prints for low-budget films. Prints can cost between $1,000 and $1,500. That means $1 million or more out of the distributor's pocket for prints. We would buy maybe one hundred or two hundred prints at first and spend $100,000 to $200,000.

Almost all our films those first two years were financed partially by franchise holders. I believe we put up 60 percent on many of the films. Then, we were doing so well it was no longer necessary to finance from the outside to diminish our risk.

Big Doll House, for example, cost about $125,000 and took in $3 million in rentals. Our distribution fee, if it was 30 percent, came to $900,000. We shared that with the franchise holders, and after deducting distribution expenses and production costs, we shared the profits with them. After a while, as our confidence and our retained earnings grew, we financed almost all our films ourselves.

After Larry left, I hired Frank Moreno as sales manager. Frank had a lot of experience in the art film business as well as exploitation films and that helped us enormously later on. After a year, our profits were so high we were closing in on AIP as the biggest distribution company in the United States. Nobody could believe what we had done. With our second picture we were getting booked sight unseen, which was virtually unheard of for an independent. Independents usually have to test films in small towns to see how well they will do. That's cumbersome. It lengthens the distribution process, and you're eating more interest on your negative cost. We were now able to say, like the majors, "Here's the next New World picture on a certain date; book it."

Other companies start up with a giant staff, spend $500,000 a month on overhead, go into heavy debt, and then look for a project. I had played it more cautiously. I had commissioned a low-budget picture while I was still shooting *Von Richthofen* and didn't open up my office with Larry until two weeks before releasing our film. And it went into profit immediately.

I was like a kid who had never played minor league ball hitting one out of the park in the big leagues with his first swing.

We discovered a youth-oriented market between fifteen and thirty years of age. Each film had an element that could be advertised, or "exploited." Certainly action and sex sold. Also, the liberal or left-of-center political viewpoint was a third element worth "exploiting" and it made me happy to put some social point of view in. It improved the films, too, because it added a coherence usually lacking on low-budget films.

It also helped attract a special kind of young director. Many of those who came to me then had leftist, antiwar sympathies from the 1960s. On the walls of my office they saw the French posters depicting the May 1968 rioting in Paris. They were given to me by a producer friend, Pierre Cottrell. They were in a semiabstract and somewhat harsh style that fit us quite well: revolutionary students at the barricades, tearing down the French conservative traditions, battling police with clenched fists in the air. It told anyone coming to us where we stood and which side of the barricades they had better be working on in Hollywood.

One of those early "discoveries" who fit right in was a young, intensely dedicated filmmaker from NYU's film school named Marty Scorsese. He directed a classy, hard-hitting film called *Boxcar Bertha*, his first commercial feature. That film was also the first of some twenty projects my wife, Julie, has developed or produced. She was associate producer this time. She had gotten hold of a book that caught her eye, *Sisters of the Road*. It was a true story about a young woman named Boxcar Bertha Thompson, a Depression-era hobo who meets up with a pair of railroad workers and gets involved in a spree of petty railroad robberies and prostitution. Julie found her a most intriguing character, a strong, assertive woman but outside the upper middle class of the women's movement.

That was the first time we worked directly together. We called it *Boxcar Bertha* and we signed Barbara Hershey for the title role. Her boyfriend, David Carradine, played Big Bill Shelley, a railroad worker who turns union organizer. AIP signed to release it. They felt they were getting something akin to a *Bloody Mama* sequel.

★ **MARTIN SCORSESE**

I was twenty-eight then and I had just done *Who's That Knocking at My Door?* which was neither mass market nor underground. It was done out of NYU. There's no such thing as studying film at NYU. At NYU they made you study *Wild Strawberries*. I studied *Wild Angels* in movie theaters. Every morning at NYU you had to light a candle to Ingmar Bergman.

They had little shrines to Bergman all over the place. I love Bergman pictures but it was Corman's movies we studied in those strange dives all over New York.

Knocking came out as *J.R.* I was in L.A. as a supervising editor and associate producer on a movie called *Medicine Ball Caravan* at Warners. I met Roger through my agent and he said he had seen my movie and enjoyed it. He said he wanted me to do the sequel to *Bloody Mama.* I said sure. I was saying yes to all these guys out there. Anything they wanted me to do I did, trying to get that first commercial one going.

I didn't hear from Roger for six months. The old story.

What happened was Roger got married, went away, came back. By then I was helping John Cassavetes with sound effects on *Minnie and Moskowitz* at Universal. My agent called me at John's office, saying Roger was hiring me to do my first feature. John's people, who were all my friends, thought someone was playing a joke on me and hung up on him. The message finally got through.

Roger sent me the script he had promised me. The credit went to Joyce H. and John William Corrington. But I rewrote it myself. This was the end of 1971 and I shot the picture in Arkansas. I had to join the DGA to make the movie. The budget was under $1 million and I got scale to direct it. I don't think I was paid for the rewriting I did. But I would have *paid Roger* to do my first feature.

Roger came out and stayed a week in Arkansas during location scouting, preproduction, and the first days of shooting. This was not a plush or luxurious location either. Julie came down as associate producer. I had expected in Roger a Harry Cohn type, a rough, very crude person who was a genius at knowing what people wanted and how to market it. Instead I found him a very courteous and gentlemanly guy, but a very stern and tough customer who was quite polite as he explained these outrageous tactics of exploitation in cold, calm terms. It was very funny. Roger is, despite himself, the most remarkable type of artist because, while not taking himself too seriously, he was able to inspire and nurture other talent in a way that was never envious or difficult—but always generous.

He once said, "Martin, what you have to get is a very good first reel because people want to know what's going on. Then you need a very good last reel because people want to hear how it all turns out. Everything else doesn't really matter." Probably the best sense I have ever heard in the movies.

I made sure I was completely prepared. I went to Arkansas with about five hundred drawings after two weeks of preproduction. Roger looked at them and said he didn't need to see the rest. He knew I was prepared. I also got a lot of organizational and technical help from Paul Rapp, the

key man down there who knew Roger's way of working quite well. I
then used him on *Mean Streets.*

After *Mean Streets*—*New York, New York* to *Raging Bull* and
through *The King of Comedy*—I got up to one-hundred-day shoots. To
force myself back into the Corman mode, I fell into a low-budget picture
called *After Hours.* All that toughening up seemed to pay off. When I
did *The Last Temptation of Christ,* I shot a biblical epic in sixty days,
cutting all day and night and utilizing time the way I learned from Roger.

★ SAM ARKOFF

I gotta say something about *Boxcar Bertha.* Roger doesn't crowd a
young director. But if he sees anything wrong he'll let him know right
away. All the rushes were coming in from the first four or five days of
shooting and there was nothing but train wheels going around and
around, train wheels going this way, train wheels going that way. I
called up Roger right away. I said, "For Chrissakes, Roger, what have
we got here, a fornicating documentary on trains?"

★   ★   ★

There were people at AIP who wanted me to fire Marty and direct
myself. They became absolutely convinced that he was incompetent.
I told AIP no. They sent someone to pressure me. "There is no reason for this trip or to replace Marty," I told the guy. "The picture is
on schedule, on budget, Marty's getting excellent footage." All this,
I believed, was a function of internal politics at AIP. Nicholson had
died, and there was a big executive production staff trying to make
points and advance their careers.

I see this nowadays in the studio system and at the independents.
Certain people, for purely political motives, will try to create a crisis
or problem and then solve it so they look like heroes. I was the last
one left from the "old days" at AIP. I was convinced this was an
attempt to discredit me so that the new regime could take control of
all films and I would cease to be a threat. Ironically, I had no intention of doing any more films with AIP. I did *Bertha* only because Sam
had asked me.

As for standing behind Marty, history has vindicated me. Marty
Scorsese has become a major director. After Marty, we became a
filmmaking Mecca for untested, ambitious talent.

★ JULIE CORMAN

The first film I produced at New World was *Night Call Nurses.* It was
the first film Jonathan Kaplan directed. Jon Davison (who later went on

to produce *Robocop*) showed up on the set wearing a button that said
ROGER CORMAN.

I asked Danny Opatoshu, who cowrote the script, who he was. "Oh,"
Danny said, "Jon's a great friend of ours. He put himself through school
by pirating Roger's films and showing them on college campuses."

That night Roger and I were having a drink at home and I told him
about Jon. "What do you think?" I asked.

Roger, without missing a beat, smiled and said, "Well, I think I've got
a spot for him in distribution."

★ JONATHAN KAPLAN

I had graduated NYU in 1970, having won first prize in the 1970 National
Student Film Festival. I said, Well I've won this, now Hollywood will be
calling. Of course, Hollywood didn't call. Julie Corman called. "Hello,
Jonathan," she said, "this is Julie Corman. Martin Scorsese has rec-
ommended you to direct *Night Call Nurses.* Can you come to California
Monday and direct this picture we start in a couple of weeks?"

"How am I gonna get to California?" I asked. "I don't drive. I live on
the Upper West Side of Manhattan."

"I don't care if you can drive. I'm not asking you to be my chauffeur.
I'm asking you to direct."

"Yes, I can direct. I can direct."

"The deal is, you will get $2,000 plus a round-trip ticket. Your agent
will negotiate the rest of the deal."

"I don't have an agent."

"You can use mine. Oh, and the script will need some work. Martin
says you write. And edit."

"Oh, yes."

"Good. Then you can rewrite and edit the movie too. See you
Monday."

I called Jon Davison, who was working at the Fillmore East with me.
Danny Opatoshu lived downstairs from him. We all went to NYU. They
were very excited for me. I got Jon and Danny to come out and rewrite
the script. We shared a place in Hollywood. I locked them up for two
weeks while I cast the film. I borrowed this 1959 red Chevy convertible,
had no license, barely knew how to drive, and took them out for occa-
sional rides to let them see light and people.

Roger expounded on the formula for me—nudity, action, violence,
but not much violence. A humorous nurse plot, a kinky nurse plot, and
a socially conscious nurse plot, which was usually the ethnic one. He
showed me the poster for the other nurse pictures but the new one had
our title and the copy: "It's always harder at night for the Night Call

Nurses.'' Why don't numbskulls at the studios think like he did: Why make a movie if you don't have a campaign?

Before shooting, Roger gave me some incredible advice that has stayed with me since then.

Always ask yourself when you approach a scene: From whose point of view is this scene shot? Who is this scene about? Which characters does this scene affect? In whose head do you want the audience to be? But that didn't imply a subjective shot from their eyes with a hand-held camera panning around. The way the character sees the world is the way the audience sees the world. This was priceless stuff that he just threw off because he knew how to make movies.

We screened the first cut for Roger five days after the thirteen-day shoot wrapped. He hadn't seen a shot since the first day of rushes. I thought the first cut was a disaster that made *Student Nurses* look like a masterpiece. I thought I'd never work again. But Roger was wonderful. He had a yellow pad with about thirty neatly written, very specific notes on it. He read me his notes and that was the last time I've gotten specific notes from anybody on a movie. He suggested places where I could speed the film up by double-cutting between two people in a dialogue. He told me places where we could cut three frames. Find me one executive in the studios who would know the difference.

I was seduced by the nurturing, noncompetitive family atmosphere of New World. Jon and his friend Joe Dante, then an editor of *FilmJournal* in New Jersey, worked on a script together that never got made. But Roger hired Jon—who desperately wanted to work for Roger—to be head of advertising and promotion. *Night Call* broke the house record for a theater in Chattanooga, as Julie told me on the phone from Paris. So they hired me back to do *Student Teachers*—Danny and I wrote it and Jon brought Joe Dante out to edit the trailer.

Roger also knows the bottom-line distribution business as well as anyone. I did *White Line Fever,* which was really a Roger Corman truck driver movie, in 1974. It came out on a Wednesday. On Friday at four P.M. he called and said, "Your picture is going to do $35 million worldwide. I'm always right within $100,000." The pictured ended up doing $35 million.

* * *

Fairly early on, I began to worry that New World Pictures might become too closely associated with exploitation films. I had begun to feel we should move the company in an utterly different direction—the domestic release of art films from the finest directors in the world. I wanted to go after the art films because, first, I knew my sales manager, Frank Moreno, knew how to handle that field. Also, we were growing very rapidly and being taken quite seriously. The distribution side started as a small investment next to production but had quickly turned into an extremely successful and strong element of New World.

Our first effort was a resounding success—Ingmar Bergman's *Cries and Whispers* in 1972. Once we hit with that, Frank and Barbara Boyle, who joined the staff in the fall of 1974 after being on retainer for two years at New World, traveled all over the world to buy foreign films.

Frank knew Bergman's agent and learned that Bergman had had disputes with Svensk Filmindustri, the major state-subsidized film company that had backed most of his work. But he had financed *Cries and Whispers* himself. I heard a story that he had divided up the world into its normal percentages of grosses. For example, Australia, he might have computed, was a 3 percent country—that's how much of world grosses came from there. And so he wanted all his money back from distributors in each country.

I never negotiated. I met Bergman's agent, Paul Kohner, for lunch at Scandia, which, like the Cock 'n' Bull, was a film industry watering hole where all kinds of projects were discussed and deals struck. I made my deal there over fine Scandinavian cuisine. Paul offered to screen the film for me first. I told him I'd release the film sight unseen.

Subconsciously, I must admit the change in image was for myself as well. I did not want to personally be identified, even stigmatized, by exploitation filmmaking. But I was running the company, I owned it, and to a large extent, I *was* the company. So the new image for New World reflected on me.

Historically, the works of great directors like Bergman, Kurosawa, and Fellini were usually distributed by small companies run by art film aficionados who didn't really have the muscle to market them properly with the right terms or squeeze out a fifth theater week if the fourth was poor. Or they were distributed by the "classics" divisions at the majors who simply did not understand the market, perhaps because the smaller grosses weren't so crucial to the studios' survival. Moreover, I had built a reputation in distribution and could book these films into a broader circuit than the small art houses.

So I figured: The majors don't understand, the smaller players aren't strong enough. There's a market here for us.

Our foreign imports turned New World into a schizophrenic company. Who else could release *Cries and Whispers* in the same year as *Night Call Nurses*, or *Amarcord* with *Caged Heat* two years later, or 1980's *The Tin Drum* and *Humanoids from the Deep*?

This odd dichotomy got us lots of publicity. It seemed hip, smart, rather amusing. We had exploitation and we had art and we were the leaders in both across the United States.

We paid Bergman $75,000 against profits for U.S. and Canada distribution rights. The percentage split was roughly 70/30 for us from dollar one—a formula Barbara used for many of the two dozen or so acquisitions we made through the years. The film did incredibly well in the States and won an Oscar. It was, by far, Bergman's biggest success yet in the U.S.

We were the first to get Bergman into drive-ins, the first to book him in multiple cinemas in the same city, as we did on Manhattan's east and west sides. We knew the drive-ins were suffering from a product shortage, whereas ten years earlier and ten years later they had a product glut. So it made sense and it made money.

The film took in $1.5 million in rentals, or a profit of close to $1 million. Advertising and print costs were low because we made very few prints. We had a fancy but not formal premiere at an art cinema in Westwood. Yellow roses were part of the symbolism of the picture, so I had two of my good-looking young women staffers wear long gowns and hand out yellow roses to the lady guests as they came out of the film. We did things like that deliberately, to treat the film as a unique art object, an event. The majors would never think of that for an art film.

When I finally met Bergman years later, he mentioned that he thought it was great that we put his film in the drive-ins. "Nobody ever thought of that before," he said. "I've always wanted my pictures to get the widest possible audience. That's an audience that never saw my pictures before New World."

Over the next year we also released *The Harder They Come*, the popular film from Jamaica that helped introduce reggae music to the States, and a stunning animated science fiction feature called *Fantastic Planet*. Frank had seen *Planet*, a truly extraordinary animation by René Laloux. Julie and I saw it at the Cannes Film Festival on his recommendation and I decided to buy it. We made a deal right there with the producer. We drew up a little deal memo, the producer brought out a bottle of champagne as we closed this deal and gazed out over the Mediterranean from the hotel room. The film got nominated for an Oscar and made a couple hundred thousand dollars.

We eventually acquired such great foreign works as Fellini's *Amarcord*, one of our most profitable releases, François Truffaut's *The Story of Adele H.* with Isabelle Adjani and *Small Change*, Alain Resnais's *Mon Oncle d'Amerique*, Kurosawa's *Dersu Uzala*, and, a few years later, *Breaker Morant*, by Australian director Bruce Beresford. We made back not only $350,000 for a nonexclusive HBO deal but

$1 million total in pay TV sales and something like $3.5 million in film rentals on *Breaker Morant.*

The most we ever paid for the rights to a foreign import was $400,000 for Volker Schlöndorff's *The Tin Drum.* Barbara handled those prolonged on-off negotiations quite effectively. They came in wanting $750,000 and we came in offering $300,000. It drew over $2 million in rentals in the U.S. and Canada.

The last foreign film we handled before I sold the company was, fittingly enough, *Autumn Sonata* from Ingmar Bergman, who had given us our first. It was nominated for an Oscar. During the ten-year period from the early 1970s to the early 1980s, more pictures distributed by New World won the Academy Award for Best Foreign Film than all the other companies combined.

★ BARBARA BOYLE

It was amazing at Cannes, the way people would tug at me, shove fliers under the hotel room door because New World had such a reputation. People wanted to go with us because of Roger's renown as a filmmaker in Europe, particularly France. Just to be with Corman's New World was perceived as a major plus. In that sense he was the godfather to filmmakers abroad.

Just after I joined the staff in October 1974 I went to the New York Film Festival. Our New York guy got me to a screening of Truffaut's *Adele H.*

Afterward, I called Roger. "I've seen this picture and just love it," I said. "I really think you ought to look at it. They're asking for a hundred thousand dollars. I want to send it to you."

"Don't bother, Barbara," he said. "I trust you." And he hung up.

I called him back. "Look, what do you mean? I'm your lawyer, not a film buyer."

"You've seen the movie. I have not. There is no reason for us to have this conversation—and stop spending money like this. Buy the movie." And he hung up again. Of course, by "spending money" he meant the long-distance call, not the $100,000 for acquisition.

Of course, as we grew, all the majors jumped in with their own little "classics" divisions that bumped the purchase price of foreign films way up because they'd open in New York with $300,000 in advertising. And today, those classics divisions are just about all gone.

Then there's *Derzu Usala* and the positive, artistically committed side of Roger.

Roger says, "I want to buy this film." And I say, "Roger, three people

in the world want to see this film and two of them are sitting in this screening room." I was sure we'd lose a fortune. They wanted $75,000.

"I don't care, Barbara. Derzu Usala deserves to be bought for the American market." I was scared stiff but Roger was absolutely determined that this picture be seen. Derzu Usala did over $400,000 in rentals and won an Oscar for Best Foreign Film. Roger's instinct was absolutely on the money.

★   ★   ★

Not even Frank and Barbara could "insulate" me when an early Corman "graduate," Francis Coppola, cast me in *The Godfather II*. I played a member of the Senate committee out to nail Michael Corleone. There were close-ups on me, harsh, blinding lights. Big stuff. Practically every member of that committee was either a writer, producer, or director, all friends of Francis. Francis told me at lunch beforehand that he chose us because, having watched old Kefauver Committee hearing newsreels, he found senators are intelligent and dignified but awkward in front of TV cameras. "I asked myself," he said, "How can I achieve that effect? I'll pick writers, producers, and directors, all thinking men but untrained as actors. They will be uncomfortable in the lights."

He was right. I was behind those lights for two days. Really heavy banks of lights pouring down on us. You couldn't see a thing on the other side. Just before we started, I heard a voice yelling at me from somewhere out of the darkness. I shaded my eyes and saw it was Jack Nicholson. He was shooting a film on an adjoining stage and heard I was on the set. He came by just to needle the guy who had hired him to play the dentist's masochist in *Little Shop*. It was just before my first speaking part in a big-budget feature.

"Don't get nervous, Rog," he yelled through his mischievous grin, "but your entire career in Hollywood depends on how you say your lines."

Chapter 15

What had started as a hobby during my directing sabbatical was quickly turning into the major independent operation in the film industry. To run my own studio, I had to resort to some new tricks to keep the New World schedule rolling. I knew what I wanted to make and what made money. I also had to feed our expanding distribution network to keep it going and cover our overhead. More and more young driven directors came to us as apprentices, committed to working for next to nothing in order to get that first credit and break into the business.

It was a period of rapid expansion and intense creative energy at New World. We found new ways to make and release low-budget

Top: Cloris Leachman in *Crazy Mama*
Bottom: Ron Howard in *Eat My Dust*

films, as well as acquire product from abroad. And as the network, pay TV, and cable markets opened up for presales of films, we were discovering new ways to recoup our production costs. We functioned outside the mainstream but boasted a strong profit margin on many projects, enabling us to become known as a "studio" that paid off on profit participation when it was offered. The tradition of never seeing profits in Hollywood simply did not apply to New World.

The first job in running your own studio is to find material worth producing. Yet, if I were a young, aspiring screenwriter the last place I would send my script to would be an independent low-budget operation like Roger Corman's. It would first get read at Universal, Columbia, Paramount, Fox. This makes sense. The majors will pay more money, make a bigger film, confer greater prestige, and make you a star screenwriter—if and when they make the movie. That's the catch.

More likely, they will all pass, and when they do, then I'd send it to Roger Corman. The scripts that come to us—and this was true back then as well as today—are discards of the studio system. In that sense, independents are script-recycling plants. The studios, despite all their faults, are not run by stupid people. They reject very few really good scripts. Their problem is that, to protect themselves, they buy virtually all the good ones and a lot of the bad ones. Each major has a vast library of unmade scripts because they will buy anything that seems to have a chance.

That system was clearly not going to keep us adequately supplied with product, and since I was not a screenwriter, we had to do something. In those first few years I imagine three fourths of all our films came from ideas of my own. I would scribble down ideas—a paragraph or two—in the middle of the night or after driving home from work. I often bounced my ideas off my ace story editor, Frances Doel, who would then help shape them into treatment form as we went after a writer.

Obviously, we had to generate in-house projects or be imaginative and resourceful in tracking down outside "pickup" projects. I'd have an idea to do a film, say, about models. We'd done nurses, stewardesses, inmates, teachers. Okay, models. I would have a meeting with Frances and we'd come up with a rough outline or treatment and then bring in a writer. And the writer would do the screenplay in about two months.

The company was then a signatory to the Writers' Guild contract so I had to pay their scale. Then I didn't renew my option to resign because they had raised the scale to the point where it didn't make sense for low-budget films. Their minimums crawled up to $30,000 in the 1980s, and when you throw in residuals and other costs, it was more like $50,000. Similarly, the Directors' Guild scales are prohibitive, except for big budgets.

Many early New World films were developed by our production staff. Very few came in over the transom. Besides the art films, we also released domestic and foreign exploitation films through various "pickup deals"—*Lady Frankenstein, The Cremators, Scream of the Demon Lover*—produced by others or cofinanced with us in exchange for distribution rights.

We got films other ways too. Just as the Bruce Lee/kung fu craze started, for example, I acquired a Chinese dynasty period film with martial arts action sequences from the Shaw brothers for very little money. It was called *The Water Warriors* or something like that. A Chinese actress friend of mine, Lisa Lu, who had worked with the Shaws in Hong Kong, helped with the English translation and looping. We recut it and tightened it way down to emphasize the action because it was very long and talky. Then we turned it into *Seven Blows of the Dragon*. It was a nicely profitable little film.

We set *I Never Promised You a Rose Garden* in motion when Ed Shereck, who had the rights to Hannah Green's best-seller, came in with the script. He had partial financing and asked if we would co-produce it. It was a different kind of movie for us—emotional, dramatic, serious—and we went ahead. The film was highly praised and commercially successful. Its screenplay was nominated for an Academy Award.

Another unorthodox project was *Hollywood Boulevard*, which started out as a bet that Jon Davison made over lunch at Cyrano's. He bet me that he could produce a picture—it would be his first for us—for $90,000, cheaper than anything New World had done. "The bet's on!" I told him.

The deal was that Joe Dante and Allan Arkush, two young future directors who were cutting trailers for me, would direct it. Chuck Griffith and Danny Opatoshu each wrote a draft. Part of the deal was that Jon could have free use of stock footage from New World Pictures, so it was obvious the story would involve low-budget filmmaking. They had ten days to shoot. Paul Bartel was going to play the director of low-budget exploitation films.

★ **JOE DANTE**

Anyone who was committed, willing to kill himself and go crazy all night to figure something out, would make it with Roger. That was me. I had known Jon since we were teenagers in Jersey. He got me the trailers job in 1974 after I worked at a film trade paper in Philadelphia. The first trailers I did were *Student Teachers* and Demme's *Caged Heat*. I had

never cut 35 mm. I had no idea what to do. Through the process of simply not getting fired, I learned.

For *Boulevard,* we obviously didn't have enough money to shoot real action scenes, plus I didn't know how to direct *anyway.* We could only afford to shoot people talking. And we couldn't very well make a film of people talking. We had grown familiar with all of Roger's films by working on these trailers. So by making it a film about a film company like New World, we could use stock footage from those pictures. Why else would there be constant shots of Filipino people falling out of trees?

So before we shot *Boulevard,* we cut all the footage we wanted from the other films. Then we took this stock footage and shot material to match scenes in the stock material. We had shots of people skydiving— hence, the three actresses in our movie skydive into the Philippines to their movie location.

Then Roger read the script and said the skydiving girls didn't make sense. "How would they get through Customs?" he asked. His knack for the logical sometimes blunted his own sense of humor. That's why people have sometimes had trouble doing comedy with him. The film cost $80,000. The three of us and Amy Jones all edited it together. The film barely broke even. Still, we made a movie. It was astounding. Great learning experience.

★   ★   ★

One of the wildest "pickup" projects that led to a New World release was *Tidal Wave.* I bought a Japanese disaster film that obviously could not play in the U.S. as it was. There were some acceptable special effects and the picture had a big production value. We edited and tightened the Japanese sequences, with the producers' approval, reshot ten to fifteen minutes with Lorne Greene as the representative to the U.N. who wanted to help save Japan, cut them into the film, redubbed it all into English, and sent it out. Amazingly enough, this film *didn't do too badly.* It surprised all of us and made money. This was not typical. Most films we distributed exactly as given to us. *Tidal Wave* was probably the most outrageous example of reediting a film for domestic release.

★   ALLAN ARKUSH

The movie Roger bought was called *Submersion of Japan.* It was made by the same people who had done *Godzilla.* An ecological disaster causes Japan to sink into the ocean. Three hours long. It was actually pretty good. Roger said, "Cut it down to seventy minutes, and drop as much Japanese dialogue as you can. I want an American movie called *Tidal Wave.*"

So he got Lorne Greene to be the head of the United Nations and we shot Lorne in the studio looking worried, asking dumb questions. It was dubbed into English by Joe, Jon, secretaries in the office, all doing Japanese accents.

We'd shake the frame and make loud noises so it looked like he was in an earthquake as well. We had guys shaking down flour to look like dust and debris. We took all the Japanese people out of the trailer to make it look like an American disaster movie. We used outtakes for the trailer where his arms are in the air, like, "What do I do now?" That really sold the picture.

★ FRANCES DOEL

It didn't take Roger long to figure out that if I was going to work on all these outlines for the movies anyway I might as well do the first drafts myself. This happened first on *Big Bad Mama*. He and I figured *Bloody Mama* had done well for AIP; why not do another female gangster—fictional this time—but on a crime spree with daughters instead of sons? Roger gave me an idea of what he wanted—what she should rob, that she should be more provocative than Ma Barker, what kind of action—and I came up, as I so often did, with the story line. I was all set to find a writer. It was a Wednesday morning and Roger came in with my outline, which he invariably added to or deleted stuff from.

"This is fine," he said. "Now, Frances, it is exactly nine-thirty. Stop whatever you are doing. I want a first draft of this by Friday six P.M. It need be no more than a hundred, hundred-ten pages. Movies, remember, are a visual medium. Not too much dialogue. Figure you'll work eight hours a day, which means thirty, thirty-two pages a day, which breaks down to four pages an hour. That's about a page every fifteen minutes or so."

This was agony for me. I stayed at the office until midnight. I handwrote my pages. I didn't type well at Oxford and I still couldn't. So Roger hired a typist and I gave her the pages in the morning and she'd call me every night and say, "This is shit. I can do better than this."

The next phase of this masochistic exercise was having to meet with the real writer assigned the rewrite, William Norton. I thought my draft was so bad and embarrassing that I pretended that Roger had given the script to one of our young film students, who, I lamented so convincingly, had really mucked up. I urged Bill to feel free to totally revise it.

Then Bill started quizzing me—as New World's story editor—on every aspect of the offending article—the characters' motives, the bond between the daughters and mother, strange sexual goings-on in the script. Suddenly he got into the project. "I'd like to meet with the writer, your film student."

"Well," I said, "he, she, uh, he's gone. Left the country. He's not here anymore." By the time he finished the draft he figured it out. "You wrote this, didn't you?" He was really sweet about it. He insisted I share a screen credit with him and Roger agreed. After about six scripts for Roger I just went to him and said, "Please, no more!"

★ ★ ★

Despite our numerous successes there were some disappointments. *Cockfighter* is one picture I thought might work but didn't. The film was adapted from a novel that had intrigued me. The author was a writer named Charles Willeford. The story of a Southern man who owns a stable of fighting cocks, I thought, would provide a rich visual context for a solid film. Monte Hellman was directing and I hired Nestor Almendros as cinematographer. This was his first American feature. I knew Nestor's brilliant work from *The Wild Racers*, which I produced and Danny Haller directed. Pierre Cottrell, a French producer friend of mine, recommended Nestor. I figured: Can it cost any more to fly him from Paris to Georgia than to fly out a cameraman from Hollywood? Besides, Nestor got less money and he was better than most of the cameramen we were using in Hollywood. He won an Oscar for the 1978 *Days of Heaven.*

To my knowledge, no one had ever made a picture about cockfighting. Now I know why. No one *wants to see* a picture about cockfighting. The picture failed. I thought it was an interesting, commercial film about the dark side of rural America. What can I say? I was wrong.

But there we were, Julie, Nestor, Monte, and me, scouting locations in the backhills of Georgia. We found this old cockfighting arena that must have been fifty or a hundred years old with rotting broken-down boards, corrugated iron roof with rusted holes. Inside, beams of light came through the holes and caught the dust filling the place. There were old chewing tobacco signs everywhere, and these craggy old Georgia farmers in overalls, drinking beer and moonshine whiskey. They were sitting in wooden bleachers around the dirt pit, throwing down their bets, yelling and screaming for their cocks.

I got myself in on the action and started betting, drinking, and talking to the locals. I lost. I should have seen that as an omen. Chickens all look the same to me. I can't, in all honesty, look at a chicken and say, "This one's a better fighting chicken than that one."

Julie and Nestor were watching me. Nestor said to her, "You know, this is wonderful." I agreed. "This is really going to look sensational on film."

"Where's Monte?" Nestor asked. We found him in the parking lot. "Monte, what are you doing out here?" I asked. "It's so incredible in there." Monte didn't agree. He was thoroughly repelled. "I don't want to look at anything like that," he said. Well, I thought, there goes my cockfighting picture. The director hates cockfighting.

Monte shot a good film, with Warren Oates in the lead, but he pulled away from the action, the bloody stuff, and we never got the graphic close-ups that we should have had. I knew we'd have to shoot them second unit later.

For the postproduction shoot of a dirt floor with the fighting cocks, the film's editor, Lewis Teague, volunteered. "I can direct that." And did he direct it. He and a cameraman had to go to Arizona, one of the states, like Georgia, where cockfighting is legal. Lew just got in there with the camera. This was his chance. His stuff was so good, with such bloody close-ups of the action, that we had to cut back on it in the final cut. People looking at dailies in the projection room had to turn away. Nobody wanted to see what he had put on the screen, including me. It was too rough. Lew went on to bigger and better work—*The Lady in Red* for Julie, which John Sayles wrote, and then the highly commercial big-budget action/adventure hit *The Jewel of the Nile.*

I really thought this picture would turn out to be a fascinating look at a subculture of American life. But I believe when I use the word "fascinating," many other people would use the word "disgusting."

We lost some of our money on the picture, then tried to save it and rerelease it as *Born to Kill.* I asked Joe Dante to help in the salvage operation. The beauty of Joe then was that as a trailer editor he was never limited by the movie he was doing.

★ **JOE DANTE**

Cockfighter was really more of an art film. Warren Oates takes a vow of silence until he wins the Cockfighter of the Year award or something like that. Bizarre movie. I'm doing the trailer and I've got Warren doing sign language, a bunch of chickens, no action, what am I gonna do?

I make a fairly good trailer, the movie opens in Georgia, where Roger is sure it will be a hit. Roger's in Europe. Well, in Georgia it turns out that cockfighting is an embarrassment. It's like *child molesting.* It's not something people talk about. So no one goes to the movie. It gets terrible reviews and it's a disaster. Roger's stuck with a film that cost more than usual.

I'm editing another picture when I get a call from Roger in Europe. "Here's what we're going to do," he says. "I want you to go into *Night Call Nurses* and I want you to take out the dynamite truck chase and then go into *Private Duty Nurses* and take out the bedroom scene and I want you to cut all these things together into a one-minute montage. I want you to take some lines from the picture that Warren says to the girl—when he was talking—and put some weird music over them. Cut it into the movie right after Warren goes to sleep and when he wakes up. And it'll be a dream sequence."

I say okay. "Now," he adds, "we're going to call the picture *Born to Kill* and we're going to make a new trailer and we're going to put all these new scenes into the trailer and make it look like a picture with trucks and girls and tits and guns and all these things that really aren't in the movie. And we'll try to save the picture."

He also cut out fifteen minutes. To Roger's credit he tried to save it. But in saving it, he lost some of the best scenes, the more thoughtful ones. But the wonderful part of it was the way Roger refused to give up on a movie. Guys at the big studios give up, even on the expensive films, after two days. Roger, never.

We did all kinds of things in trailers to help sell films. We had a famous exploding helicopter shot from one of those Filipino productions that we'd cut in every time a trailer was too dull because that was always exciting. We'd take a shot of a guy shooting a gun and cut in the air and cut to the exploding helicopter. No one ever remembered it wasn't in the movie, but by then they've paid for the ticket, anyway. As an ethos, of course, this wasn't right, but it was fun. It was all tongue in cheek.

Roger was just unable to help himself. Thrift was like a congenital condition with him, a compulsion, almost, that at times impaired his judgment. He was a self-made millionaire but he could hurt himself and his movies by not spending money.

One way Roger saved money was to print and edit the color films in black and white—except for one interior and exterior shot to make sure the stock wasn't defective. Black-and-white-dailies were much cheaper back then and this went on until 1978. So we often edited trailers without knowing what was really in them. When I cut the *Big Bad Mama* trailer we got our MPAA approval for the black-and-white version. When we screened the final, color version, we discovered all these shots with people covered in blood. And the trailer got turned down because it was so violent-looking. We just thought they were wearing black or something and had no idea that stuff was blood.

People wanted to please him. Making him happy meant making Hollywood happy and that meant going on, hopefully, to something else. There was a real feeling of being part of the movie business without selling out—a late 1960s, early 1970s thing. Without working for the studio system and being safe and making pictures with Sandra Dee. Everyone wanted to get in. It was the place to get hired when you didn't know anything.

To us, Roger was an iconoclast with his left-wing posters all over the office as he counted his money. And there was the classic father/son or counselor/camper or mentor relationship: On one hand, you needed to please him; on the other hand, he was a wonderful figure to rebel against.

★ ★ ★

I met Jonathan Demme when he was living in London. Through UA he became my unit publicist for a month or so during *Von Richthofen*. He came with a background in publicity, commercial production, and some film writing. After offering him the job I asked if he liked motorcycle movies. He did. "Well, in that case," I told him, "let me tell you what else is going on with me. I'm starting up a company in the States. I need to have eight films in production by the end of the year. I'm stuck in Ireland with just a few scripts. Maybe you could write a motorcycle movie for me."

"Love to give it a try," he said.

He and his close friend Joe Viola, a commercial director, knocked out a script in eight weeks that Jonathan described as a motorcyle *Rashomon*. When I next got to London we met in the bar of the Hilton International. They gave me the script and turned to walk out. "Where are you going? I'll read it here. Just wait a minute and have a drink." I looked at it quickly.

"Okay," I said. "Joe, you've directed commercials. Jonathan, you've produced them."

"Right," they nodded. They couldn't believe it. We were there less than an hour.

"I want you guys to come out to L.A. in two months. I'll give you my script notes for the changes. Joe, you'll direct; Jonathan will produce."

They ended up calling it *Angels Hard as They Come*. Then they teamed up immediately afterward on *The Hot Box*, which they wrote from Joe's treatment. I had a production deal in the Philippines with a young producer there named Cirio Santiago. He was coming to town and I told Joe I needed a story outline the next day to show Cirio. He did it in an afternoon.

In the Philippines Joe had Jonathan shoot battle scenes and convoys as second unit director, just as Coppola, Bogdanovich, Hopper, Teague, and others had started. Soon after they wrapped, Demme asked if he could direct a feature. I liked both movies and they both made money. "Sure," I said, "come up with a women-in-prison picture."

Demme spent a year working on the script, getting a lot of guidance from Frances Doel. I decided not to finance the project because the cycle had peaked. But I liked Jonathan's work. He got his own financing—$180,000—and I agreed to distribute the film, which came out as *Caged Heat* in 1974.

★ JONATHAN DEMME

The obligatory first-director's lunch before *Caged Heat* was the most extraordinary hour, just amazing. Not because Roger picked up the tab—although it was a free lunch at Cyrano's—but for the way he just machine-gunned the rules of directing at me. Like: Find legitimate, motivated excuses for moving the camera but always look for ways to move it. The eyeball, he said, was the organ most utilized in moviegoing. If you don't keep the eyeball entertained, no way you'll get the brain involved. Use as many interesting angles as you can. Don't repeat composition in close-ups. Don't remind the eye it's already seen the same thing. Make your villain as fascinating as your hero. A one-dimensional villain won't be as scary as a complicated, interesting one. It was amazing. When I did *Something Wild* years later, I felt I was making a 1980s Corman picture.

Roger liked *Caged Heat* a lot and immediately put me to work on *Fighting Mad,* designed to cash in on the redneck revenge motif of *Billy Jack* and *Walking Tall.* He suggested strip-mining and independent disenfranchised farmers as the social backdrop and I got into it. I was looking at a $600,000 budget this time.

My first day in Arkansas, we were doing pass-bys of these eighteen-wheelers. While waiting for the truck to turn around this very unusual dog, a Texas spotted leopard hound, came by and smiled, hung around, did all these cute things.

So I asked the cameraman to take the camera off its tripod and get some kind of reaction shot of this dog for a cutaway I could cut in somewhere. So the truck is turning, the crew and cast are waiting, the cameraman's trying to make this dog smile for the camera. And now a car pulls up and out steps Roger Corman, making his traditional visit to the set on day one. A man who feels saying "Thank you very much" after each setup is optional because it wastes two seconds. Everyone looked around and KNEW how ugly this would look to Roger. It was a real freak-out moment. "Wh-wh-what exactly's going on here?" he asked.

"Just trying to get a quick cutaway of this dog here."

Roger looked at this animal and sort of chuckled.

"Well, that's a good idea," he said. There was always that surprising twist to Roger. He helped us get the shot of the dog and seemed quite gracious, amused, and cute about the whole thing.

★ ★ ★

As we moved along in the 1970s the budgets crept up to $300,000 and beyond but we enjoyed some solid, and often unexpected, successes. I acquired the rights to a futuristic, violent short story by Ib Melchior and went into production on a movie released as *Death Race 2000* in 1975 with David Carradine as the "hero," Frankenstein, and Sylvester Stallone as the lead heavy. It was only his third part. He'd been in *The Lords of Flatbush* and Paul Bartel, an actor/writer who had also done second unit work in a film of ours, recommended him for the Frank Nitti role in *Capone*, which I produced for Fox that same year. Paul also suggested him for the lead heavy in *Death Race* and brought in Mary Woronov as the female lead. She had been in *Hollywood Boulevard* with Paul.

Not every story can be a true original, but this one was. It concerned a cross-country automobile race from New York to Los Angeles. The drivers were scored on how fast they could drive and how many pedestrians they killed. I was interested in tying in the notion of gladiatorial games and an element of potential or sublimated death (as in boxing and football), then bringing it back to real death involving spectators.

When I read the story I thought: You can't do this as a straight and serious film. I wanted a dark, socially pertinent, Strangelovian comedy that would comment on matter-of-fact, institutionalized violence in our society. This idea recurs from *Kelly* in 1958 through *Bloody Mama* in 1970, *Death Race* in 1975 and then *Crime Zone*, my own idea, in 1988. The creators of the *Mad Max/Road Warrior* series stated in an article that they got their idea when they saw *Death Race 2000*.

Bartel directed the film after drafts were written by Robert Thom, Chuck Griffith, and Paul himself. It cost roughly $300,000—one of our biggest films up to then—and became one of our most successful pictures. Carradine, who negotiated a percentage of the profits, has come back to me and done a half-dozen pictures over the years because he knows we pay off on our back-end commitments on percentages. Paul went on to do the highly acclaimed quirky comedy *Eating Raoul*, which was a starring vehicle for him and Mary.

Stallone, whom I paid about a thousand dollars a week, asked for the right to rewrite his dialogue, and we let him. A year later he was *Rocky*, with another Corman "graduate," Talia Coppola Shire, as Adrian. Talia had been in *The Wild Racers*, which I produced in Europe, and proved a worthy member of the Corman ensemble. I still remember how she helped save money with props on that film. She took some drapes, lamps, and other items from our hotel rooms to dress a set when we had nothing else for it. The hotel manager caught her red-handed—bringing it all *back into* the hotel.

Five years later Stallone was getting $10 million per picture. Sly was an excellent actor right off the bat, even though many people failed—or refused—to accept that about him. I ran into Sly shortly before *Rambo* came out. I knew he had worked with some friends of mine on it. "How'd it go?" I asked. "Fine, but I looked at the rough cut and it goes on and on. You fall asleep watching this picture." He told me he went to the editor, who had worked on some of my films, and told him, "Cut it down to the action—the way Roger cuts his pictures."

We were in postproduction and needed shots of Frankenstein's car on the winding roads outside St. Louis—actually around the Paramount Ranch in the Valley. Chuck Griffith went out to direct. I decided to go out myself. For the futuristic cars I bought a half-dozen used rear-engine VW's at auction. They're cheap and reliable, and the rear engine allows you to more easily build a fiberglass body around the shell. We designed some bizarre bodies.

Once we got there, none of the stunt drivers would drive Frankenstein's car. Carradine wasn't around because this was all second-unit, nonspeaking footage. "It's got no license, no headlights, no bumpers, can't pass any of the laws," they told me. "You can't drive it down a city street. You'll be arrested."

It was necessary to get this shot, so I said, "The hell with it, I'll drive the car."

I told the assistant d.p. to under-crank the camera to make the car seem faster on film. I was going to cruise around the corner through town and traffic and everything at about fifty miles an hour. "I'll wait for a break in the traffic and I'll be the only car on the road."

To my utter amazement, damned if there wasn't another film company shooting a couple blocks away, with cops all over the place to halt traffic. Here I was in this insane futuristic alligator-shaped racing vehicle with no plates, no lights, no horn, nothing. A completely illegal car about to go fifty miles an hour through the business section. I drove by and the cop paid no attention to me. We got the shot in two takes and it's in the film.

Jackson County Jail in 1976 was one of the rare scripts that came to us from the outside and became a big picture for New World. A dynamic but disillusioned woman advertising executive quits her job in L.A. and decides to see America by driving home to New York. She ends up in a small-town jail overnight in the Southwest somewhere. When the drunk jailer tries to attack her, she hits him over the head with a stool and kills him. A drifter in the next cell persuades her to steal the dead man's keys and let them both out. The picture then turns into a chase. A nice story structure. Mike Miller did a fine job of directing. The pair on the run were Yvette Mimieux and Tommy Lee Jones, in his first feature lead. It got strong critical notices and became a huge success.

Part of the backing for *Jail* came from a Chicago-based real estate syndicate called Balcor. They wanted to invest in films as a tax shelter. I could see that sharing the investment would protect my own stake as some of our budgets crept up beyond $600,000. Balcor also backed *Grand Theft Auto*, which would be Ron Howard's first directing job. It was a loose sort of spin-off from *Eat My Dust. Eat My Dust*, written and directed by Chuck Griffith, had been a giant success, a teen action/adventure picture that earned us millions in rentals on a $300,000 budget. Ron got about $100,000 of that plus a percentage as the star. He brought it in on time after twenty-two days for $600,000. The film earned close to $6 million in rentals. Ron had a healthy share of the profits on *Dust* and *Grand Theft*.

And despite my lingering doubts on *Jail*, though I liked the script, it got strong critical notices and became a huge winner. Both pictures, in fact, took Balcor right to the limit of their allowable profits; we just about tripled our own investment on both. Balcor was delighted. They couldn't believe this went on in motion pictures.

By the late 1970s the other kind of "imaginative funding" we resorted to was presale of our films to the three networks and to the pay TV cable systems like HBO. Our biggest single sale, which Barbara negotiated for a year, was with Viacom, which bought TV syndication rights—U.S. only—to sixty of our films for $6 million, the largest single advance we ever got. The opening offer was $3.5 million, so Barbara did a stunning job for me.

In that case the payment was in cash, but sometimes we got guarantees from major companies that enabled me to borrow against them on our line of credit from Bank of America. I had been with them for over twenty-five years and had a very good credit line. They would have loaned me money without such guarantees, but I wanted to know I had a guarantee before borrowing to go into production.

I remember Julie and I were at a Colorado ski resort to begin shooting on a disaster film called *Avalanche* with Rock Hudson and Mia Farrow. By the time cameras rolled we had presold all the rights for $1.8 million, considerably more than the film's negative cost. So at the end of that first day of shooting in Colorado, Julie and I broke out a bottle of champagne. I had faith in the director and the production manager. All we had to do was finish the picture and our profit was locked in.

These kinds of presales helped recoup or offset negative costs in an industry where no one ever sees "profits." The actual expenses involved with distributing a film are extremely high in today's industry of huge breaks with up to 1,500 prints. So you've got to gross three or four times your negative cost to break even. But without question there is also deviousness in the accounting.

This once got out of hand when I produced *Capone* at Fox. I saw a report indicating that the total advertising costs were to be deducted twice from the gross. That's a lot of money. I called them on it. "That's the way we interpret the contract," they told me. "Look at page such-and-such."

I blew up. Sure, on a fifty- or sixty-page contract there may well have been an obscure clause buried on the bottom of page fifty-three between two commas. But I wasn't in the mood to discuss it. "I have absolutely no intention of looking at that page or honoring the statement that you find any justification for a double deduction of $1.2 million. That's a deduction of $2.4 million against my share. I don't want to see the contract or talk about it. I want to put everybody in jail for fraud."

That double deduction—which happened *not* to be in the contract—was subsequently withdrawn. Perhaps this was an extreme case and this was not the rule by any means. But it happens and it's another reason you have to find ways to be insulated and guaranteed a better chance at going into profits.

By the late 1970s, as we had some major low-budget hits with huge profits, we also had earned a reputation for paying off and for being honest. We have never been sued—or even threatened with a suit—over profit participation; our books have been audited numerous times and the books always pass inspection. We have paid off more consistently, I believe, than any other company, and I believe too that our company has often had the highest profit ratio in the industry—profit in relation to money invested. Actors like David Carradine and Ron Howard came back and worked again for us because of this.

★ RON HOWARD

Eat My Dust seemed goofy, a lot of car crashes, not a great acting job. But my father, Rance, and I had a script called "*'Tis the Season*" that I had wanted to direct, and I knew Roger's reputation for giving chances. I went to see him and asked my agent not to come because what I was going to ask for had nothing to do with money or billing. It had to do with opportunity. "I'm not that wild about this project," I told Roger, "but if you agree to make my movie I'll be in yours." I handed him my script and left.

Roger called back and assured me it was not what he wanted to make. Young people on the run was the current formula. "But if you do *Eat*

My Dust I promise you can write a treatment for a movie and if I like the script I'll let you direct, provided you'll be in it. If not, I'll give you a second unit directing job.''

I agreed. I worked ten days on *Dust* while doing *Happy Days* half days. We shot the film over Christmas. When it came out it was one of Roger's biggest to date. Roger saw we had a hit so he asked me to pitch him story ideas. He got a big kick out of them—a sci-fi idea, a hard exploitation cop movie, a character comedy. ''Boy,'' he said, ''it's a lot better when an actor pitches a story. But I don't really want to do any of those. I'd like to get young people on the run again. You'll star. I'd like you to come up with a movie that can be called *Grand Theft Auto* and make it a comedy/car crash/action youth movie.''

The cop phrase came from *Eat My Dust* and apparently Roger's people had tested it, as they often did, among moviegoers on line. It tested strongly. My father and I worked out a story line in a day or so and I pitched Roger by phone. After ten minutes, he gave me the green light. We were in preproduction by Christmas, and on March 2 the day after my birthday, we started shooting.

I showed up at my director's lunch prepared—with ninety diagrams of shots. He said to shoot for at least twenty setups a day. Thorough preparation, discipline, toughness in editing, rigid about scheduling— that was Roger's way. I still approach complicated sequences the way I went into that first one. The last thing he said over lunch was, happily, prophetic: ''Conditions are rough, not much money. But if you do a really good job on this picture, you will never work for me again.''

When we had a black-and-white work print Roger asked me to come to this place called ASI, an audience survey firm. They tested demographics for TV pilots and commercials on walk-in audiences. Each person's seat had buttons or knobs wired into it and they pressed or twisted it when they liked or disliked something and their responses were all fed into a control room computer for a read-out. That way you could track audience reactions as the show moved along. Roger used this method to make cuts and changes in films.

It scared me a little. There were no sound effects. I wouldn't be seeing the color until we had an answer print. We got there and the room was filled with elderlies, people leaning on walkers, women with blue hair. And this is a raunchy wild youth comedy. At least 70 percent of the audience is over fifty.

''Audience is kinda old, isn't it?'' I said.

''Oh, an audience is an audience,'' Roger answered. Jon Davison, who produced the film, came over. ''Roger made this deal with ASI so he could show his movies here for free and they'd test them for him. It usually costs fifteen thousand dollars. These people come in thinking they're seeing a movie or TV show and after ASI shows them two or three commercials, the people get pissed off because they thought they were going to see a movie. So they show them movies. Sometimes,'' he added, ''you just don't get the right demographic group. Roger factors that in.''

The screening was a disaster. I went away feeling sick. But the real audiences came through and gave Roger one of the biggest hits he had ever had with over $6 million in rentals. Again, I had points on the net profits as the star and wound up making quite a bit of money on both pictures from my share of the profits.

A while later Roger called me. ''Congratulations,'' he said, ''we just sold *Grand Theft* to a network for a million dollars. It's the first time that's ever happened.''

''Wow, that's great!''

''That sure makes your seven and a half percent look awfully good.'' ''Yeah, it sure does,'' I agreed. ''And,'' he said, ''it makes *my* ninety-two and a half percent look even better.''

★   ★   ★

Chapter 16

wning almost 100 percent of all my films and their profits, I
have never felt an incentive or desire to put my company up
for sale. But the fact is that *any* company is for sale if the
price is right. In the spring of 1982, I was made an offer I
couldn't refuse and I sold New World Pictures. I kept my
entire film library, however.

I had no way of knowing that the sale would lead to a series of
bitter, startling events culminating in the only major lawsuit of my
entire career so far. But as traumatizing as it was to be sued and
brought into court, I came out a winner and discovered once again
that it is possible to go up against the system and win.

The irony of the sale and its painful aftermath was that by the end
of the 1970s the company had reached its high-water mark. We con-

Top: Scene from *Piranha,* written by John Sayles
Bottom: Scene from *Slumber Party Massacre*

tinued to flourish with youth-oriented hits, surprisingly commercial art-film imports, and an eclectic crew of new directors and screen-writers to provide us with a widening array of genres. New World was a powerful, well-oiled production and distribution machine, with up to a dozen features a year. By almost any standard, we were the biggest independent in the industry, worldwide. We had a full decade of incredible growth before things finally slowed down in the early 1980s due to changes in the market, the industry, and the increasing costs of distribution. Until then, the notion of selling the company I had created and built into an independent power was inconceivable.

I never even seriously considered giving up any control of the company by going public, despite compelling arguments by my attorney and negotiator, Barbara Boyle. She felt the period 1977–78 was the golden moment to raise between $50 million and $100 million in capital and move to bigger pictures and higher stakes. As she would point out, the pay and video markets in Europe were about to explode. Perhaps at certain times over the years I probably would have gone public had my company been losing money. But I was seeing multimillion-dollar returns on surprise hits like *Dust*, *Grand Theft*, *Avalanche*, and *Piranha* in 1978, which was directed by Joe Dante from a script by a first-time screenwriter named John Sayles.

Going public wasn't the way, I felt, to benefit. She came to see this decision as the one great lost opportunity for the company to expand. I knew Sam Arkoff cursed the day he and Nicholson went public because suddenly they had to deal with scrutiny and account-ability and run a company with the public's money. You hire some-one who accounts to the Securities and Exchange Commission and to stockholders for your expenditures. And besides, bigger budgets meant further risk.

★ **BARBARA BOYLE**

I told Roger, "You only want to move and grow so much." We talked about this endlessly and I grew discontent. I just wanted to lock in Rog-er's wealth and never have it at risk again. Going public could do this and put us in a more important part of the business, but Roger would always back away. Disclosure, scrutiny—he didn't want it. He couldn't give up any control and control meant manipulation of revenue in a com-pletely personal way. Also, he'd have had no patience for the procedural nonsense and bureaucracy.

We were so much out of the mainstream. There's never been a Stan-dard & Poor's, no credit rating available on Roger, you can't look him up. Which he likes. There's nothing. But he has absolutely never hidden anything. We were never sued, never did anything devious. Everything was conservatively, scrupulously within the law. That would be a terrible fear for Roger—to be so rigid and so control-oriented and have something or someone hanging over his head.

★ ★ ★

By not going public, I could keep budgets down and take the company in any direction I wanted with utter autonomy. As long as it was my money at stake—even in the best years—I was there to instill the virtues and tactics of quick, efficient low-budget film-making.

For example, when we needed a revision of the screenplay for what was eventually called *Piranha,* I offered $10,000 to John Sayles. Every now and then I asked Frances Doel to find some young novelists or story writers who might want to earn some money in Hollywood. She had read John's short stories in *The Atlantic.* He had also published a novel, *Union Dues,* and was in L.A. trying to sell a screenplay called *Eight Men Out.* That script got him an agent and a first rewrite assignment with me.

He had done two drafts when I offered the movie to Joe Dante in our trailer department. Joe shot ten minutes of preproduction footage in L.A. on a Friday for the opening scene, but the cost was too high and I met with Jon Davison and Joe that weekend, telling them that I would stop the picture if we couldn't cut the budget. Actually there was no chance that I'd stop the picture, but I knew the budget had to be cut immediately.

★ BARBARA BOYLE

Jon called me from a gas station in Pacific Palisades Sunday afternoon, which was rare. He said Roger had threatened to cancel the picture. Jon had showed him the *Piranha* budget. Jon worshipped Roger and was obviously shaken. "It came to seven-fifty," Jon said. "Roger said he wanted to keep it at six-fifty. Then he told me he didn't care how I cut the budget, but it had to be done."

So I called Roger. I reminded him that we were still negotiating a deal with UA—they'd get international distribution for putting up half the negative cost. That softened Roger. "They'll put up another fifty thousand," I assured him.

"You're sure?" Yes, I said. "Okay, then tell Jon—I know he's called you—he can come back up here."

This was in a period where, indeed, budgets were creeping up to

$600,000 and regularly spilling $50,000 over. Roger was very concerned about losing control.

★ ★ ★

The picture was another success for us, with $6 million in rentals domestically—despite opening in New York during a newspaper strike—and millions for UA abroad.

We were still hitting home runs with first-rate foreign imports like *Mon Oncle d'Amerique* and *The Story of Adele H.* and were on a hot streak as the 1970s ended. Even when I screened a rather bizarre Japanese film and decided rather whimsically to acquire and release it in 1980, we ended up with another surprise money-maker.

This one was called *Shogun Assassin.* It was part of a fantastically successful series in Japan called the Baby Cart Films. It was about a samurai and his baby son and it just pushed everything to the absolute limit and beyond. I still remember the early key scene. While the samurai is away, his wife and everyone else in the palace is killed in an attack. Only the baby son, who's too young to walk or talk, survives. The warrior returns and swears eternal vengeance on the perpetrators of this crime. So in a moment of high passion, he puts the crawling baby on the floor between a toy and a sword. He tells the baby, who obviously cannot understand *either* Japanese or English, "If you crawl to the toy, I will kill you because you will be a hindrance on my mission of vengeance. But if you crawl to the sword, I will take you with me."

Of course, the baby starts moving toward the toy. Just then, however, the sky opens up, a shaft of sunlight comes down and flashes on the silver blade. When it catches the baby's eye, he quickly reaches over and grabs the sword. I said to myself, This is absolutely wonderful. I could never have thought of a scene like that if I tried all my *life.* The man who came up with this is an insane genius!

In my own search for inspired madness right at home, I was giving plenty of assignments to first-time and second-time directors, including several women. The Corman School had an unusually high "enrollment" of promising women writers, producers, editors, and directors in part because historically the industry had been and still was very difficult to crack for untested women. But I always felt inclined to give women an equal shot, even though not many women were eager to work in exploitation in those days. Barbara Peters did *Humanoids from the Deep.* Amy Jones, a quite talented editor who had worked with Joe and Allan in the trailers department, was unusually resourceful in getting her first directing job, *Slumber Party Massacre*, a New World film that in a sense defines exactly what we did best.

The script came to us as "Don't Open the Door" by Rita Mae

Brown. I had offered Amy an assistant's job when I heard she had won honors in film at Wellesley and MIT. She declined. She was editing when she called a year later and asked if there was any directing work. I told her that our schedule was filled, but Frances gave her some scripts to read and she picked out Rita Mae's horror story. Without my knowledge, Amy went out with some UCLA students as actors, a crew of four, and a bunch of "short ends"—the cheap remnants of unused film on short rolls. She shot the first seven pages of the script, edited it on Joe Dante's moviola as he was finishing *The Howling,* and put some music and sound on it. She showed Joe the reel and he immediately called me. "You should look at it. It's seven minutes of a script you own and it's pretty good." I said, "Joe, I only have one question. Did she shoot sixteen millimeter or thirty-five?"

"Thirty-five." The next day Amy came in. The reel was very good. "Tell me, what did it cost you to do this?" I asked. "A thousand dollars," she said.

"Well, you have a future in this business. What's the least you can do the rest of this script for?"

"Two hundred and fifty thousand." I offered her $10,000 to direct and she was on her way. After *Massacre* I asked Amy if she wanted to do another one. "You can make an art film with some exploitation or other salable elements and still make money on presale," she said.

"Write me one," I said. She wrote *Love Letters.* Frances helped her with this spec script as a story editor. Within a month we were in preproduction.

★ AMY JONES

That's, like, nowhere else in the business. The budget was between $500,000 and $600,000 on a six-week shoot. We got Jamie Lee Curtis for $25,000 when she was getting a million for *Prom Night* and *Halloween.* She loved the script and she took a brave gamble. Meg Tilly was our first choice. I'm thrilled she didn't work out. She loved it too and said, "I beg you, let me do it. I'll do it for nothing."

Her agent tried to get her $30,000, but Roger's ceiling was $25,000. The agent said to me, "You have to prove to me you can make Roger go to $30,000 for Meg."

"Look," I said, "Roger's given me a lot of breaks and I'm not going to make Roger do *anything.* That's not the way it works around here. It's his movie, his money."

★   ★   ★

That film was unusual for us, a moody, dramatic love story that got only fair reviews in New York but raves from movie critics Gene Siskel and Roger Ebert and good reviews in the rest of the country. More often, we stuck to New World conventions, even as we ventured into different types of films. As the resident "professor" of film, I was dealing with all kinds of problems faced by our novice directors. In the case of *Rock 'n' Roll High School*, my "students" taught me something about cashing in on the thriving music late-1970s record business. The film featured the New York punk band the Ramones and was directed by Allan Arkush, Joe's partner in our trailer department. Allan was eager to do a rock movie, as was Joe. When I offered *Piranha* to Joe, Allan got the music movie. I thought we were going to cash in on disco, which was hot at that time, but we ended up cashing in on punk rock.

★ **ALLAN ARKUSH**

Originally, Roger wanted to make "Girls' Gym," a movie with girl gymnasts. Joe and I did the first draft, but Roger cooled on the idea. Then it was "California Girls" and then "Disco High."

Mike Finnell, a producer who later became Joe's producing partner, and I worked for a year and a half to get the movie done. I was getting ready to start when Roger asked me to spend four days "fixing" a movie that had wrapped. There had been lots of trouble on the set. The first-time director had been threatening the woman lead, calling her in the middle of the night, getting paranoid, carrying a .45 under a ski parka in the desert. Plus they were trying to do stunts with street Yamahas.

I spent four months "fixing" this movie. I completely recut it, planned new stunts, straightened out the plot, cut out the mutants, which were terrible.

"Try another chase scene," Roger said.

"Only four cycles are still running," I noted.

"So what? The others—just blow them up. I want big explosions." I had done second unit chases on *Grand Theft* for Ronnie Howard, which was wonderful. This wasn't. We found this deserted Nike missile base in San Pedro where we could do explosions. "It looks futuristic with silos and concrete bunkers," I told Roger. "A great place for a chase, but it's T-shaped and only fifty yards long. You want a four-minute chase."

"I've seen the Polaroids," he said. "I want you to make it look like *Ivan the Terrible*."

"Part One or Two?" I asked. He laughed. "Part Two. It's in color. Go buy a book with pictures from *Ivan the Terrible*. They used the same castle for all the different locations. I did that in my Poe films. You can make the same location look different by putting different foreground pieces in front of the camera." Then he mapped out the whole thing right there off the top of his head.

"Have a couple sheets of thin plywood, painted with cement paint. Put them in the foreground and it'll look like different turns and alleys. Paint them different colors. We'll get some barrels, paint them red and white, paint DANGER symbols on them."

"Shoot a drive-by and then put the concrete thing in front. Shoot another drive-by and then put the barrels in front. Shoot *another* drive-by, then set the barrels on fire and shoot another drive-by. Before you know it, you'll have enough drive-bys and footage to put a chase together. Whenever a motorcycle stops running, throw it against one of the walls and blow it up."

I finished on a Thursday, showed him the film on Monday. It was awful. He said, "Very good."

I started work on "Disco High," and when Roger told me to put disco music in it, that's when we decided to make *Rock 'n' Roll High School.* Students defy their rock 'n' roll–hating principal and blow up the school. Roger, during preproduction, was the only one who thought it was still "Disco High" because his script was the only one with that title still on it. Every other script said *Rock 'n' Roll High School.* What rock 'n' roller's gonna read for a movie titled "Disco High" in 1979? Two weeks before shooting we broke it to him that the Ramones were not a disco band but punk rockers. "But why can't they be disco?" Roger asked. We said, "You can't blow up a high school to *disco* music."

★   ★   ★

When *Piranha* made a lot of money for UA in its international release the studio wanted to make another deal. But UA had been acquired by Bank of America and came under the control of TransAmerica, which owned B. of A. Suddenly, UA's Hollywood bosses were expected to take their place within the TransAmerica hierarchy. Mike Medavoy, used to being around Jags, Rolls-Royces, and Mercedeses, found out that his company car was a Buick. He said, "No way I'm driving to the lot in a Buick." He also found out the president of TransAmerica made less than he had at UA. After *Piranha* Mike and UA's three other top executives—Arthur Krim, Bill Bernstein, and Eric Pleskow—said to hell with the corporate mold and quit UA to form Orion Pictures. Because they had been very successful backing half the costs of two New World films for foreign rights, they wanted to continue the same deal at Orion.

The result was *Battle Beyond the Stars,* which, in 1980, was the most expensive production I had ever financed at $2 million. It was an idea I had that was sort of "The Seven Samurai in Outer Space" with a nod to my own *Five Guns West* and George Lucas's *Star Wars.* Five space cowboys try to save a demilitarized planet from the evil

Sador. John Sayles wrote the screenplay; Jimmy Murakami directed. Richard Thomas, George Peppard, and my one-time teenage caveman, Robert Vaughn, starred. Some of the special effects were ultimately handled by a twenty-three-year-old whiz named Jim Cameron, who went on to write and direct *The Terminator* and direct *Aliens.* His producing partner—and eventually his wife—in those huge hits was Gale Anne Hurd, a Stanford Phi Beta Kappa whom he met when she was my assistant. In fact Jim later said after doing *Terminator* that all he did was "take everything we did on *Battle* and just do it all bigger."

It was while doing *Battle* that Jim met Gale. I hired her after reading a film criticism she wrote that was superb. It was clear she was brilliant. We were in production on *Humanoids from the Deep* when Gale moved up to production assistant. She quickly became assistant production manager for *Battle.*

I went to effects houses with my script and heard bids of $5 million and $7 million. This was a $2 million film. Effects were a big business after *Star Wars.* They didn't know they were talking to a Stanford engineer, trying to convince a presumably ignorant producer that a single shot would cost $800,000. "Sure, show me your sketches," I'd say.

The best bid we got was from a likable guy named Chuck Kaminsky who worked at one effects house. I offered him a raise over his current salary and asked him to head a whole new in-house special effects company owned by New World. It was Chuck who hired Jim Cameron.

We used a very complex and sophisticated system called the Elicon. It was a computerized remote-control motion repeat system costing $200,000. It won an Academy Award that year for best technical invention. Jim functioned as model builder, effects cameraman, and art director all on the same shoot. He concocted his own powders, blew up his own models, and designed the pyro effects for a spectacular climax—demolishing Sador's spaceship—at our Venice studio in the middle of the night. He did it much the way I had gotten my last shot for *The Intruder*—on the fly and with split-second precision.

In all we made about 350 effects shots for a little over a million dollars. Audiences cheered, critics praised the film. It was profitable for us in rentals and sold to network TV for $2 million. But despite the encouraging results of our biggest production to date, there were some disturbing trends. Growth was slowing. The New World formulas—art films from abroad, youth-oriented action/adventure/comedy—weren't working as well in the changing theatrical and pay markets. I was still making money but for a year or two in the early 1980s profits began to slip. During one year in that period we actually lost money. It was the first and only time I ever had a losing year.

We still had a sizable net worth. But we were making fewer movies. The market for low-budget exploitation films was shrinking because the majors were making the same kind of films—science fiction, sword and sorcery, action/adventure, youth comedy, horror films—at an average cost of $15 to $20 million and getting much bigger production value on the screen.

Then in mid-1982 I was approached with a very substantial offer to buy the company. The offer was made by three Hollywood attorneys. Harry Sloan and Larry Kuppin were partners in a law firm that specialized in television negotiations for star clients; Larry Thompson was the other attorney and he was also a TV producer.

Harry, Larry, and Larry, as we began to refer to them, wanted to buy a going production and distribution company, the film inventory included, which then was about a hundred films. Film libraries do have some worth, and I put a very high price on mine. The talks fell apart over that. Larry Kuppen was an extremely tough negotiator. Harry Sloan, the smiling one, invited me to lunch. "Let's just the two of us sit down without lawyers and accountants, nobody else. We'll have lunch. We know your stand. You know ours. Let's see if we can work this out."

"Harry," I said, "there will be a lawyer there. You." We went to Gatsby's down San Vicente in Brentwood. I'd always had good luck making movie deals over lunch in the old days with Jim and Sam. Harry and I had been stalemated and sure enough, we reached a compromise. I agreed to a little less than I was asking; he agreed to a little more than they were offering.

But by then the terms had changed. They bought the company but I retained the assets—namely, the films. So in February 1983, we signed the contract very late at night in a Century City law office. We broke out the champagne and Larry Thompson said, "Well, Roger, you've sold us the right to feed the dinosaur." That was the most significant statement anyone made the whole time. Larry realized I had a large overhead, with offices throughout the U.S. and Canada and a staff on salary. That was the dinosaur and I knew what it took to keep it fed.

I sold the company for more than I thought it was worth. The announced figure was $16.5 million, but that included some intangibles such as the value of the distribution contract, which didn't turn out as well as planned. Yet it was a good deal for them: they got a turnkey operation. They were overnight operators of a going and internationally respected concern. They wouldn't have to start from scratch and spend five years building.

I gave up nothing but distribution and the name. I planned to start producing again the next day with a new name. The deal was structured to encourage that. They had bought the dinosaur of distribution, leaving me with the film library and production staff. I sold New World one night and the next morning I was in business as Millennium Pictures.

Harry, Larry, and Larry rented my offices in Brentwood for six months and I took my people across the street to a large office building. I didn't like the high-rise so I cleared some space and moved Millennium to our studio, a former lumber yard on Main Street in Venice. The New World people eventually cleared out, as agreed, and rented very expensive space in Century City.

Then I moved back into the old offices on San Vicente in Brentwood. There were no interruptions or changes whatsoever, except that the distribution albatross was removed from around my neck. I was deeply relieved.

I did have a guaranteed and quite favorable distribution deal with the new New World. In the midst of negotiations, I picked a very low fee of 15 percent; they were so anxious to buy that they agreed to release our pictures for, I believe, six years at that fee. Normal would have been 25 to 30 percent.

This was cheaper than the cost of distributing myself. I agreed to stay out of theatrical distribution for several years. Why would I go back into distribution?

There was even some talk of me directing a feature for them. Kuppen was quoted in *Variety* as saying, "I'm sure Roger will come up with something interesting for us."

With the overhead gone, the losses were behind us and production picked up. We started seeing profits by the end of 1983 and through 1984. I was back in the ball game. Meanwhile, the new owners of my former company presented quite a different image. Their plan all along had been to go public and raise millions in capital. Two months after the deal, they were in force at the Cannes Film Festival throwing a bigger party than I had ever thrown. Their agenda had more to do with the stock market than with film production, and they were using the company's established name to stimulate interest on Wall Street.

The deal, however, came back to haunt me. It was just too good. They never gave my pictures a full release, and they never paid me the money the pictures earned.

Larry Thompson sold his share of New World to his partners, and, shortly after, they complained that they weren't making any money distributing my films. "It's in the deal," I said. "You paid me partially in cash and partially in an extremely favorable distribution fee." It was obviously a waste of time for them to distribute these films. For me, it was an absolute necessity, backed up by an iron-clad contract. We had given them four, maybe five, films and they continued to owe me more money.

This seemed a simple straightforward matter. I had hired a young lawyer named Brad Krevoy when my prior in-house attorney, Paul Almond, stayed with New World. Brad, a graduate of both my alma maters, Beverly Hills High and Stanford, started as our lawyer and eventually branched into foreign and video sales as well. I told New World, "If you aren't paying me, you've broken your contract with me and therefore I am no longer bound by my agreement not to go into distribution." The last thing I wanted to do was get back into distribution, but I had no choice. My pictures needed distribution and I needed the revenues.

In early March 1985, I sued New World for the money they owed me and they sued me for going back into distribution. After some very tense hearings and meetings, we went to trial. I had never been in a trial before in my life. After two days in court, it was clear they had no chance and we agreed to suspend the trial and seek a settlement. Within two days we had our settlement. They paid me the money they owed and agreed that I could go back into distribution.

This was an unhappy experience. I was forced back into distribution, a business I did not want to be in. I was so dead-set against it that I proposed a formula to a group of four well-financed independent producers to jointly start a distribution company.

I had chosen the name Concorde Films. I had read a book this time that said hard C's were the most significant sound to sell products—like Kodak, or Coca-Cola. Concorde not only had two hard C's; for extra measure the dictionary described it as a harmonious grouping of similar entities with similar goals. We had meetings and arranged a cooperative distribution company. These men were all well known and presumed to have a lot of money behind them. The plan was to share the overhead and distribute each other's films.

But when it came time to start up, every one of them backed out. I was amazed. Not one of them could come up with the money. And these men, I thought, were the best. Each was to put up $200,000. People you might presume are the most successful, most famous, really don't have that much money.

I had been around Hollywood most of my adult life and I was surprised by how *thinly capitalized* so much of this industry was. If these men couldn't pull it off, why dip to the next level? I should have been more knowledgeable. So I went back into distribution alone as Concorde.

Chapter 17

Just before I graduated from Stanford in 1947, I was given a daylong test that measured both aptitude and interest in various careers. There were ten categories. The day after the test a woman called and said, "This is one of the most unusual scores I have ever seen. In nine categories you scored ninety-nine or one hundred out of one hundred. In the tenth you scored an eleven."

"Which category was that?" I asked.

"Bookkeeping and Accounting. According to the test results," she went on, "you can succeed at anything you want to do in the world that requires intelligence provided it doesn't have anything to do with bookkeeping or accounting."

Top: Julie and Roger Corman at the 1972 Cannes Film Festival
Bottom: Roger (center), Christmas 1989, with his family (left to right):
Catherine, Roger, Mary, Julie, and Brian

Some thirty-five years and two hundred plus films later, nothing much has changed on that score. I am, I admit, one studio executive in Hollywood who does not believe—or, for that matter understand—everything in his own books.

Unlike most studio heads, I still get involved in every creative stage of filmmaking—from concept to story development, script, and all the way through to rough cut, answer print, advertising design, and videocassette packaging. But those tiny numbers, those long narrow ledgers, those little forms, all that green light coming off those dark computer screens with a million flickering figures, are not for me.

There are other, more direct, ways I can help the company stay ahead of the pack in independent low-budget filmmaking in the late 1980s than staring at computerized ledgers. The biggest task has been to position us well in the presale of features to the booming home video market. In 1987 and 1988 alone we produced forty-four films, more than any of the major studios for that two-year period. The majority of those films were presold and every one was successful.

As we have grown, we have become a truly international force, with multifilm production deals in Europe, Asia, South America, and Canada. I have financed films through "dead-equity" swaps—buying Third World currency at a discount so I could get up to, say, one third more production value by promising to spend that currency on productions in those countries.

As for genres, we have continued with youth comedies, action/ adventure, horror, and science fiction films. But we have expanded very successfully into several fantasy and sword and sorcery "series" derived from original titles like *Deathstalker*, *Wizards of the Lost Kingdom*, and *Barbarian Queen*. After my own *Bloody Mama*, we have successfully done crime-family sagas with *Big Bad Mama I* and *II* and *Daddy's Boys*. Recently we've moved into family films with *The Dirt Bike Kid*, *Munchies*, and *A Cry in the Wild*, and into film noir with *The Drifter*, *Overexposed*, and *Body Chemistry*.

We have tried to concentrate on improving story development and scripts, but by mid-1987 I was getting bogged down. I was spending too much of my time on my two lifelong nemeses—contracts and bookkeeping. We were in production on *Big Bad Mama II*. The inefficiencies and overwork were driving me nuts. I was just getting angrier and angrier. I couldn't stand it anymore.

I sat in my office one floor above San Vicente Boulevard near Wilshire and said to myself, There's no reason for me to be doing this. I don't need the aggravation anymore. I got up out of my chair and stormed out, walking across San Vicente into the park adjoining the huge Veterans Administration complex. The only good thing about the whole day had been starting the morning with dailies from *Mama II* sets that looked good. But the film was spilling over budget and that upset me. I was so tired of all the legal and mathematical junk. Make a film, get away from the hassles and aggravations, I told myself. It will be like therapy. Legal and accounting fill half my waking life. And theatrical distribution and administrative stuff I dislike *intensely.*

I thought back to when we did *Little Shop* and *The Terror* simply because I saw nice standing sets and created a movie to fit them. I missed that kind of wild, creative abandon. So I figured: The *Mama II* sets are good and more are still being built. They cost a fair amount of money. We've got the cars, the wardrobe, and all this 1930s period stuff paid for and in a few weeks it'll all be gone. But it's here now. I should get a script written almost overnight and shoot another film right *behind* this one. Once a set is built and the scenes shot, it's lit, it's dressed, ready to go. Another crew and cast should go in the next day and follow through. The second picture would cost virtually nothing.

These thoughts excited, enlivened me. This was what it was all about. Making movies. I wandered through the park among the vets on benches and on the lawn and made up a rough story line. I came back to the office an hour later, called in my two top production people, Matt Leipzig and Anna Roth, and announced: "We're making a film." They both had their hands full with our outrageous production schedule. "Don't we already have enough films?" they asked.

"I don't care. I just want to make a film. I'm tired of all this stuff. Here's what it is." We talked it through—a 1930s rural gangster film. I called it "Mama's Boys." "I need a writer/director," I told Anna. "I need pages immediately to get shooting in a few days to use the *Mama II* sets. We've got to be following this film, set by set."

Anna called Joe Mignon, a friend from NYU and a very sharp, talented young writer. He'd written *After Hours* for Marty Scorsese. I knew his work. I had offered him $200,000 plus a percentage to write, coproduce, and direct "Vampire's Kiss," his own story. The most money I ever offered anyone. Then he sold it to a studio for more money, but the picture was never made. I told Anna to offer Joe $5,000, but to guarantee that we'd be shooting in ten days. I heard his studio deal was stalled. He was on a plane and in the office in a day. He brought in Darel Haney to help write and play the lead in the movie, which eventually underwent a gender switch and became *Daddy's Boys.* It cost about $300,000 and went pretty much the way I figured it would behind the other film. It did quite well in

Europe before it was released here on home video, where it did well enough to make a small profit.

But the point was: I had *done* something.

What have you got to show for shuffling papers in an office for forty years aside from a huge stack of invoices? What has actually *taken place*? Has anything been *produced*? Is there tangible proof of your existence? When you make a movie, at least there is tangible proof. You create something. At the beginning there is nothing. You get an idea. At the end is a finished motion picture—a story with a beginning, middle, and end.

I once was a pretty good deal maker, but I lost patience for negotiating. I could not hang in there long enough to wear the other guy down and swing deals anymore. I have been more of a coach, sending in plays and discussing strategies from the sidelines for Brad Krevoy, as I had for Barbara Boyle. He has done particularly well in locking up foreign sales and major deals with virtually all the top video firms.

Home video has been the key to our survival. The reason is simple: low-budget films—ours rarely exceed $3 million—do not do as well in theaters as they once did. But they often do exceptionally well in video. TV and video have become the venues for today's low- and medium-budget pictures.

Psychology and image obviously play a role in deal making. Media Home Entertainment had taken three films at $500,000 each for the U.S. only. While discussing a ten-picture deal with Steve Diener of Media Home he said they were paying $1.5 million for domestic rights to bigger-budget films. And these were films we had *outgrossed* in video sales. Brad and I looked at each other, like, "We must be *idiots*! How can this be?"

Clearly Steve's perception of our films' commercial impact was wrong. The numbers proved it. The people getting $1.5 million had guaranteed perhaps $1 million in ads for a costly release with lots of prints, but their video sales were less than ours.

The result was a one-year ten-picture deal with Media Home that required an absolutely minimal theatrical release. And they bought them *sight unseen* for a rather large amount of money. Ten new films from any one independent is an extraordinary deal. Independents don't *make* ten pictures a year. And we still had enough other product to close deals with MGM and others. Often, advances for a picture from video and other markets recoup its negative cost before we even go into production. The trick with theatrical exhibition nowadays is no longer to make big money on rentals as in the 1970s. Instead, you make *some* money theatrically, but use the release as advertising so you can get the video profits.

We've done quite well this way. Our MGM contract is our most important deal. Recently they've expanded our original commitment, added another two years and offered us an almost unlimited outlet for our films.

The MGM deal requires a minimum of six hundred play dates. A play date is one screen for one week, usually Friday through Thursday. Other deals have lower requirements, the smallest being just a few play dates to barely satisfy the definition of theatrical release. On almost every home video deal, the producer guarantees to spend a certain amount—say $3 million—on negative cost. I have *never* quoted or guaranteed the cost of a picture to the video purchaser. I say, "We have our own studio, we shoot all over in Third World countries, we do our own accounting." Instead, we show previous films and guarantee their approximate comparable production value. I prefer to rely on our track record—which, in a sense, is a reflection of my own performance as a player over the past three decades."

Ironically, I have never parlayed my success in home video into made-for-TV network films or series. Clearly, there is staggering money to be made in TV but the odds against that success are almost as staggering. The creative process for network is notoriously communal and derivative, as I found out when NBC approached me in 1988 to develop a science fiction series.

My first meetings were with some agents and Brandon Tartikoff, the dynamic head of production. Brandon's best "high-concept" idea was: father and son go to space. I said okay. Why not? Brandon made NBC the number one network. I made a deal, wrote a treatment for the pilot. Tried to get Michael Crichton as scriptwriter. But his agents wanted so much money, so fat a cut, and so much control that there wasn't much left for me as the producer and financial backer. I wasted months. Then his agents finally indicated to me that if I became a client of their agency, they could probably work out a more favorable deal for me. That's when I realized how the "packaging" machinery works. "I'm already paying a commission to one agent," I said. "The last thing I want is to pay a second one to you, especially since this all started because Tartikoff came to *me*."

After another writer got sick, NBC asked me to work with a highly touted young writer who had some success on other series. I did not like his ideas as much as the network did. Still, I figured, these guys are Number One, they're bright men, they know their business.

We had some discussions with their writer. It was soon evident that every idea discussed was derived from one hit series or another. I had nothing to say while everyone else was congratulating each other for these brainstorms. "I love it, I love it," they all kept saying. Here I was the producer, clamming up and apparently not thinking much of these new ideas. I did feel they were wrong for the show. I had to say *something.* But what? I asked myself: What's the top show around? *Cosby.* Okay, so, if I'm picking up the beat here, what I should really say is, "Make the astronaut and his son black." High concept.

No, I thought. If I say that, I'm undercutting the whole thing and insulting everyone in the room with such an obvious put-down. So I made up some innocuous response instead. A few minutes later, the writer broke in with an idea. "One other possibility I had for the show," he said, "was to make the astronaut and his son black."

I couldn't *believe* this discussion. It was like ordering from a Chinese menu. I had great admiration, actually, for the executives in the room, as they diplomatically sidestepped these ideas without demolishing them. Another idea was that this distant planet where the father and son live was somehow tuned in to a radio station in Miami that played 1950s hits. Things like that. I thought, What about indigenous culture on this faraway planet? Don't they have music of their own? Why should 1950s American rock reach this planet at the outer reaches of the galaxy?

Why? Just *possibly* because 1950s music was enjoying a trendy renaissance and could maybe be worked into a soundtrack LP for a show about a planet in deep space. Why Miami? Just *possibly* because of *Miami Vice.* And these were not stupid people but a top-of-the-line network production team, functioning in a world they all understood. When I expressed some reservations about the writer, the network helpfully mentioned to me that the original producers of *Cosby* had similar qualms about some of the changes taking place in that show's early development before they went forward with the pilot. And that each one of those once-skeptical producers stood to make over $100 million for his share of the show when it goes into syndication. "That can happen, you know," the executive assured me.

It can but it didn't. Their writer eventually turned in a first draft and the network decided his ideas were, indeed, wrong. So the project, I was told, was put "on hold." "On hold" has never been a comfortable place for me.

Once or twice, when problems get to me, the studio head in me tells the director in me that my original decision to stop directing was a major mistake. Frankly, it might have been a nicer life. I might not have made quite as much money but it might have been more satisfying. I just never found anyone else to run the company the way I felt it had to be run back in the early years of New World. In that sense, the immediate success of New World was unfortunate.

Who knows what would have happened had I gotten back to directing a year later? I had a reputation, I had offers to make bigger films. But once New World built up momentum, there was no getting out.

Did I quit out of fear? Did I let myself get wrapped up in the business of New World so I wouldn't have to confront any insecurities I may have had about my worth as an artist, as an auteur? I had gone as far as I could in low-budget exploitation, and it was time for me to make my move up into better, more sophisticated films. The Updike novel was offered to me. It was time to see if I could really make it in the majors. Staying behind a desk instead of a camera certainly protected me from the risks of artistic failure.

Was New World a way for me to remain master of my own limited universe and reject a mainstream system that would only compromise my creative freedom and financial autonomy? I still get angry thinking of the ways AIP and the studios exerted censorship over my last few films as my themes became more radical and anti-Establishment.

Should I have gone public and financed bigger, riskier pictures? No real regrets there. Cannon, De Laurentiis, and other independents, including the new New World, raised hundreds of millions of dollars among them and overextended themselves. They all got into deep financial trouble, with stock drops of 75 percent or more. They just couldn't generate the consistent winners needed to cover their giant overhead and debt.

By the end of the 1960s, I was exhausted. I was not the only one to be worn out by that decade, but I had made picture after picture, had lived out of suitcases from location to location all over the world. I was, though perhaps not consciously, more disposed to the allure of a more settled, stable home life. As for bachelorhood, enough was enough. I quit directing, got married, and started New World the same year. A couple of years later, in 1975, Julie and I started raising our family. Now we have four wonderful children—Catherine, Roger, Brian, and Mary.

Materially, our desires are limited. I have never wanted to own a private jet or a yacht. My idea of a great perk is world travel—to locations where we're shooting or film festivals and vacation spots. I've gone around the world to every continent as tourist and filmmaker.

My one indulgence has been a string of fast cars—Mercedeses, Porsches, Jaguars, a Jensen, an Alfa Romeo, even a Lotus.

We have a spacious house with a tennis court, a swimming pool, and a couple of acres. Julie and I never needed a beach house since we are a few minutes from the Pacific. For five years we owned a Manhattan condominium over the Museum of Modern Art, but we never used it enough. We lent it to friends and associates but then let it go.

★ JULIE CORMAN

The two words that come to mind when I think of Roger are "conservative" and "outrageous." When we first met, we went out to dinner and I remember him saying, "I'm on overload right now. My life is a little out of control but in about two weeks I'll have everything under control." And that's been Roger's statement ever since. The only thing he varies is the length of time it's going to take him to get it under control. It's never less than a week or more than a month. But it's still on overload.

As a father, Roger is extremely concerned about every aspect of our four children's well-being. He was the boys' basketball coach for two years and they won the Brentwood League championship both seasons. They had no alternative but to win. He was so intense the parents came to watch him coach. It was as if he was directing a movie and four hundred people were standing around waiting to see what he would do next.

Basketball was our life for the whole season. He'd come home from practices in despair: "The boys' concentration is off, I need a new strategy." The next year he had a physically handicapped boy on his team. He wasn't satisfied until he worked out a play for that boy that allowed him to score. And they won the league championship again that year.

He has never once called in a favor or enforced an option. The people who worked for him are still his friends. When they've gone on to greater things, Roger has never traded on the friendships.

★　★　★

We did acquire a five-hundred-acre vineyard in the San Joaquin Valley in central California when times were very good up there. We made quite a bit of money for a while, selling grapes in bulk to Gallo. This was before lots of Californians bought vineyards and the state got overplanted with grapes.

We bought it sight unseen. We never had time to inspect it. The vineyard had been owned by the Hughes Aircraft Executive Retirement Pension Fund and they offered to fly us up there in a Hughes jet. But we never went. We were the only vineyard in the area that signed with Cesar Chavez and the United Farmworkers Union. We went up there for the first time for a signing ceremony and a very moving luncheon party with Chavez and union executives.

I had had visions, somehow, of early California Mission architecture, white gleaming stucco with arches, the red tile roofs and the vineyard stretching out to the horizon. The land was divided into two parcels. The vineyard manager, after lunch, showed us around. My daydreams were a little off. Château Corman turned out to be a big corrugated iron shed to store the harvesting equipment. It was midsummer, maybe 105 degrees in the endless fields, blazing sun beating down on this iron shed.

"Well, we can always *add to this*," I told Julie. "Maybe a vacation house. Won't it be nice. A summer place in the vineyard." We drove up and down looking at vines. "You want to look at the other piece of the land?" the manager asked.

"Actually, I don't," I said. "I can't tell a good vine from a bad one." I looked at Julie. "If we leave now, we can be back in L.A. for dinner."

We bought two other working farms up north—they call them ranches. Again, sight unseen. But by the late 1980s these three ventures were not doing well at all so I decided to sell them.

To own a vineyard for status is, of course, ludicrous, as I found out when I met Baron Rothschild. A friend of ours, Elin Vanderlip, had a party for the Baron, who was a good friend of hers. This was around 1986. He owns Château Rothschild, one of the great vineyards and wines of the world. She introduced us and said, "Roger has a vineyard himself up in the San Joaquin." "Well," I said, trying to be as friendly and modest as possible, "it's true. But in all honesty, my vineyard to your vineyard is like a Volkswagen to a Rolls-Royce."

I could see the Baron was getting a big kick out of this. He smiled and said, "No, no. Not a Volkswagen. It's as a *Deux Chevaux* is to a Rolls-Royce." The two-horsepower Deux Chevaux is maybe the least substantial car on earth. I stood there with my drink in hand and thought: You know, the swimming pool is just over there. I could push him right in.

Clearly, my only cash crop remains film. As Julie once said of the land and other such extravagances, "We have what we need. Beyond that, money is just a series of marks on paper."

In Hollywood those can be big marks. All of us in this business are overpaid when you compare us to the real world. Compare Menachem Golan paying Sly Stallone $12 million plus points for *Over the Top*—both of them had started with me—to what a teacher gets in L.A.'s school system. Hollywood's an easy target; it's glamorous, it's sexy, it's flamboyant. It's all about supply and demand.

It's also been about fulfillment, goals, and some regrets. I've made quite a bit of money but I might have made as much or more if I'd stayed as a director and moved on to bigger films. My career has been moderately, not completely, fulfilling. I don't know anyone who fulfills all his goals. Maybe that isn't such a terrible thing. I've had a good career. I have come reasonably close to my goals but not achieved all of them.

★ JONATHAN DEMME

Let's face it, Roger is arguably the greatest independent filmmaker the American film industry has ever seen and will probably ever see. He has been the presence behind a massive, *endless* outpouring of product with a fairly consistent high level of imagination from essentially new people in virtually all areas. Roger simply characterizes this immense body of work. He's just a humongous filmmaker. A wildly gifted, masterful director—when he chose to be—in complete command of the medium: superb casting, camera work, and editing; graphic and brilliant use of the frame; amazing storytelling. There are hundreds of people who gained careers in the movie business as a result of being given an opportunity by him. He is a giant in all these areas. His contribution to motion pictures has been absolutely awesome.

★   ★   ★

In some of my films there is a theme of an artist who must destroy or be destroyed in order to create. *X-Ray Eyes, Bucket,* and *Little Shop* come to mind. Clearly, there is something of me in those films. The creative process is very difficult for me. I have always envied those directors who can just walk out onto a set and shoot a film. John Boorman, a friend and brilliant director who did *Hope and Glory* and *Excalibur,* said each time he finishes a film, he doesn't know how he got through it. He can't imagine doing it all over again. But even as I felt that I might have overdone it, made too many films in too short a time, I found myself getting increasing recognition from the critics. If some people thought of me as a cult director, some of the awards reflected that thought. You can't take them seriously. When I was awarded an engraved hubcap from Joe Bob Briggs at the Dallas Film Festival on behalf of my contributions to the drive-in film industry, I assumed the hubcap was stolen, and made my acceptance speech accordingly. I received the Saturn Award from the Academy of Science Fiction, Fantasy and Horror Films. More in the mainstream, I began winning prizes at major film festivals and was the youngest director to ever have retrospectives at the Cinémathèque Française in Paris, the National Film Theatre in London, and the Museum of Modern Art in New York. Yet I have the sense that serious critics have never really been able to pin me down. As Penelope Houston, the editor of *Sight and Sound,* the most influential of the intellectual cinéaste magazines in the 1960s and 1970s, once put it: "Roger Corman has become, if not the darling of the critics, at least their mascot." More recently *Le Monde,* the leading Parisian newspaper, referred to me as "the Pope of Pop Cinema."

By running my own studio, of course, I have played neither darling nor mascot but mentor, working closely with the young writers, producers, and directors assigned to my films. I still go into our small screening room at the end of the hallway and watch rough cuts and first cuts with my legal pad and pencil. I make notes about everything from major structural changes to trimming a few frames here and there. The Corman School is still the place to break in and we are besieged with applicants who want to come and learn how to produce, write, and direct. If they don't have a student film or spec script to show, I rely on the American university system to prescreen them for intelligence and motivation. Many of my assistants have come from leading universities—Mary Ann Fisher, Gale Anne Hurd, Laurette Hayden, Virginia Nugent, Matt Leipzig, Cheryl Parnell, and Kevin Reidy from Stanford; Frances Doel and Rupert Harvey from Oxford; Rodman Flender and Catherine Cyran from Harvard; Alida Camp and Anna Roth from Columbia; and Sally Mattison from Yale. My story editor, Beverly Gray, holds a Ph.D. in English from UCLA and was an assistant professor at USC before opting for films. Many are still with me and most of the others have gone on to head their own companies or to become producers or executives with major studios or television networks.

Somebody once said that my company should be called The Corman Graduate School of Film. People know that a "degree" from Corman is recognized in Hollywood. Director hopefuls design projects specifically for us so that I will give them a go-ahead. The film schools do an adequate job of preparing future directors and I have occasionally given immediate assignments to film school graduates. More commonly, I hire someone for six months to two years in production and then give him or her a film to direct.

★ **GALE ANNE HURD**

One extraordinary aspect to Roger is that he is and has always been, without question, a great champion of women in film, 100 percent. I went on to produce *Aliens, The Terminator,* and *The Abyss* in the studio system. When I left Roger, I thought all of Hollywood was going to be like that, that women would be given opportunities and even considered better candidates for the job than most men. I think Roger prefers to work with women. I never even realized sexism *existed* in Hollywood until I got outside New World. Roger had no problem, continues to have no problem, hiring women directors, women editors, women art directors, producers, writers. Through my experiences at New World, Roger

gave me this naive idealism that this was an industry with no barriers to sex or age. Initially, when I went to studios after Roger, I got a lot of ''How can a little girl like you expect to do a big movie like this?'' which is a comment on my age *and* my sex.

★ ★ ★

By the end of 1988, I had spent about as many years behind the desk as I had behind the camera before I quit. I had a standing offer from Universal to direct a project called "Roger Corman's Frankenstein." They offered me the highest fee I'd ever made plus a percentage of the profits. It took a long time to get the right script together, with several drafts. But by mid-1989, it finally looked like a go-ahead as *Roger Corman's Frankenstein Unbound,* with Thom Mount coproducing with me. Twentieth Century–Fox was distributing domestically and Warners overseas. The budget was set for about $9 million on a two-month shoot outside Milan. It was going to be by far the biggest production of my career.

The story and theme evolved into a gothic, high-tech Frankenstein picture, set in the twenty-first century and moving back through time.

Of course, Frankenstein's would hardly be the first monster I had brought to the screen. To what extent did I put myself on-screen through my own characters? Is a producer/director an auteur? I believe he is, if he is the one whose passion for a story brings it to the screen. Are his movies projections of his personality, his fears, dreams, and obsessions? I tend to believe they are, because we work from both the conscious and unconscious levels of the mind. The very selection of themes and stories tips your hand somewhat; there are parts of me in all of my films. But which parts?

There is the bleak madness of Roderick Usher; the tortured, self-blinded Dr. X, who sees through all physical reality and right into the center of the Universe in *Man with the X-Ray Eyes;* the twisted Little Guy in *Bucket of Blood* who craves notoriety and acceptance and then becomes a celebrity sculptor by covering his murder victims with clay. There's Seymour Krelboin, the Little Guy in the florist shop who crosses two plants and inadvertently becomes a star by creating a man-eating monster. There's Paul Groves, the Peter Fonda character in *The Trip,* who takes acid and drops out of his life as a director. And there are the Wild Angels, outlaw bikers snubbing Establishment conventions and living free on the fringes of society.

I've thought that the Baron von Richthofen, the proud, fearless aristocrat in a passing age of warfare, *and* Roy Brown, the nervous factory worker with superior reflexes and cunning who shoots him out of the skies in World War One, both reflect "warring" aspects of my character: the elitist-artist and the hustler-maverick destined to defeat him.

Those two characters, in a way, sum up my view of Hollywood and the culture of film: It's a compomised art form. It's a 50–50 split, art and commerce. Maybe that's why Americans are so good at it. In a time when American industry is falling behind other countries, the American film industry is by far the most successful in the world. That's what we're good at—art and commerce, compromised.

It's been suggested that *Creature from the Haunted Sea* is my most personal film. That's actually not a bad suggestion, considering it's got my favorite ending of them all—a last scene I invented on a whim and literally phoned to Chuck Griffith from Puerto Rico. This was the story about a band of Batista's generals making off with a treasure chest of gold from Cuba. The man they hire to captain their boat is a mobster. He murders the generals and covers up the crimes by inventing a story about an undersea monster who devours people. But there *is* an undersea monster. "We have always killed off our monsters with fire, electricity, floods, whatever," I told Chuck. "This time, the monster wins. The final shot in this picture," I insisted, "is the monster sitting on the chest of gold at the bottom of the ocean floor. The skeletons of all the people in the picture are scattered around him and he's picking his teeth. That's it. The monster wins."

ACKNOWLEDGMENTS

The authors would like to express their deep gratitude to the cast of characters whose voices and reflections so generously aided the research for this book. In no particular order, they are: Francis Ford Coppola, Jack Nicholson, Jonathan Demme, Vincent Price, Jon Davison, Frances Doel, Beach Dickerson, Peter Bogdanovich, Brad Krevoy, Julie Corman, Peter Fonda, Bruce Dern, Barbara Boyle, Gale Anne Hurd, John Sayles, Ellen Collett, Jim Cameron, Allan Arkush, Joe Dante, Chuck Griffith, Ron Howard, Gene Corman, Samuel Z. Arkoff, Beverly Garland, Dan Haller, Kinta Zabel, Abby Dalton, Tina Hirsch, Mike Connors, Mel Welles, Dick Miller, Paul Rapp, Tamara Asseyev, Jack Bohrer, Richard Shupe, William Shatner, Leo Gordon, Lynn Cartwright, Deborah Brock, Joanne Freeman, Robert Alden, Amy Jones, Anna Roth, Jim Wynorski, Matt Leipzig, Paul Bartel, Linda Shayne, John Alonzo, Shelley Winters, Nestor Almendros, Diane Ladd.

Jim Jerome would especially like to cite: Jon Davison for lending original prints from his film collection; Samuel Z. Arkoff for permitting access to his AIP film library; Beverly Gray, Cheryl Parnell, Sally Mattison, Catherine Cyran, Pam Abraham, Pam Vlastas, Mike Elliot, Alida Camp, and Germaine Simiens at Concorde–New Horizons; Jean Brown (New York) and Jeri Staley, Linda Kamberg/Jill's Secretarial, and Pat Fleming (Los Angeles) for their expert tape transcriptions; and authors Ed Naha, J. Philip di Franco, Gary Morris, and Mark McGee for their books on the Corman oeuvre.

The authors would also like to thank their literary representatives, Frank Curtis of Rembar & Curtis and Amanda Urban at International Creative Management; and, of course, a special thanks to their wise and tireless editor, David Rosenthal.

ABOUT THE AUTHORS

ROGER CORMAN has been America's preeminent independent filmmaker for nearly forty years. He lives with his wife, Julie, in Los Angeles.

JIM JEROME is the co-author of John Phillips's memoirs, *Papa John*, and has written more than fifty cover stories on show business personalities for national magazines.